LEARNING WITH PERSONAL COMPUTERS

Harper & Row Computer Science and Technology Series

Barclay: *Using Graphics to Learn BASIC Programming*
Bartee: *BASIC Computer Programming,* Second Edition
Bellin: *The Complete Computer Maintenance Handbook*
Bork: *Personal Computers for Education*
    Learning with Personal Computers
Chou: *Microcomputer Programming in BASIC with Business Applications,* Second
    Edition
Gallier: *Logic for Computer Science: Foundations of Automatic Theorem Proving*
Garavaglia: *PROLOG: Programming Techniques and Applications*
Greenwood and Brodinski: *Enjoying BASIC: A Comprehensive Guide to*
    Programming
Halpern: *Microcomputer Graphics Using PASCAL*
Huelsman: *Engineering and Scientific Computations in PASCAL*
Jackson and Fischer: *Learning Assembly Language: A Guide for BASIC*
    Programmers
Jones: *PASCAL: Problem Solving and Programming with Style*
    Modula-2: Problem Solving and Programming with Style
Keller: *When Machines Teach: Designing Computer Courseware*
Lamprey, Macdonald, and Roberts: *Programming Principles Using Pascal*
Lin: *Computer Organization and Assembly Language Programming for the PDP-11*
    and VAX-11
Mason: *Learning APL: An Array Processing Language*
Newell: *Introduction to Microcomputing*
O'Shea and Eisenstadt: *Artificial Intelligence: Tools, Techniques, and Applications*
Passafiume and Douglas: *Digital Logic Design: Tutorials and Laboratory Exercises*
Rafiquzzaman: *Microprocessors and Microcomputer Development Systems: Designing*
    Microprocessor-Based Systems
Shumate: *Understanding ADA*
Touretzky: *LISP: A Gentle Introduction to Symbolic Computation*
Ural and Ural: *Introduction to Programming with Modula-2*
Weir: *Cultivating Minds: A Logo Casebook*
Wood: *Theory of Computation*

LEARNING
WITH
PERSONAL COMPUTERS

Alfred Bork
University of California, Irvine

1817

HARPER & ROW, PUBLISHERS, New York

Cambridge, Philadelphia, San Francisco, Washington,
London, Mexico City, São Paulo, Singapore, Sydney

Sponsoring Editor: John Willig
Project Editor: Susan Goldfarb
Text Design Adaptation: Barbara Bert
Cover Design: Wanda Lubelska Design
Cover Photo: Paul Conklin/Monkmeyer Press
Text Art: Fineline Illustrations, Inc.
Production: Willie Lane
Compositor: Donnelley/Rocappi, Inc.
Printer and Binder: R. R. Donnelley & Sons Company

Learning with Personal Computers

Credits begin on page 237.

Library of Congress Cataloging-in-Publication Data

Bork, Alfred M.
  Learning with personal computers.

  1. Computer-assisted instruction—Addresses, essays,
lectures.   2. Education—Data processing—Addresses,
essays, lectures.   I. Title.
LB1028.5.B616   1987   371.3'9445   85-27293
ISBN 0-06-040868-5

86 87 88 89 9 8 7 6 5 4 3 2 1

CONTENTS

PREFACE

This book is a collection of papers, most previously published, about the work of the Educational Technology Center at the University of California, Irvine. The selections cover the period from 1980 through 1984.

These papers were written after those in my earlier collection *Learning with Computers* (Digital Press, 1981). Except for minor editorial changes, the papers are in their original forms.

For convenience, this collection is divided into seven parts: "Overview," "Computers and Schools," "Scientific Reasoning," "Physics," "Production and Design," "Videodiscs," and "Computers and the Future of Education." The papers can be read independently, in any order the reader desires. Often, further detail on a given topic may be found in another of my recent books, *Personal Computers for Education* (Harper & Row, 1985). I will now review briefly the papers in each part, with the intent of helping the reader make decisions.

part one: *Overview*

The two papers in this first part provide a general introduction. The first paper, originally prepared for a conference at the University of Oregon, looks at a wide variety of uses for computers in education, with particular attention to the school system. It argues, as does a later paper, that BASIC is an unsuitable first programming language. It ends with a set of suggestions aimed primarily at teachers beginning to work in this area.

The second paper has a much narrower focus. It concerns the use of computer-based learning material as a learning aid in a variety of subject areas. This paper emphasizes the quality of learning units and points out common errors in developing such units.

part two: *Computers and Schools*

The first two papers in Part Two are concerned with how teachers confront this new learning technology. These teachers are often poorly prepared. Further, I regard most of the programs for training teachers about computers as worse than useless.

The third paper concerns the evils of BASIC, the junk food of computer languages. The problem is a major one, given the widespread teaching of unstructured BASIC in our schools. Again, teacher training programs bear a large part of the blame.

The last paper in this section was originally prepared for the meeting of an IFIP (International Federation of Information Processing) subgroup in Working Committee 3. It outlines a k–16 computer curriculum for science and engineering majors. But we are a long way from such a curriculum; we do not have more than a small fraction of the learning materials necessary to make this curriculum practical. The discussion at the end of the paper addresses the issue of how such a curriculum could be implemented in the future.

part three: *Scientific Reasoning*

Part Three moves from general discussion to specific material. The modules described in the papers in this section were all developed at the Educational Technology Center at the University of California, Irvine. Two grants supported this work, one from the Fund for the Improvement of Postsecondary Education, the other from the National Science Foundation. About twenty hours of computer dialogues were developed.

The purpose of these modules is to help students begin to think and reason the way a scientist thinks and reasons. Students are placed in "environments" in which they must think and act like scientists. These environments are friendly and supportive, giving help when appropriate. As their titles suggest, some of the papers concentrate on individual programs, while others look at groups of programs.

part four: *Physics*

The two selections in Part Four are very different, but both reflect my long-term interest in the problems of learning physics.

The article from *Physics Today* might be described as a survey, a review of various ways of using the computer to teach physics. It gives examples of various modes of usage and should apply equally to high school and college courses.

Newton, the subject of the second paper, has had a long history in our group. Our initial proposal to the

National Science Foundation, in 1967, described such a program. The version we describe in this paper is the second one developed. The notion is to provide a rich collection of experiences about motion controlled entirely by the user. By this procedure we hope to improve students' understanding of physical laws.

part five: *Production and Design*

For many years I have argued that the key to successful use of the computer in a wide variety of learning modes is a thoughtful, effective production system. A major emphasis of our work at Irvine has been the development of such a system. All the papers in this section are about our production system.

The first paper is an extensive overview of the system, looking carefully at each of the stages involved. Three aspects are discussed: pedagogical design, technical implementation, and evaluation. The SADT charts summarize the process.

The rest of the papers in Part Five look at more specific issues in developing an effective system. Several are concerned with screen design.

part six: *Videodiscs*

When I first saw prototype videodisc players about a dozen years ago, I was struck with their potential for educational use when coupled with powerful personal computers. But I am frustrated with the lack of progress in this area and with the low quality of most existing materials. The papers in Part Six address this situation. The underlying theme is how to develop more effective learning material using the computer-videodisc combination.

part seven: *Computers and the Future of Education*

We are at an early stage in the educational involvement of computers, and the equipment is still evolving rapidly. So it is critical, if we are to use computers wisely, to think carefully about future directions for education.

Although the computer is being used increasingly in our learning environments, at all levels, it is not clear whether this use is improving education. The computer *can* lead to an improved educational system, but only if we work with care toward a better system. The papers in this final section discuss future pitfalls and possibilities.

ALFRED BORK

LEARNING WITH
PERSONAL COMPUTERS

one

OVERVIEW

The Fourth Revolution— Computers and Learning

ALFRED BORK

Of all human inventions since the beginning of mankind, the microprocessor is unique. It is destined to play a part in all areas of life, without exception—to increase our capacities, to facilitate or eliminate tasks, to replace physical effort, to increase the possibilities and areas of mental effort, to turn every human being into a creator, whose every idea can be applied, dissected, put together again, transmitted, changed.[1]

The theme of this paper is that we are on the verge of a major change in the way people learn. This change, driven by the personal computer, will affect all levels of education from earliest childhood through adult education. It will affect both education and training. It will be one of the few major historical changes in the way people learn. The impact of the computer in education will not produce an incremental change, a minor aberration on the current ways of learning, but will lead to entirely different learning systems.

This massive change in education will occur over the next twenty years. Schools will be very different at the end of that period. There will be fewer teachers, and the role of the teacher will be different from the role of teacher in our current educational delivery system. I use "schools" throughout this paper in the general sense to include any formal schooling activity, whether it be the primary school or the university, or any other level of education; for emphasis particular types of schools will be mentioned.

I hasten to say that this change will not necessarily be a desirable change. Any powerful technology carries within in it the seeds of good and evil, and that applies to an educational technology. One of the major goals in making presentations of this kind is to nudge us toward a more desirable educational future rather than a less desirable one. Our efforts in the next few years are particularly critical for education.

The full long-range implications of the computer in our world of learning are seldom discussed. Indeed, people are often overwhelmed by the technology, delighted with each new toy which they receive. Yet these implications must be considered if we are to move toward an improvement in our entire educational system. The strategy of this paper will be to first look at the "why," then to look at the "how," and then to return to present action. Many of the issues are discussed in more detail elsewhere.[2]

3

WHY WILL THE COMPUTER BECOME THE DOMINANT EDUCATIONAL DELIVERY SYSTEM?

In making a brief case as to why the change I am suggesting will take place, I first look briefly at educational factors in modern society. Then I will consider aspects directly related to the computer.

Current Status of Education

First, it does not take any great effort to see that our educational system is currently in trouble. We are being told this constantly from all sides. The daily newspapers, the popular magazines, and recent books are full of descriptions of the problems of our current educational systems. Perhaps the most interesting and critical information is the decline in faith in education in the United States. We can see this very heavily reflected among politicians at all levels. At one time for a politician to speak out against education was suicidal. Now we find that it is often politically effective. Indeed, our current president campaigned on the notion that we had no need for a Department of Education. The entire science education division within the National Science Foundation was at one point abolished simply by cutting its budget effectively to zero. The politicians know that education has little support in American society and that, indeed, it is politically expedient to cut educational funds. Education has few defenders and many detractors.

I do not wish to imply that these problems with education are simply a matter of public relations. Indeed, education has very real problems in this country and elsewhere. In the whole history of the American educational system there has seldom been a time when there was greater turmoil and where the status of teaching, in both the schools and universities, has been lower than it is now. All indications point to the fact that this decline in popular support of our educational system will continue. Few positive factors other than interest in the computer can be pointed to.

Coupled with this declining appreciation of education, perhaps even a consequence, is a factor which affects education even more directly, the factor of increasing financial constraints. The schools do not raise enough money to run an adequate educational system in this country today. Any adequate science or mathematics teacher can earn far more money outside of the schools and universities than that individual can earn within the schools. A few teachers will be dedicated enough to stay with the schools or go to schools in spite of this. But many competent people will *not*, and many people who are not competent to do anything else will teach. These are harsh statements, ones that are not pleasant to hear, but I think they must be made.

Financial constraints manifest themselves in other important ways in education beside teacher salaries. We have had no new major curriculum development at any level in the United States for over ten years. I am referring to sizable curriculum development projects, the type which could lead to improvement in our educational system. Indeed, since the development of the MACOS (Man—A Course of Study) course in the early 1970s, federal funding in curriculum development stopped almost entirely. Ironically, we were just becoming skillful in such development when the funds vanished. What we learned is now being used in large-scale curriculum development in *other* countries.

Another dismal factor in American education is the current classroom environment. Even young children frequently show little interest in education, reflecting widespread parental attitudes. High school classes often seem more like battlefields than educational institutions. This is in stark contrast to what one finds in many other countries at the present time. Hence, American education, and to a lesser extent education everywhere, is in trouble at the moment. It needs new approaches and new ways of doing things. Much of the pressure on education is from the outside, and this is the type of pressure which can lead to real change:

> The teaching profession is caught in a vicious cycle, spiraling downward. Rewards are few, morale is low, the best teachers are bailing out and the supply of good recruits is drying up.[3]

Computers

When we move from this dismal picture of what is happening in education today to look at the computer situation, the picture is entirely different. The computer, the dominant technology of our age and still rapidly developing, shows great promise as a learning mode. It has been said that the computer is a gift of fire with all the attendant advantages and problems. First, a few hardware comments. Personal computers will be dominant in education. But it is a mistake to believe that computers currently around are the ones I am talking about. We are only at the beginning stage of computer development, particularly with regard to the personal computer. Today's Apples, and even today's IBM Personal Computers, considerably more sophisticated than the Apple, are hardly a shadow of the types of machines that will dominate learning. Central processing units are becoming cheaper and more sophisticated, and memory of all types is rapidly dropping in price.

The integrated circuit technology is only at its beginning, and we can expect a long, steady decline in prices, increase in capabilities, and decrease in size. Going along with this will be increased educational capabilities, such as sound (both in and out), improved graphics, alternate media, such as those provided by the videodisc, and a host of other rapid developments. In planning for computers in education we must give full attention to this dynamic situation rather than focusing on today's hardware.

Technology is not learning. We can be too carried away with the technology and become interested in it to the exclusion of learning. Therefore we should not give primary attention in education to the new hardware developments. The real interest in the computer in learning lies not in its decreasing price and increasing capabilities, obvious to all, but rather in its effectiveness as a learning device.

How does one demonstrate this effectiveness? In education the traditional mode of experiment has seldom proved to be satisfactory. Neither the financial resources nor the number of subjects are adequate in most existing educational research. The difficulties arise from the many variables which cannot be controlled, so different from the experimental situations that are typical of the physical sciences. Few large-scale experiments have proceeded with the computer, and these were often flawed. Further, our skills in developing materials have advanced, and many of the studies are based on minimal early material. We can find lists of research projects that supposedly do or don't demonstrate that the computer is good in learning, but I am singularly unimpressed with most of these studies when I examine them closely.

So the use of adequate comparison studies in demonstrating that computers are useful in education is seldom practical. All is not lost, however, in demonstrating effectiveness for users. One important way to do this, very convincing in many situations, is to look at some examples of what is possible and to point out the features of those examples which lead to the computer becoming generally very effective in learning. It is this approach we will follow here. Another approach is through peer evaluation, the examination of materials by pedagogical experts in the area involved.

Educational Technology Center Projects

I will describe in this section three projects in computer-based learning from the Educational Technology Center of the University of California, Irvine. The first used a timesharing system; the others, more recent, were developed directly on personal computers.

The first project is a beginning term of a college-based physics course for science-engineering students. The key computer materials are the on-line tests, taken at a computer display. Other computer learning materials are also available. The tests contain a large amount of learning material. As soon as a student is in difficulty, he or she is given aid which is specifically related to the difficulty. Each test is unique. Passing is at the competency level; students either demonstrate that they know the material or are asked to study further and then take another variant of the test. In 10 weeks we give about 15,000 individual tests to 400 students. The computer keeps the full class records.[4]

The second project is concerned with scientific literacy. It hopes to acquaint students with some fundamental notions about science: What *is* a scientific theory or model? How is such a theory discovered? How do we use it to make predictions? What determines if it is a good theory or a bad theory? The material, currently six two-hour units, is designed for a general audience, with initial testing done extensively in the public library. The materials have also been tested in junior high schools, high schools, community colleges, and universities.[5]

The third project aims at helping pupils become formal operational in the Piagetan sense. The primary level is the middle or lower secondary school. The format for these units is similar to that for the science literacy materials.[6] A description of one of the units is included at a later stage in this book.

Computer Advantages

Given a brief view of several activities involving the computer in learning, we can now say *why* the computer is such a powerful learning device. At least two factors are critical in considering the effectiveness of the computer in aiding learning, the interactive nature of computer-based learning and the ability to individualize the learning experience to the needs of each learner.

One of the major problems in education, particularly education which must deal with very large numbers of pupils, is the fact that we have lost one of the most valuable components in earlier education, the possibility of having learners who are always playing an active role in the learning process. In a Socratic approach to learning, two or three pupils work closely with the teacher, answering questions and therefore behaving as active learners. The process is highly labor-intensive. As we had more and more people to educate it became less and less possible to behave in this way. We cannot afford or produce enough master teachers to base our educational system on the Socratic approach. But we *can* develop good computer-based learning material in which the student is always *active*. The computer may enable us to get back to a much more humanistic, a much more friendly, educational system by making all of our learners participants rather than the spectators they frequently are in our present book- and lecture-learning environments.

The second advantage offered by the computer is individualization of the process of learning. Everyone says that pupils are different, that each pupil is unique, that each pupil learns in different ways. But most of our standard learning procedures are very weak in allowing for these individual differences. They typically treat most pupils in the same way. For example, if a pupil in a particular point in a course is lacking some important background information, that pupil is swept along in our traditional approaches to teaching with everyone else in the class. The missing information is hard to acquire under those circumstances. The rational procedure would be to allow the pupil needing special help to stop the major flow of learning at that point and to go back and pick up the background information. But most of our present structures for learning have no adequate provisions for such a possibility. The actual needs vary between what can be learned in a few minutes and what can be learned in a whole course.

With the computer the situation is entirely different. Each pupil can move at a pace best for that pupil. Each pupil will be responding frequently to questions. (We have found in our recent programs that a pupil responds about every fifteen seconds.) So the computer, with curriculum material prepared by highly competent teachers, can determine what the learner understands or does not understand at a given point. Remedial aid can be given where appropriate, simply as part of the flow of the material with no break from the learner's point of view. Indeed, the pupil using well-prepared computer-based learning material does not have the impression that any "special" treatment is taking place, so no psychological stigma is attached to such aid. With the individualization possible with computers, one can hope to achieve the goal of mastery learning, where everyone learns all material essentially perfectly.

So much for "why" computers are going to become the dominant educational delivery system. The two factors mentioned, the unpleasant situation in education today and the usefulness of the computer as a way of learning, particularly in dealing with large numbers of pupils, suggest that the computer will move rapidly forward in education. But we still must look at the other side of the question, the "how" of the development. That is, how do we move from our present situation, where computers are little used in learning, to a situation in which they are the dominant delivery system? This is the subject of the next section.

HOW WILL WE MOVE TO GREATER COMPUTER USE?

Let me first recapitulate earlier information. The period ahead in education, for at least ten years and probably longer, is likely to be characterized by a series of continuing problems. The traditional methods of preserving the status quo in education, or allowing only small incremental changes to take place, such as the power of the administrators and the unions, will have relatively little effect; much of the turmoil in schools will be imposed from the general community. Often changes will be generated by financial decisions which lead to less money to the schools. The challenge will be the most serious one that has been seen in a very long time in the educational system.

The following comment by Peter Drucker gives a view of the situation from outside academia:

> In the next ten or fifteen years we will almost certainly see strong pressures to make schools responsible for thinking through what kind of learning methods are appropriate for each child. We will almost certainly see tremendous pressure, from parents and pupils alike, for result-focused

education and for accountability in meeting objectives set for individual pupils. The continuing professional education of highly educated mid-career adults will become a third tier in addition to undergraduate and professional or graduate work. Above all, attention will shift back to schools and education as the central capital investment and infrastructure of a "knowledge society."[7]

Thus, we will have a society more and more unhappy with the current educational system, a society groping for new ways to handle education. Few "solutions" to the problem will be apparent.

Home Computers

During the same period of time computers, particularly personal computers, will be decreasing in cost, increasing in capabilities, or (more likely) some mixture of these two trends. The changes will often be drastic. While the term one hears in the computer industry, zero cost hardware, is intentionally something of an exaggeration, it does reflect what is happening in many areas of computer technology.

One aspect of the rapid development of personal computers that will be extremely important for the future of education will be the increasing presence of the computer in homes. Homes will represent the largest possible market for personal computers, since in no other situation can one speak of millions of units. There are approximately eighty

million American homes; so the number of computers which can be sold for home use, provided the ordinary person can be convinced that the computer is valuable to own, is enormous. The home will be the driving force for education too, since the commercial pressures for home sales will be very great. In a sense, education is never "first" with computers. For many years we piggybacked on essentially a business or scientific technology in computers with education only a poor follower. The new situation will be similar, but with the home market the dominant one.

To sell computers for the home, it will be necessary that they *do* something. The average home owner is not going to buy a computer on the grounds that they are currently being sold to homes, primarily for hobbyists. The home user of equipment buys an *appliance,* a device such as a refrigerator or stove that accomplishes some task or tasks. They do not buy a gadget that they can put together in various ways to accomplish different types of tasks. The size of the home market will depend on the skill of vendors in convincing people that the computer in the home will be *useful* to the average person. Some estimates have suggested sixty million computers in homes in ten years.

I do not wish to imply that a single appliancelike use of the computer will drive the home market. On the contrary, a variety of such uses are likely to be important. Home word processing, for example, will be an extremely important use. Home financial systems, complete enough to keep all the financial records and write the income tax when asked to, and to aid in home financial decisions, will also be of importance. Personal record keeping systems, including class notes, lists, and similar uses, are also likely to be of major use in the home. Finally, educational material will be one of the types of material that without question will drive the home market. The size of this market will depend on the quality and quantity of such appliancelike programs.

Thus, we will find learning material based on the computer being developed for home computers, in some cases almost independently of whether it will also be usable in primary and secondary schools, universities, or other learning environments. Schools will use the material developed primarily for education in the home even though it may not be ideally suited. It may be that this material will often have more careful thought put into it than some of the earlier products developed particularly for the school environment, simply because the potential market is so much larger and users more discriminating. Schools are already desperately searching for computer-based learning material and are finding that little good material is available.

The people who are using the new learning materials in the home will be coming to our schools and universities. They will already have become accustomed to interactive learning, and more and more they will demand it in educational institutions. If the educational institutions wish to survive,

they will provide it. This may seem a very market-oriented point of view but we must be realistic in trying to plot the future. We must understand that the most fundamental issues that will determine the future are these marketing issues, not the academic issues which may be at the forefront of our own minds.

Companies

When we look at the school market, we see interesting commercial pressures. The dominant sellers of educational materials to schools today are the commercial textbook publishers. Yet commercial textbook publishing is a static domain at almost all levels of publishing. That is, it is difficult for a company to make much progress there, in the sense of increasing profits. Education itself is getting declining amounts of money. There will be declining numbers of pupils for several years. The competition between companies is fierce. To end up with a much larger share of that market at the present time, considered purely as a textbook market, is extremely difficult. Therefore it is not surprising that many of the most influential textbook publishers are now beginning to devote sizable amounts of effort, attention, and money to computer-based learning. They see this as a new market, where it is not at all clear at present who will become dominant. Thus, a minor textbook publisher could see the possibility of becoming a major computer-based learning publisher, or a major publisher could see that computer-based materials would very much increase revenues. Or a new company could see this as a particular opportunity for advancement, allowing them to leap over the established companies. All these situations are happening now.

The list of textbook publishers putting sizable resources into computer-based learning is a distinguished one. It includes such names as John Wiley, Harper & Row, McGraw-Hill, Longmans and many others. The type of involvement is different in different companies—this is, after all, a new market, one that is poorly understood by everyone. The degree of involvement also differs from company to company and is likely to differ in time.

In addition to these established companies, new companies, often particularly devoted to either educational software or to personal computer software more generally, are coming into existence. Sizable amounts of venture capital have been available for such companies. These companies, old and new, will be selling their wares, and so more and more school authorities will be able to easily acquire computer-based learning materials. Both old and new companies will have people actively soliciting school business. The older textbook companies may want to tie in the computer material with their existing textbooks, but the newer companies will have no need for this, and so may be open to more adventuresome activities. Some of the companies will be selling to a combination of the home and school market. In general the materials developed for the home market will be available in the school market also.

Schools

Given the financial restraints in the schools, the commercial pressures, the pressures created by the home market, and the increasing effectiveness of the computer as a learning device, more and more schools will turn to computers for delivery of learning material. One interesting sign is the fact that there are schools that do not have adequately prepared teachers to teach some of the important courses in the curriculum. Thus if we look at high school courses such as advanced mathematics and science courses, rural schools in the United States presently are often not providing these capabilities, at least not in a way that is competitive with the better large urban schools. Computers will be a mechanism for equalizing opportunity for pupils by providing computer-based learning courses in these declining areas, courses that otherwise would not be available. Hopefully, these courses will be developed by the best individuals from all over the country.

We may see a decreased role of the formal school and the formal university in our educational system. Much education will be able to take place in the home in a flexible fashion. At the university level we already see one outstanding example of a development of this kind in the Open University, but still with relatively little use of computers. The Open University has demonstrated that good curriculum material in home environments can be effective as a learning mode and economical when compared with the standard cost of education. Voucher systems, if they are enacted, will make home learning much more likely.

I do not wish to imply that all education will move to the home. Indeed, a view of the educational system such as that shown in George Leonard's book, *Education and Ectasy,* suggests that the sociological components, the factors associated with living with other people and living with oneself, will still probably best take place in small group environments within schools. But many of the knowledge-based components of learning may move to the home.

Types of Usage

We have discussed very little about the way computers will be used within the school system. Something needs to be said about this, if only to counteract some of the current propaganda. The computer will be used in a very wide variety of ways within our educational system. The notion that some "right" way exists to use the computer, and that other modes of computer usage are somehow wrong, is one that has been promulgated by a number of individuals and groups in recent years. Indeed, often staged debates at meetings comparing types of usage have been held, with the implication that there are right and wrong ways to use the computer in education. Books have been organized in such a way that it sounds as though

there were a competition for different types of computer usage.

These debates, often on philosophical grounds, have made a tacit assumption that a right way to use the computer exists, if only that way could be discovered. Mostly the authors have had a naive belief in their "right way," and then set out to try to establish a case for their beliefs. The principal problem with this type of reasoning is that it often does not proceed from instructional bases, nor does it proceed from empirical bases or experimental studies. That is, the issues that dominate are often technological issues, the nature of the computer hardware and what can be done with the computer hardware. These writers are trying to carve some unique niche for the computer among other learning media.

These technologically based and media-based arguments for a single type of computer usage are, I believe, entirely misleading. The decisions as to how to use computers—the modes of computer usage, the areas—should be made entirely on *pedagogical* grounds, the questions of what aids learners rather than on these philosophical, media, or technological grounds. Whenever decisions are made on pedagogical grounds, it will be found that a wide variety of computer uses will be employed, uses which are often adapted to the individual situation being considered. There is no single "right" way to use computers, but rather a great variety of ways.

I will give a brief classification of the various ways the computer can be used.

This list is not exhaustive, nor does it show fine detail. But it may be useful to at least consider the range.

Computer Literacy

Computer literacy is ill-defined and so much debated. It is recognized that at all levels of education, starting perhaps as early as eight or nine years old and continuing through the school system, university, and adult education, individuals in our society need to understand the various ways the computer is going to be used in that society; they need to understand the positive and negative consequences of those ways. Few full-scale computer literacy courses exist. Indeed, what often passes as computer literacy is vague history or learning to program in a simplified way, to be discussed in a moment. So this is still very much an open area for computer uses. Specialized courses are needed for each group addressed; thus, computer literacy for teachers is a pressing national issue. All these courses need to consider such important future uses as word processing, personal financial and record keeping systems, and educational material.

Learning to Program

Learning to program is already a rapidly increasing activity in our universities and schools. It represents in secondary schools the most common usage of computers at the present time. Unfortunately, where it happens at this level it is often a *disaster,* harming more than helping the pupil. The major

problem is the way programming is taught. A whole group of people is being taught a set of techniques which are no longer adequate to the programming art today. These techniques were common in the early days of computing, but they are inadequate according to today's standards. Many of the people learning to program in schools cannot overcome the initial bad habits which have often been instilled in them when they come to the universities. Many universities are now reporting this phenomenon.

The main culprit is BASIC. It is not that BASIC has to be taught in a way that is antithetical to everything we know about programming today. But it almost inevitably is taught in such a fashion. *BASIC is the junk food of modern programming.* Indeed, the analogy is close in that junk food tends to destroy the body's desire for better types of food. But the analogy is weak in one regard: BASIC is the initial language of the vast majority of these people. It is as if you started feeding junk food to babies one day old and give them nothing else until they were six! If I could leave one message, perhaps the most pressing message, it is to *STOP TEACHING BASIC.* It is becoming clear that students who learn BASIC as their first computer language will in almost all cases acquire a set of bad programming habits. These habits are very difficult to overcome, so BASIC programmers have difficulty writing readable and maintainable code.

The following recent comment by a distinguished computer scientist, Edgar Dijkstra, is relevant:

It is practically impossible to teach good programming to students that have a prior exposure to BASIC; as potential programmers they are mentally mutilated beyond hope of regeneration.[8]

What programming languages should we teach? There are a number of possibilities for both primary and secondary schools. Logo is certainly one interesting possibility, although I must confess that some features of Logo are different from those recommended in the best modern programming practices. Logo, however, is introduced in a problem solving environment, and that is very much to its advantage. Often its main intent is not to teach programming but to teach more general problem-solving capabilities or some specific area of mathematics. But its general problem-solving effectiveness has yet to be demonstrated in our mass school environments with ordinary teachers.

Another possibility is Pascal or a Pascal-like language. The material developed at the University of Tennessee and sold by McGraw-Hill under the name of *Computer Power* is an excellent example of an approach of this kind. If one looks for print materials that are usable at the secondary school and perhaps even at a lower level at the present moment, the *Computer Power* material seems to be one of the best possibilities. Another approach is to develop some interesting capability based on a structured programming language. For example, the recent *Karel, the Robot* from Wiley follows such an approach.

Turtle geometry, in Logo, is the best known example.

Learning Within Subject Areas

Undoubtedly the largest use of the computer in schools at all levels will eventually be not the categories just discussed but rather the use of the computer as an aid in learning mathematics, in learning to read, in learning to write, in learning calculus, and in all the other tasks associated with the learning process.

One person may work alone at a display or several may work together. When one looks at these learning tasks in detail, again one finds a great variety of computer use, ranging from tutorial material, to intuition building, to testing, to aids in management of the class for the pupil (feedback on what is needed and how to go about getting it), and the teacher. The three projects presented earlier show something of the range of possibilities.

Unfortunately, much of the material now available of this type is very primitive. We are, however, rapidly learning to develop better material to aid learning.

Production Process

If we are to move to meet this new future, where the computer will be the dominant educational delivery system, a critical aspect will be the generation of effective learning material. We need new courses and entire new curricula, spanning the entire educational system. Hence, the development we are talking about is a nontrivial process. It is the degree of success of the development process that will tell whether we will improve or damage education. We must convince the likely distributors that it is important to develop quality materials, not the poor quality resources mostly available today.

The development of curriculum material in any field and with any medium and at any level is a difficult process. It cannot be done by amateurs who are doing it simply as a spare time activity. Many new observers in this field, looking at the problems quickly, tend to underrate these problems of developing effective learning material. Hence, some of the solutions which have been proposed are solutions which are simply not adequate to the problems. Some of these solutions assume only small incremental changes in the curriculum structure and do not understand the magnitude of the development necessary.

Several critical points concerning products should be made to give the reader a reasonable overall viewpoint. The production system is a complex system, one that should involve many types of people with many different skills. If one looks at the production of any educational material, one sees that that is the case. We can learn much by examining effective curriculum production systems, such as that currently in use in The Open University, that used in producing the major curriculum efforts in the United States more than ten years ago, and that involved in such areas as the development of textbooks. We need to resist the notion that one person, perhaps a teacher in his or her spare time, will do it all. I do not believe that any sizable amount of good curriculum material will be produced by this method. Furthermore, I do not believe that the devices which are being urged for these teachers, such as simple-minded authoring systems based on toy languages (Pilot) will be effective. Nor do I think that languages such as Tutor will be effective, because they do not meet the reasonable criteria associated with modern programming languages. Most of these languages are old in their design, and few of them understand the nature of structured programming. A serious professional approach is needed if we are to maintain the quality of the computer-based learning materials produced.

We can see a number of stages needed in such a professional approach, listed below:

a. Preplanning
b. Establishing goals, objectives, and rough outlines
c. Specifying the materials pedagogically
d. Reviewing and revising this specification
e. Designing the spatial and temporal appearance of the material
f. Designing the code
g. Coding
h. Testing in-house
i. Revising
j. Field testing
k. Revising

The last two stages may be repeated twice.

In the entire process, the educational issues, as opposed to the technical issues, should be dominant. The best teachers and instructional designers should be involved in stages (c) and (d) to assure the quality of the product.

Present Steps

This paper has presented an overview of some of the problems associated with reforming an entire educational system during the next twenty years. Many details are either not mentioned or treated very hastily. But I hope I have given enough details to convince you of the main directions that need to be taken.

As teachers, we are undoubtedly interested in what we should do now to work toward a more effective future for education. First, we must decide whether we would wish to be involved in the type of curriculum development suggested. If we do wish to be involved, we must take a long-range view of how to prepare for this activity.

I would *not* advise you to purchase one of the popular machines and start to use it! Nor, as you might suspect, would I advise you to take courses in BASIC. But it would be desirable to take a variety of courses, if they are accessible to you or to study on your own, in certain areas. Here are some suggestions. The first three refer to areas of learning, either through formal courses or through informal methods.

1. **Learning Theory.** Good curriculum development cannot be developed without some appreciation of how people learn, even though there is no single coherent theory there. Courses in learning theory may help, based on the research literature concerning learning.

2. **Curriculum Development.** The question of how to develop good curriculum material is one that deserves serious study. Some universities provide such courses. Some textbooks exist. Many of the issues are independent of computers, referring to development with any learning media.

3. **Modern Programming Languages.** You might wish to become acquainted with modern programming languages, such as Pascal. Again, you must be careful here. It is possible to meet these languages either in an old-fashioned environment or in one that stresses structured programming. You want the second possibility. Look at the textbook. If it does not introduce procedures until a third of the way or even further along, do not take the course. This is not the only factor, but it is a good way of distinguishing reasonable from unreasonable courses.

   Avoid the "CAI" languages—they are inadequate, not suitable for serious material. Look at the authorizing approaches based on modern structured languages.

4. **Listen to Pupils.** In your own teaching, begin to move away from the lecture mode presentation into a more Socratic mode. A critical factor is listening to what pupils say and watching what they do. This means that when you ask questions, you have to wait for answers. It also means working

more individually with pupils in groups of two to four. It is only by this procedure that you will begin to build up the insights you need for how pupils actually behave when they are learning.

People whose primary mode of interaction with pupils is through the presentation mode or through textbooks are seldom the best choices for preparing computer-based learning material. The development of computer-based learning material will need vast numbers of experienced teachers, teachers who have been listening to their pupils and who understand pupil learning problems.

5. **Personal Computers.** Begin to use a variety of personal computers, with particular emphasis perhaps on the newer machines. Read the journals that tell you about new equipment. Watch for voice input, improved graphics, and full multimedia capabilities.

6. **Critical Attitude.** Examine computer-based learning material, trying to develop a critical attitude toward it. Do not be overwhelmed simply because it is interactive or because the computer is involved. Keep your mind on the learning issues and learn to develop some sensitivity as to what existing material helps learning and what doesn't.

Most existing material is poor. Find out why. Read the journals that specialize in critical reviews.

7. **Work with Others.** The development of good computer-based learning material is best done in a group. Work with others in discussing goals, strategy, and the details of design.

8. **Future Orientation.** Concentrate on the long-range situation, not today or tomorrow. Decisions which are "good" from a short-range point of view may be undesirable in the long range to both you and to the future of our entire education system. So keep the long-range point of view strongly in mind.

9. **Visions.** Begin to think about what type of future educational system would be both desirable and possible. If you want to influence the future, you must have visions.

Developing quality computer-assisted instruction demands forethought; those of you who are unfortunately caught up in expedient movements in education need to take a closer, more courageous look at the nature of the hope on Pandora's chip. You are dealing with as powerful a tool as the gods have ever given us.[9]

May 1982

REFERENCES

1. Servan-Schreiber, Jean-Jacques, *The World Challenge.* Simon and Schuster, from The Mitsubishi Report.
2. Bork, A., *Learning with Computers,* Digital Press, Billerica, Massachusetts (1981).
3. Boyer, E., quoted in *Report on Educational Research* (February 3, 1982).
4. Bork, A., "Computer-Based Instruction in Physics," *Physics Today,* 34, 9 (1981).
5. Bork, A., Kurtz, B., Franklin, S., Von Blum, R., Trowbridge, D., *Science Literacy in the Public Library,* Association of Educational Data Systems, Orlando (February 1982). Von Blum, R., *Computers in informal learning: A case study* (November 1980). Arons, A., Bork, A., Collea, F., Franklin, S., and Kurtz, B.,

"Science Literacy in the Public Library—Batteries and Bulbs," *Proceedings of the National Educational Computing Conference,* Denton, Texas (June 1981).

6. Trowbridge, D., and Bork, A., "A Computer-Based Dialog for Developing the Mathematical Reasoning of Young Adolescents," *Proceedings of the National Educational Computing Conference,* Denton, Texas (June 1981).

7. Drucker, Peter F., *The Changing World of the Executive,* Times Books (1982).

8. Dijkstra, Edgar W., "How Do We Tell Truths That Might Hurt?," *SIGPLAN Notices,* 17, 5 (1982).

9. Quote from Burns, H., "Pandora's Chip: Concerns About Quality CAI," *Pipeline* (1981).

Compendium of Bad but Common Practices in Computer-Based Learning

ALFRED BORK

This is an exciting era for those of us who have been working for many years with computer-based learning. We are beginning to see commercially available products for aiding students to learn via computers. Many of these products are quite new. Unfortunately most (perhaps 90%) of these early modules are very poorly contrived.

At this early stage of the market, when almost any product brings sales, quality has not always been a determining factor in persuading people to market a product. Indeed, some marketers are already beginning to distinguish between their first-generation materials and their better second-generation computer-based learning materials.

Users, however, often misunderstand this distinction and cannot distinguish the better materials. If we are to demand that vendors market higher quality material, users must develop a set of standards for examining material. This paper is directed toward the development of such standards for all users. We must begin to understand that any old learning material on the computer is not necessarily "good." I hope that my comments on judging material will be useful for developers of computer-based learning materials; I discuss development in more detail elsewhere.[1]

The current situation, the poor quality of material commercially available, has great inherent danger. The problem is that the implicit inadequate standards promulgated by these poor materials may become *the* standard for computer-based learning modules. If this happens, we will lose, perhaps for a long time, the real benefits of the computer in education.[2]

My tactic is to enumerate practices in computer-based learning which are common but undesirable. Often these are practices which the novice does not note, but which are nevertheless worth discerning.

I will avoid pointing to specific examples from existing material. But readers may find it interesting and profitable to examine such examples by *applying* the ideas developed in this paper.

CONTENT

Undoubtedly the most important consideration in judging any learning material is *content*. We are interested in material that aids learning, so that should be our primary focus. Is it substantial material, intended to accomplish some important learning function? Does it accomplish this function? A surprising amount of material, both computer and other, is very vague on issues of content; it is often unclear how learning material fits into existing or proposed new sequences of learning.

The most serious weaknesses in the content are what I shall call *trivial* pieces of material, learning material which is inconsequential. Limited segments of learning material, computer or otherwise, need not be inferior, but often are. A small amount of material may suggest a very exciting new approach to a particular area or to learning more generally. But the small computer programs currently available for learning seldom do that. Indeed, they seem to have been developed primarily because the material was "do-able," easy and cheap to program, not because it has any serious learning purposes; thus, technology rather than education dominates.

One type of offender is the computer "game." At least two problems exist. First, this terminology is applied to almost anything. The word "game" is used to apply to activities that, as far as I can see, have no gamelike aspects, assuming the everyday meaning of the word "game."

Another problem is that games seldom tie in well with specific learning situations. What is to be learned in playing an educational game is often vague to both student and designer. If they are true games, they often are strongly motivational. Although motivation is certainly extremely important in learning, it is not the whole story.

One could achieve similar motivation in some cases by bringing a pinball machine into class. One could then argue profoundly about how the students are intuitively learning information about the laws of motion in mechanics, particularly with regard to colliding objects; university faculty are skillful in making such arguments. I think these arguments would be weak for sustained use of pinball machines. Educators need a clear view about what is motivational with little educational value and what is motivational with strong educational value. Materials should be related to learning.

Games, I hasten to emphasize, *can* be extremely important in the learning process, more important than they are today. We must consider motivational issues. But we must develop games very skillfully if they are to incorporate learning issues. We cannot assume that anything called a "game" is automatically valuable.

Another area in much existing material where content in the learning sense is particularly weak is the type of help offered to students in difficulty. This is perhaps the most critical capability of good computer-based learning material. Good students typically do not *need* such material. They can learn with almost any media. The real advantage of computers entails being able to give individualized aid to students who do have difficulty.

Yet much of the material one sees is inadequate for students in need of aid. The only help may be simply to tell students that they made errors, often in terms rather discouraging to the student. When "help" is offered, often it bears the guise of brief verbal advice, say, repeating a definition. Interactive help sequences, bringing users to understand the material and taking the time to determine if they *do* understand the material, are seldom available. Unfortunately, the typical help is a screen full of text, with no interaction, and details repeated that have already been stressed. "One level" help will be inadequate for many students; some may require quite different help in order to facilitate learning.

The problem of inadequate aid for the learner in difficulty is related to a larger problem, the lack of individualization of the learning material. Different students learn best in different ways. Good computer-based learning material *assumes* this, and provides a wide variety of learning sequences and styles. However, much current computer material provides only a single learning path, forcing everyone through the same approach in a lecturelike fashion.

I might summarize many of these bad practices in content by saying that much current computer-based learning material devotes very little time—far too little—to considering the pedagogical details of the material. Much of it gives the impression that a quick pedagogical idea was generated, and then most of the energy went into the coding. Serious pedagogical material demands serious attention to the curriculum details, with or without computers.

MEDIA CONSIDERATIONS

A developer of computer-based learning material sometimes may have had experience in extensive curriculum development in other media; others are new developers without previous experience. Many workers in this field will inevitably be people who have developed learning material in book form, in lecture form, or in other ways. Hence, it is not too surprising that, particularly in their early use of computer-based learning, such developers tend to employ modes similar to those which drove their earlier activities. They are often still thinking implicitly about books or some other medium.

Developing a "feel" for a new learning medium, as we must do in the case of computers, is a heroic enterprise. We can give no very definite rules, since much of this activity depends on experience. But I will indicate a few of the media factors that characterize poor practices with computer-based learning material.

Perhaps the central problem is the failure to recognize the potential of the computer as an *interactive* medium. Poor material has far too few interactions, too much for students to read on the screen before *doing* anything. Nontrivial interaction is the hallmark of good computer-based learning material.

Although difficult, it is not impossible to establish criteria for "quality of interaction," a numerical measure, giving a rough feeling for the degree of interaction. One aspect of interaction, although by no means the only issue, is the *time between interactions* for the average user. There may well be an occasional situation in which the designer wants this interaction time to be long, perhaps as long as several minutes.

Generally the average time between interactions (one interaction ends and another begins) should probably be more like 15 to 30 seconds. Sometimes we want it to be a good bit less than this. It is characteristic of poor material that the average time between interactions is too long, primarily because of excessive amounts of text.

A model can aid in developing such interactions. One can ask what good teachers do when they work individually or with a very small group of students. In such a situation most teachers will not "lecture," but will work interactively with the students, perhaps by asking questions. Learning must be an active process, if it is to be accomplished efficiently. Computers provide an excellent medium for such interactive learning. Readers interested in more details about interaction, including an early attempt to provide a numerical measure, may consult an earlier paper by the author.[3]

One bad practice, common with computers and with older learning media, is the inadequacy of visual or graphic information. Many students are not very skilled with language, and will only gradually build up language skills in courses. These students often need more visual aids in learning than are typically presented. Since teachers and developers of curriculum material *are* skilled in handling verbal information, they tend to use too much of it for many learners. We must insist, in examining curriculum material using computers and other media, on the necessity of providing sizable amounts of pictorial learning material. This information should be of direct help to the learner, not just visual "gimmicks." We *don't* want just a set of pretty pictures.

Another annoying feature of much computer-based learning material is the constant repetition of stock phrases. In both simulations and problem generators, a given section of computer code may be used over and over. This is often desirable, particularly when the material is embedded in a richer learning structure. But how undesirable it is to repeat over and over exactly the same phrase, as students progress through the program! This is deplorable because it reduces the material to a mechanical procedure, whereas computers have the potential for engaging students in friendly dialogue. A variety of simple techniques can easily avoid this impediment. For example, we can choose a phrase randomly from a collection of equally appropriate phrases for the particular situation. While this may seem to be a minor issue, attention to this can create material more appealing to students.

One media-related difficulty is the practice of solving "problems" associated with the learning material through other media. For example, my experience in making films discloses a tendency to believe that one should solve learning problems associated with the film by means of associated print material. Yet with most films, because of logistic or other problems, most students never *see* this associated printed material; so this way of trying to solve the problem is unsatisfactory. Similarly, a good unit of computer-based learning material should, in most cases, *not* be highly dependent on print material, video, lectures, or other learning media.

It is poor practice to solve a pedagogical difficulty in learning material by resorting to another medium. I hasten to say that multimedia material itself, with each learning medium playing its full instructional role, is important in the learning process. But even when various media are effectively used, the logistical problems of making certain everyone has all the components at the right time can become difficult in the real world. Thus, laboratory material in the sciences for the first through the sixth grades, as in such projects as ESS and SCIS, has proved to be very difficult to use in practice, because teachers do not want to be bothered keeping and maintaining kits of material. In looking at computer-based learning material, when I raise a pedagogical question and the developers of the material tell me they deal with that problem in the student notes or teacher notes, I have qualms.

Finally, one set of media-related problems seems important enough to discuss in a separate section. I next discuss the arrangement of material on the screen in both space and time.

SCREEN DESIGN

As with other aspects of computer-based learning, newcomers often treat the screen the same way they have treated "writing surfaces" in older media. Thus, the screen is considered like the page of a book or some other printlike format or a blackboard. Often developers do not even know about print readability since that information is not used commonly in developing print material for learning. Perhaps the only curriculum development group to give adequate attention to the research literature on readability is the Open University in the United Kingdom.[4]

In some cases the computer-driven screen allows capabilities beyond those available on a page. For example, timing, by which material can develop in time to aid the reader's comprehension of that material, is not possible on a page of a book; when the learner turns the page the new material is all there, print and pictures. But the screen situation being very different, material can develop in time. In other situations approaches possible in the book form are not *economically* desirable. One important influence upon a number of issues is that of blank space. Blank space in a book increases the cost of the book; blank space on the computer screen is free.

Let me point to a series of readability factors common to both print and screen. Then let's look at some factors unique to the screen. Various studies show that these factors hurt readability, both in print and on screen, yet they are fairly common in print and computer material. The first is the use of very long lines of print. In general, the learner handles material better with short lines, although the readability results are rather complex. Right justification, combined with left justification, the common practice in books, often cuts down on readability. Hyphenation is a negative factor too; it is common practice, usually combined with right justification.

Keeping natural phrases, defined either syntactically or semantically, together on a line also helps a learner who is not a good reader. While books have followed this practice occasionally, such as in the Leiber and Leiber popularizations of mathematics and science, it is still extremely rare in print material. It is almost equally rare in existing computer-based learning material, although newer "second generation" learning material is beginning to show it. At present, to maintain phrases on the same line typically requires some human intervention; perhaps that is why it is not frequently implemented. At least from a syntactical point of view (not a semantic point of view), it could be automatic.

A number of useful ways to *emphasize* critical words and phrases in computer-based learning material seldom appear in available material.

Some of these techniques for emphasis involve "moving" the material in some way, either turning it off and on— blinking—or oscillating it, or reversing field at some rate. Other techniques for emphasizing words and phrases will involve timing. Thus, one can pause a suitable length of time before and after a grammatical entity needing emphasis, just as one does in speaking. We can vary the *rate* of textual output for such entities, a topic we shall discuss later. Timing can also be effective in pausing after such punctuation marks as commas, semicolons, and periods.

One bad practice, almost universal with existing materials, spews text at the user at the fastest possible rate, with no consideration as to whether this is desirable. In the Educational Technology Center, for many years we have been examining this question informally and recently more formally. We find that few users other than professionals like the fast rate typical of material today. Instead, "normal" users, given a choice, use a rate much like the 300 baud rate of communications. In interviewing users, we have found that the fast rate is disturbing to many. One of our current research projects is attempting to gather more detailed information about this issue. Our previous experience makes it clear to us that text is usually displayed too rapidly for most users of the system, another very common bad practice.

Although we currently set the initial speed of materials at what we consider the best desirable rate, very uncommon in computer-based learning material, we also believe it is desirable to allow learners to *control* the rate of text output at any time. This raises an issue of an entire set of factors for user control of the screen. One of the computer's advantages is that it *allows* such reader control, which is not possible in text material. Yet developers commonly ignore this possibility and provide no more control than is available in books. Users can employ a number of controls with computer-based learning material. Bad practice is *not* to allow such controls.

The handling of input is often particularly bad. Long inputs, with much English text, frequently lead to words split at the edge of the screen. That is, when the print gets to the edge of the screen, the hardware or software shifts part of the word to the *next* line. The edge, however, is not necessarily the critical location. One might prefer a word *not* to overlap a diagram or other text, and so provide controls that prevent such overlap, while assuming that a whole word is on one line. Strategies for not splitting words are well-known in computing; they are used widely in word processing systems, where they are typically called "word wrap." Words crossing lines or words overlapping with diagrams or others, particularly on long inputs, is a frequently seen but highly undersirable practice. Like many bad practices, relatively minor increments in the software can control it. The difficulty is that input and output provided by most computer languages is quite inadequate.

Perhaps the worst among a number of bad practices associated with student input are the types which allow a program to bomb because of a mistake, such as typing a letter instead of a number. Such typing mistakes are common, particularly with a novice likely to confuse the numbers one and zero with the letters *1* and *O*. Fingers resting lightly on the keyboard can "add" characters not intended. For some time special "font ends" for novices have provided coding for input which supersedes the rather crude input now provided in most computer languages. Many current materials do not provide such user-friendly front ends.

Another useful but rarely available feature for student input is the timed read. In many situations it is undesirable to let a learner sit indefinitely long before the computer does something. Learners may not really understand that they are expected to type something at that point or may have no clear view of what to type or may have typed something without pressing return. In all these cases timed input can carefully handle the situation.

Weak underlying software is likely to generate bad practices in computer-based learning by poorly designed placement of text on the screen. Most computer languages make the booklike assumption that text should always start at the left-hand margin. I consider this a very bad practice, seldom desirable. Text should appear on the screen by conscious design to best aid learners with that particular component of text.

Finally, text should frequently *disappear* from the screen without erasing information which is still relevant. Text no longer applicable to the situation at hand shouldn't be there. Modern systems allow parts of the screen to be removed, without affecting other parts of the screen. In much current computer-based learning material, at any one time the screen shows a past history of what has happened, often with irrelevant text for the current situation. The practice of removing superfluous text, concentrating the student's attention on what is currently relevant, relates to the frequent use of blank space mentioned earlier.

OTHER FACTORS

Other issues should be mentioned which fit either loosely or not at all in the classifications developed. Some have to do with tactics used in the materials. A number of tactics are poor tactics, but commonly used.

One such undesirable tactic is multiple-choice questions, particularly in on-line quizzes. In some cases this is a subconscious choice. People know that multiple choice has something to do with computers, so they focus on it when they start to develop interactive computer materials. Some computer quizzing systems for both off-line and on-line employ primarily multiple choice.

Multiple choice should, I believe, almost *never* occur in computer-based learning material for two reasons. First, multiple choice is a poor way of determining what a learner knows. Guessing factors play too sizable a role. Further, this mode of quizzing fell into education as a tactic of desperation, using relatively crude early technology to handle large numbers of students. It has little to recommend it at present. Better technology renders it obsolete. It is not needed with a computer, for we can ask a much wider range of questions which avoid guessing factors, and so lead more quickly to reliable information about what students do and do not know.

A number of departures from ordinary English also fall into the category of bad practice. Some are hard to understand. For example, often *immediately* after the question mark, with no intervening spaces, the computer pauses for a reply to a question. The display is certainly not characteristic of the way we teach people to write English!

Also common is the widespread use of Ys and Ns, or even worse 1s and 0s, in place of "yes" and "no." While some use of single-letter mnemonics may be useful,

it is an undesirable tactic to follow in most computer-based learning material. Future displays, such as those currently in use in Sesame Place, may build "yes" and "no" keys directly onto the display. At least in this case the full word is there, not some computerized abbreviation.

As stated earlier, I urge upon the developers and publishers of computer-based learning material some standards of quality. And I wish to suggest to users of computer-based learning material the possibility of reasonable judgments concerning the quality of that material. Many important positive issues in the development of computer-based learning material are not tapped. For further details the reader can consult a recent book by the author, *Learning with Computers.*[5]

I welcome comments about bad practices from others to add to my list.

April 15, 1983

REFERENCES

1. Alfred Bork, *Production Systems for Computer-Based Learning,* study commissioned by the U.S. Office of Education, July 1982.
2. Francis Fisher, "Computer-Assisted Education: What's Not Happening," *Journal of Computer Based Instruction,* 9, 1, Summer 1982, 19–27.
3. Alfred Bork, *Textual Taxonomy,* July 1981.
4. Alfred Bork, *Interaction in Learning,* National Educational Computing Conference, June 1982.
5. Alfred Bork, *Learning with Computers,* Digital Press, Billerica, Massachusetts, 1981; Alfred Bork, *Personal Computers for Education,* Harper & Row, 1984.

two

COMPUTERS AND SCHOOLS

Teachers and Computers

ALFRED BORK

Computers are appearing rapidly in schools all over the world. There are now [in 1985] approximately one million computers in American schools, although estimates disagree. This means about twelve computers per school. They are, however, unequally distributed. Some schools have no computers, while others have many.

The United States is not a leader in using computers in education. For example, in England every school, through government policy, has at least one computer.

In all countries, a major problem is training teachers how to use computers effectively. Given the rapidly increasing number of computers in schools, the question becomes: what happens with the computers when they reach the schools? There are two problems: (1) preparing teachers to use the hardware, and (2) providing adequate learning materials on the computer. I won't address the second problem, although I consider it the major one. Nearly all the material currently available to teachers is of poor quality.

Traditionally, the training of teachers in the United States and many other parts of the world has been a three-pronged venture. First, schools of education give the initial training to teachers and perhaps more advanced training later in their careers. Second, we

find in-service courses offered in the afternoon, evening, weekends, and summer. In-service courses may be given through schools of education too, through extension programs or as part of the standard programs of universities. And third, informal teacher education, where the teacher assumes the major burden of learning the material either individually or working on an informal basis with several other teachers, is also important.

England's coherent program for training teachers involves curriculum development at the Open University and regionally taught courses for teachers, the Microelectronics Program in Education. France also had, with its ups and downs, an elaborate teacher training program with seven centers in different parts of the country. Extensive study leaves were granted to teachers.

In the United States, we have no coherent program. What we have are many informal programs in many parts of the country. I wish I could say these programs are mostly good, but my experience in looking at many is that they are poor, both in schools of education and elsewhere. There are a few outstanding exceptions. When students ask me where they can go to school to learn about computers, particularly teachers looking for master's or doctoral programs, I am hard put to name many programs whose quality I know to be high. The good programs are few and far between.

Most teachers simply *do not have access to any decent programs* concerning the computer in education. This isn't accidental. Schools of education have no tradition in this area. Computer science departments, on the other hand, have no experience working with teachers and no understanding of their problems. It isn't surprising, therefore, that many of the courses in both teacher training and in-service are harmful instead of helpful.

For example, teachers are advised that they should study an elementary programming language. I see absolutely no merit for any teacher learning anything about BASIC, given its deficiencies. Yet that is probably the most common direction taken by teachers who are interested in learning more about computers. Even a course in a better language, such as Pascal or Logo, can still inadequately serve the needs of teachers. Also, a teacher lacks a basis for choosing between such courses.

Another problem is the *magnitude* of the problem. We aren't talking about a few teachers located in large cities near important institutions. We're talking about teachers over the entire country, often long distances from any institution that has qualifications in computers in education. Given the magnitude of the problem in numbers and geography, the route of in-service education is entirely inadequate.

I do not wish to imply that the teacher training problem is unsolvable. I think there is a good solution receiving little attention at present. It is the direction we are pursuing at the Educational Technology Center at the University of California, Irvine. So far, we do not have adequate funding for the full-scale program we would like to develop.

We have been arguing for years that the only solution to the problem of teacher training is to develop very good computer-based learning material *on the computer,* just for teachers. This material, running on personal computers, could be used within schools of education or in a variety of other educational settings, including the teachers' own schools or homes. The low cost of personal computers and their widespread and increasing availability makes this a practical direction to take. The best people in the country could be brought together to develop these materials. The results would be better than anything available through local sources in conventional courses. Teachers would learn *on the computer, not about the computer.* They would see first hand the possibilities for learning with computers. They could *see instead of being told.*

At the Educational Technology Center, we developed two units like this out of a dozen we think will eventually be needed. Our funding was from the Developments in Science Education Program of the National Science Foundation. We are seeking additional funding to go farther with this development. I will be glad to describe our approach to those interested.

September 1983

Computer Literacy for Teachers

ALFRED BORK

The term "computer literacy" has been much bandied around in recent years. It derives from a wide use of the term "literacy," as in "reading literacy," "math literacy," and "science literacy." Unfortunately literacy, in general, is one of the words that almost everybody "defines" differently. Often the implicit definitions used, reflected by what kind of courses the individuals teach under such titles, are very limited. Furthermore, a great number of variables may affect what type of literacy one is talking about—who the individuals are, the level of literacy required, the objectives of the program.

Computer literacy as a composite term is derived from the general term "literacy," as applied, among other areas, to being able to read and write in a competent fashion, being able to do essential arithmetic, and understanding science in a general sense. The implication is that these tools are needed for a reasonable level of survival and participation in modern society. If we extend the term to cover computer literacy, we should have a similar set of requirements. In all cases literacy implies the ability to *do* something—vocabulary is not enough.

My concern in this paper is for computer literacy as applicable to one group, teachers in elementary and secondary schools in the United States. We are concerned with teachers *as* teachers aiding students in the learning process. So we can focus on their use of the computer in their own classes. Nevertheless, we cannot neglect the wider issues of computer literacy with such a group. The subject of computer literacy for K through 12 teachers has received special attention through one of the subcommittees of the Association for Computing Machinery particularly concerned with computers in elementary and secondary education. The reports of that subcommittee deserve special attention in giving a variety of details, more than is possible with a brief paper such as this. The reader is referred to those papers.

THE CENTRAL PROBLEM

One of the most startling developments in education the past few years is that schools are purchasing small computers at a very rapid rate. The number in any one school is often small, but a study (Chambers and Bork) of fifty states indicated that over 90% of the districts responding to the survey (over 60%) claimed to have some computer capability at the present time. But less use it for instruction.

Because computers are rapidly

becoming widely available is not to say that the computers are well used in the schools. Often a school which purchases several personal computers, with considerable fanfare, discovers that there is little direct use of the machines when they arrive. The computer frequently becomes the personal possession of a relatively small clique of students and faculty. With such groups, game playing often turns out to be one of the major activities, or a few students learn simple programming techniques, often developing a set of bad programming habits.

We can confidently expect the rate of purchase of computers to accelerate in schools. As more personal computers are purchased for home use, there is more pressure from parents and students to have equivalent capabilities in schools. The major problem is, what are the teachers to *do* with these newly acquired computers?

Few teachers currently in the public school system have any deep acquaintance with computers. While a *few* excellent in-service and pre-service programs in certain parts of the country provide teachers with introductions to computers, these programs are few and far between. Teachers typically find that they get little or no good advice from local universities, because the university faculty are often even more backward than the schools in the use of the computer directly within the educational process. In most cases the vendors also are of little help. The pressure of vendors to sell their own particular equipment is the dominating force.

The problem is that of training a large number of teachers to make effective instructional use of the equipment that they will confront, the modern computer equipment of today and the immediate future. It is a national problem, one that should be met as soon as possible if we are to aid our teachers. For the teachers who will teach computing directly, the problem is less severe, as they have several sources available.

Typically the way of solving problems involving teacher training is with in-service and summer programs. Thus, many of the new curriculum developments in the 1960s led to workshops for teachers. But the prognosis for this approach, given past experience, is very poor. Not all teachers are close to institutions offering such training. Further, the amount of training available is often inadequate. For example, the programs available to elementary teachers in the "new mathematics" was quite insufficient to overcome their previous approaches and biases in the area. Hence, major curriculum developments failed because the teacher training activities were completely inadequate. Bold new approaches to aiding our teachers are needed to solve the problem of computer literacy for teachers.

THE COMPUTER AS A VEHICLE FOR COMPUTER LITERACY FOR TEACHERS

The key is that the *computer* itself provides a possible and feasible solution. The computer *is* an excellent learning device and can be used to aid teachers in learning as well as to aid students in learning. Interactive computer programs, plus problem-solving access to the computer, can provide a range of possibilities not attainable in any other way. The individual can be treated as an individual, with all of the features which distinguish that person from another one taken into account. Each person can proceed at his or her own pace. Furthermore, the learning experience can be an *active* one, with the learner a participant rather than a spectator.

Small personal computers of today can easily be made available in any school in the country as well as in various public institutions and learning institutions. Thus, a school district interested in acquiring computers could offer materials directly to their own teachers. Credit arrangements would be possible if desired. Thus, a new mode of teacher training is possible and feasible. And the computer material *could* be used in in-service courses also.

LITERACY DETAILS

To expand on the comments so far and move to the details of what computer literacy for teachers involves, I will discuss a number of specific areas that might be included in any program of this kind.

It should not be assumed that all teachers will need all aspects of this work. For example, while the material on designing computer-based learning materials would certainly be helpful pedagogically to teachers, whether they would or would not actually be involved in developing such materials, it is not

reasonable to expect that all teachers would develop these competencies. Nevertheless, the material to aid teachers should be available as part of any full program in computer literacy, because some teachers will want to pursue this direction. The needs of the individual teacher must be taken into account; a monolithic approach which assumes that all teachers will be given the same material will prove to be unsatisfactory.

Learning Theory Background

As we are addressing computer literacy for teachers, we should place the discussion in a context of *learning*. Hence, initial discussion of learning theories seems critical. One might like to believe that all teachers have this background; but many relevant approaches to learning, such as developmental psychology and cognitive psychology, are not by any means well known by teachers today. Therefore, some modules of this kind are important.

We would not expect to make teachers experts in this area, but rather to make them aware. A mixed presentation, looking at various approaches to learning, is desirable. Research relevant to computer use in education should be introduced.

Types of Computer Uses in Education

The emphasis is on the broad spectrum of ways the computer can be used in education, not ruling out *any* possibilities. We would stress the very different pedagogical roles which these different types play in learning. The teachers must see (that is, interact with) *many* examples of each such type of use, rather than viewing them in an abstract fashion. Some of this material would be area-dependent; thus, a mathematics teacher needs to focus on how the computer can be used in math courses. The Association for Computing Machinery work mentioned earlier discusses specific areas.

We would include both the problem-solving uses of the computer, where the computer is used as a tool to amplify intellect, and also tutorial and dialogue uses of the computer, with many different variants of each. Representative material from major projects should be represented in this panoramic perspective of types of computer use. Projections for the future are essential.

A goal will be to make teachers sensitive to the advantages and disadvantages of the computer as a learning medium. A comparison with other media is a reasonable approach. This discussion might well be extended to more general societal issues oriented to the computer.

Developing Computer-Based Learning Material

Although not all teachers will be developers of computer-based learning material, they will find it desirable to understand the process. Many teachers in the years ahead will participate in such development. So this should be an important component of a program for teachers. As an important component of

such an activity, teachers should be brought to an understanding of the advantages and disadvantages for learning of the computer medium.

There is not a single developmental strategy presently, so a discussion of this kind should show a variety of strategies. This section of the teacher training material should emphasize strategies that look to the future, toward a time where considerable material can be produced.

As an optional activity, it may be possible to get people to *produce* some small amount of computer-based learning material. This may be difficult to do in the environment that may be necessary in many places.

Structured Thinking and Programming

The recent work on both problem solving (with and without computers) and effective programming has indicated a variety of desirable strategies. These important strategies should be clearly understood by the teachers who are to use computers in the problem-solving mode with students. They are also important in the preparation of learning material to aid students to become better problem solvers.

Algorithms

The notion of an algorithm is still one that needs to be stressed and presented to the teacher, perhaps initially in noncomputer form. The notion of a rule for doing something and the ability to carry out that rule is an important intellectual concern.

Introduction to Programming

We need not make expert programmers out of teachers in a computer literacy program. But we should give them enough programming experience so that they can understand the *process* of programming and be able to *read* programs in an effective and powerful language. My bias as to language would be Pascal, although in the near future Ada may be an important competitor. There is something to be said for providing the possibility of several languages presented together; Logo, now on personal computers, is a good possibility for another language.

The choice of languages to use with teachers is an interesting one. There is no question that the most commonly used language at present is BASIC. But BASIC has many flaws as a beginning language. Recent speculation indicates that first language has a considerable effect on later programming. There are a number of features that one should look for in language design, even for beginners. These features are generally grouped under the name "structured programming."

Pascal is a desirable language as a beginning language. In this regard, it is comforting to note that Pascal is now available or soon to become available in almost all the small, inexpensive personal computers. Hence, its practicality for situations below the university level is rapidly increasing.

In aiding the teacher we must always be thinking ahead; the student will not be out of school for many years. Education is often guilty of teaching outmoded technologies. In this situation we can easily avoid this problem.

It should be emphasized that one would not want the teacher to see *all* aspects of a language. One of the beauties of a good computer language is there are capabilities one can "grow" into. Thus, in a language such as Pascal, concepts like pointers and records would probably not be necessary in this introduction.

The most desirable method of learning the language would be through examples. These examples should start at the beginning with the notion of structure, so that *procedures* should be one of the first concepts that the learner sees. An environment such as Turtle geometry might be a good beginning point. Experience in a number of different levels at Irvine has indicated that the "whole program" approach is very effective. That is, one does not start by expounding grammar, but starts by developing full programs, showing the grammar in connection with these developments. Structured programming ideas should be emphasized in such a development.

Teaching programming in an interactive environment such as suggested, where there may be no human teachers around, will be a challenge. But previous experience indicates it will be possible.

The areas indicated as necessary for teacher computer literacy are not complete. Other areas might well be added to the list. But they form a core program of this type. It will be noted that there is no emphasis on computer technology. This is not an accident.

CONCLUSIONS

In developing any new technology, it is important to bring the users of that technology to the realization of its *best* uses, not just its *possible* uses. Any technology can often have harmful uses, unthought-through activities that are carried out simply because they *can* be done. For example, the widespread advent of computer editors and word processing has led to much use of right justification in typewriterlike documents, without any thought as to whether this is a good or a bad thing. Readability research, and the views of very competent graphic designers, would in this case both agree that it is a poor choice.

It is a thesis of this paper that older modes of teacher training, based on in-service strategies, are inadequate for the problem at hand. There are simply too many teachers, and not remotely enough possibilities for training these teachers by conventional means. This is not to say that in specialized locations in-service training could not be important, just as it has been in the past. These materials would also be important in that environment, but they address the wider problem too. Very few schools of education in the country and also relatively few computer departments are willing or able to provide the in-service activities needed.

If the computer is to be widely used in education, we must aid teachers to attain a reasonable approach to educational computer use. The penalty we would pay, if the teachers do *not* develop such an approach, would be deterioration of our educational system. We cannot allow poor use of this powerful aid to learning.

The author has discussed these issues with a number of other people, particularly Robert Taylor, Richard Dennis, and James Poirot. Although I have benefited from these discussions, I do not want to attribute any of the flaws of this paper to my helpful colleagues.

December 1980

Don't Teach BASIC

ALFRED BORK

This column proposes that it is a mistake to teach BASIC. At least I claim that it is a mistake as a first language, and perhaps it is a mistake more generally. (Actually, I know of few examples where BASIC is taught as a second language, except for self-teaching.)

This anti-BASIC position will undoubtedly be viewed as heresy by many readers, as BASIC is a very commonly taught first language at the present time. In the first section I will comment on why I believe this is an important step to take at the present time. In the second section, I will comment on some possible objections to this position.

WHY SHOULDN'T WE TEACH BASIC?

When languages such as BASIC and FORTRAN were developed, there was little experience with programming, particularly for large, complex activities. However, this is no longer the case. Today we have much experience with writing elaborate programs. Our experience has led to a series of strategies which make it easier to write such programs with fewer errors, and easier to revise these programs. While not everyone is going to write complex programs, many people in the future will

be involved in this activity. Indeed, projections indicate that we will not have enough programmers, given our current ways of producing programmers, to meet this need.

The set of ideas that has evolved for good programming practice sometimes goes under the name of "structured programming." A variety of factors are involved, which I will not attempt to review. Components of software engineering also play a very important role.

BASIC, because it does not lead easily to structured programming, tends to develop poor programming habits, particularly as it is almost universally taught. These programming habits are very difficult for students to overcome later. We have not done students a service if we teach them fundamental ideas and ingrained ways of working which they later must destroy, particularly if these are the *first* ideas that they encounter in the area. It is difficult to correct such early habits. So BASIC hurts students in the long run, in spite of any short-run advantages (and, as will be seen, I claim that there are not really any short-range advantages either!).

We have seen many students at Irvine who have learned BASIC in high school or on their own who have considerable difficulty in the beginning programming courses. Our situation is not unique. For example, I have heard of very similar cases at the Air Force Academy in Colorado Springs. It is not easy to overcome some ingrained habits, particularly if they have been ingrained for a long time.

Another factor to be considered is the lack of standardization in existing BASICs. Although there is a BASIC standard underway, I do not see any widespread move of existing BASIC, or even newly developed BASICs, to conform to that standard. In fact, it seems extremely unusual that a standard for an existing language should depart so much from the current implementations of the language.

Finally, and perhaps the most critical point, *there are better languages for the student to begin with.* The languages in the ALGOL family, such as Pascal, do allow a natural approach to structured programming. They too are not always taught in this fashion, unfortunately, because often the textbooks are written by people with the same bad habits I referred to above! But the percentage is certainly much better; that is, more people learn to program in a satisfactory fashion with Pascal, for example, than with a language such as BASIC.

The coming likely importance of Ada is also an important factor to consider. If Ada becomes as widely used as seems likely, given the strong interest of the Department of Defense, it is likely to require a whole new generation of programmers to work on it. It is very hard to imagine that students brought up

on BASIC are likely to become good Ada programmers.

COMMENTS ON POSSIBLE OBJECTIONS

There are a number of comments which I feel are likely to be made about the position I have just taken. As I indicated, it certainly is not the common position; these views are likely to bring down the wrath of many BASIC users. I will consider some of the criticisms that may appear.

The first argument that is often made for BASIC is that it is common, particularly on small microcomputers. This is true. Most microcomputers have some version or other of BASIC. But these versions differ widely. As already indicated, BASIC is one of the least standardized languages around, with widely varying dialects. This is particularly true when one gets beyond the most elementary level.

But I do not feel that this is a good argument. If we always stuck with what was common in a particular time, a new and better idea would never be used. That is, we would never make any progress. Certainly, at one time FORTRAN was extremely common, when BASIC was first being introduced. The same argument could have been used at one time by FORTRAN users to persuade people not to study BASIC. Other languages, including Pascal, are increasingly available.

The second reason one often hears for teaching BASIC as a first language is the belief that BASIC is easy to teach. I believe that this is an old wive's tale, a position not supported by empirical evidence. As a teacher who has taught many different programming languages, it seems to me that for almost any language a reasonable subset is relatively easy to teach to beginners. The ease depends not so much on the language but on two quite different factors. One of these is the implementation. There are clearly some advantages in teaching an implementation which is based on an interpreter, rather than an implementation that is based on a compiler. Whether one has interpreters or compilers has little to do with the nature of the language in most cases, but only the nature of the implementation.

The second important factor in how rapidly beginners become acquainted with the language is the *method* in which the language is taught. Users can become familiar with the language in widely different amounts of time, depending on just how the language is introduced. Many methods of teaching languages, particularly those based on grammatical approaches, waste large amounts of student time, independent of the language being used. But this is a separate topic that cannot be adequately addressed here.

Perhaps the most important objection is the one I have left for last. It is often argued, correctly, that one *can* teach BASIC in a structured fashion. This can certainly be done to some extent. But the truth is that it is *almost never* done! One can find very few examples of teaching BASIC in this way. Certainly, in the commonly available books which students usually use in learning BASIC, one sees almost no teaching of BASIC in a structured fashion. There are some exceptions to this, but very few.

One cannot even introduce BASIC in a structured fashion with many BASICs; that is, one can achieve some aspects of structure with these BASICs, but not others. Many BASICs, for example, have no adequate procedures. The notion of teaching top-down programming without a powerful procedure concept is, it seems to me, ridiculous. An expression that says "GOSUB 982" is no substitution for an adequate procedure. A few BASICs do have adequate procedure mechanisms, such as some of the Digital BASICs. But many do not.

Another problem with many BASICs, which prevents them from being taught in a structured fashion, is the use of single letter or single letter plus number identifiers. Thus, one cannot give meaningful names to identifiers, and one teaches students to call identifiers by such names as X42, which have no meaning and which lead to great difficulty when one tries to revise the program at a later time.

FINAL CONCLUSIONS

I would certainly welcome any comments about these arguments. Perhaps I have missed some critical points. But it is important, particularly given the growing need for competent computer programmers in our society, to give some very careful thought to these issues. We are about to be flooded with new high school courses involving BASIC. There are some alternates to this. There is at least one quite good high school course, *Computer Power,* based on a variant of

Pascal, available from McGraw-Hill. So perhaps there are some rays of hope in what appears to be a generally dark night.

April 1982

Informatics for Everyone: A Proposed Curriculum for Math, Science, and Engineering Students

ALFRED BORK

The following outline suggests a future computer literacy program for students who intend to be science, mathematics, or engineering majors.

The theme of Informatics for Everyone is an interesting one, implying that computer education is important for everyone now, and that it will become increasingly important as we move into the next few years. In the United States the term "computer literacy" is sometimes used in this sense.

This conference is restricted to the university. My assignment is further restricted to mathematics, science, and engineering majors. It should be understood that the needs for computer literacy are dependent on the subject area involved; people coming from different application areas need to know different things about the computer in order to carry out their jobs reasonably.

I interpreted my charge for this talk in a literal sense. That is, I asked what education about computers should a scientist (please consider this term to include mathematics and engineering) receive? But I found that when I considered this problem for the university only, I had great difficulty;

depending on what background I assumed in pre-university education, different things were required at the university level. Hence I have chosen to present in this paper a curriculum that begins with a five- or six-year-old child, and carries this child through the university. Although I am considering the education of the scientist, in the early stages of education we do not know the eventual career of the student. So the curriculum I am suggesting there could be considered as a *general* approach to computer literacy for all children.

As will be noted, some of the components of this curriculum already exist, or are under development. Others could be developed in only a few years. Nothing suggested here would be possible only in the distant future. In fact, the curriculum I suggest would probably not be adequate for more than a ten-year period. By that time we can expect the computer to have changed greatly the contents of our traditional courses, because of the powerful new intellectual tools available for society; it is very difficult to predict all these changes at the present time.

GENERAL IDEAS

A number of principles and themes govern the curriculum as presented in this discussion. In this section I mention these briefly.

1. I assume that computers will be much more widely used in learning than at the present time. Further, this use will not be monolithic, but will reflect many different ways of using the computer in education. A corollary to this is that I expect computers to be increasingly available in schools and universities during this time, quickly approaching the level where every student has his or her own computer, for home as well as school use.

2. I shall assume that during this ten-year period the school and the university will still be the main arenas for learning. This assumption may well not be accurate if we look more than ten years in the future. Even during the ten-year period we may see, particularly toward the end, some shift of certain educational functions from the school or university to the home; such institutions as the Open University in the United Kingdom already indicate the possibilities.

3. Mastery learning approaches, in the sense described by Benjamin Bloom and his colleagues, will become more common in education. The emphasis will be on *all* students learning *everything* well. We will not allow the student to leave a topic until it has been demonstrated that the student is fully familiar with the topic, can perform at the mastery level. Alternate learning approaches will be available in all areas, particularly for students who have had difficulty with the original approach.

4. Different students may move through the material at different rates. The fixed pacing characteristic of most of our current learning environments will no longer be necessary, given the flexibility of the computer. Further, insistence on mastery will mean that some students will take longer to learn than other students. For example, a student in a physics course may need to spend some time filling in missing mathematical information; variable pacing allows for such a possibility.

5. Increasing attention will be given to increasing the insight and intuition of the students. We currently are much better at teaching information and techniques, but increasingly the student of the future will need to understand the area in an intuitive sense. A key factor is providing experiences for students that are relevant to an area to be studied.

6. In a similar vein the new education will emphasize approximation far more than is done at present. In the computer age it will become increasingly less important to be able to carry out long division, or addition of fractions, but it will be

very important to know if the result obtained from a calculator or a computer is reasonable.

7. Powerful intellectual tools will be introduced where they are appropriate.

8. Much of the learning that takes place directly at the computer will occur in groups of two or three students working together. Thus peer learning will be an important part of the learning activities.

THE PROPOSED CURRICULUM

As the reader will see, the curriculum presented is little more than an outline. I use the grade designations common in the United States, as they are the ones that are familiar to me. Readers should consider the outline as incomplete, but furnishing a basis for further discussion.

Grade 0—Preschool

The most important topics of early education are reading, writing, and arithmetic. Full computer-based approaches to these topics are an essential beginning for my new curriculum.

An impressive but inadequately publicized introductory writing and reading course is currently under development, with very sizable support from IBM. The developer is John Henry Martin, and the course is called Writing to Read. The premise is that young children, provided with reasonable tools, can learn to type what they can say, and can learn to read what they type. A phonetic system is taught, using digitized voice and attractive color graphics. The course had been tested with 25,000 students, in both preschool and first grade.

To the best of my knowledge no similar course for arithmetic is under development. Currently only fragments are available, often only imitations of the drill and practice material developed many years ago by Patrick Suppes. But such material could be developed, based on our present knowledge.

Some interesting, but not extensive, material available from The Learning Company indicates possibilities for general intellectual training, even at an early age.

Grades One Through Six

The focus on reading and writing would continue for the remainder of the primary school. Word processing, with specially designed word processing systems that would "grow" with the student, would be increasingly the focus of this activity. Computer aids would also assist with the prewriting and postwriting activities. Much of this material remains to be developed.

The arithmetic material already described would also continue. As suggested, approximation and intuition would receive major attention.

Grades Three Through Eight

The arithmetic-mathematics context would be employed to introduce the student to powerful intellectual tools for learning mathematics, such as Logo and Boxer (now under development at MIT as a successor to Logo). Although these languages are partially available, their successful use will demand, I believe, considerable curriculum development. We can also expect the invention of other powerful tools for learning about mathematics.

Learning about science should also begin during this period. The emphasis should not be on vocabulary, as is so often the case in teaching science to young children, but rather should focus, implicitly, on the deep issues concerning the nature of science. Thus such questions as the nature of scientific theories, the process of discovering scientific theories, the empirical basis of science, and the issue of correct and incorrect theories, should be the focus.

Some of the necessary science material has already been developed by my group, the Educational Technology Center at the University of California, Irvine. These interactive graphic computer-based learning modules are each about two hours in length for the average student; about twelve modules are available. The modules have been extensively tested and revised, not only in schools at a variety of levels, but also in public libraries and science museums. The general strategy is to place students in an environment in which they must behave like a scientist or engineer, gathering evidence, forming hypotheses, testing hypotheses, and revising these tentative theories. Much help is provided. Testing in the library assures that the units work well with a wide range of users, and assures that they are motivationally strong, as we can easily spot the places where many people leave and then improve these spots.

Grades Nine Through Twelve

Computer-based learning in mathematics would continue, using intellectual tools as appropriate. Coverage would include algebra, trigonometry, and calculus; most students in most curricula would take all of this. As with the other work in mathematics, intuition would be stressed. All of this material is yet to be developed.

Grade nine is also about the right place to begin the formal study of programming. Our future student of science is likely to need to learn to program, but I doubt that all secondary students need this course. The programming activities would emphasize modern programming and problem-solving philosophy, using a structured language such as Pascal or Modula 2. The proposed new Advanced Placement course suggested in the United States might be a basis for the programming activity.

It seems unlikely that most secondary schools will be able to attract, or hold, teachers who are fully qualified to teach this course. Hence the curriculum material developed must be entirely usable by itself, without human aid. Such a course does not yet exist, but it is within our capabilities to develop it. It might occupy several years, and it probably should be integrated within the science and mathematics courses also taken during secondary school.

In addition to using the growing student programming skills in the physics, mathematics, and biology courses, these courses need to be completely redesigned in other ways to take into account the new technology. Graphic capabilities should be widely and routinely used in these courses. Both computer-based learning sequences and intellectual tools should be widely used. Thus in physics the course should use simulation languages such as DYNAMO; this course should also include a brief introduction to numerical methods, again in applications contexts.

Finally, it is important that the student in secondary school begin to be aware of the social and ethical consequences of the computer. Of all the development suggested by this paper, this may be the most difficult to accomplish well; our current educational systems around the world are seldom successful in working in areas where values are critical. This material should be future-oriented.

University—General Courses

I should expect that all the university courses taken by our science (and mathematics and technology) students would use computers in many different ways.

As an example of a course of this type already in existence, I shall describe briefly the introductory physics course developed, and taught for about six years, at the Educational Technology Center. This mastery-based introductory mechanics, 10 weeks, is based on 27 on-line exams; students have a choice of content, so each takes about 15 different exams. An exam is usually taken several times; students cannot continue to the next unit until they complete the exam more or less perfectly. We never give the

same exam twice. The exams contain a large amount of direct aid for the students, and they are often very perceptive in identifying a student error and giving immediate relevant aid. In one of the versions of the course the student is also involved in programming as a method to solve $F = ma$ problems. An intuition-building module, with associated workbooks, is also available.

Courses of this kind could be developed throughout the curriculum. Computer uses important in the sciences should be introduced as early as possible to the student, when appropriate.

University—Special Courses

In addition to the courses already present in the curriculum, a number of new courses are needed for our newly computer-literate student.

Relatively early in the curriculum the student should have a numerical analysis course, building on the experiences of the secondary course and of the subject-area courses which used numerical analysis. It should emphasize modern methods, including extensive graphics and the use of the latest packages for calculation.

We also need a follow-up course to the earlier one on social and ethical consequences of computers. The thrust of the activities would be similar to the earlier ones, but at a more advanced level.

Another critical course, seldom taken today by the students I am considering, is software engineering. An interesting practical course of this type is now under development at the Open University.

In addition to these courses, intended

for all science, mathematics, and engineering students, some courses might be particular to the area involved. Thus we would expect engineering students to take a CAD/CAM course. And the advanced student should use the computer in research in the area, using the latest computer-based techniques.

DISCUSSION

Wolbers: How do the old Suppes programs compare with what you are proposing here? And do you deal with questions of cross-cultural differences?

Bork: The drill and practice programs developed by Suppes have been very influential and are the only ones to have actually made money! They have been widely criticized, yet have been shown to be effective. At the same time, transferring the Suppes materials outside North America has proved difficult. The most extensive experiment was in Glasgow: it was eventually stopped, but that was probably due to political changes in the education system. In the case of reading and writing, the early computer-based attempts were feeble compared with what we do now— although there is still no agreement on the best way to teach reading and writing. Whether these programs can translate to other cultures I am not sure.

Van der Mast: As the schools introduce more and more teaching in informatics, do you predict that

university programs will need to change?

Bork: Yes; my proposal may work for the next 10 years. And of course the computer will become more common in the home. Perhaps there will be no schools at all in 10 years!

Fiedler: You propose informatics for everyone. Is there in fact a common base of theory that would enable us to develop an informatics curriculum for all students?

Bork: My proposed curriculum is common only to a certain extent, largely the younger years. For example, at the secondary school level I do not recommend teaching programming to all students. However all students *should* be exposed to social and ethical questions. There are some things that it is not even necessary to teach at all—for example, the vocabulary of informatics, which students will pick up themselves as needed. I should also stress that 90% of my proposed curriculum can be taught within the disciplines themselves.

Fiedler: Could I restate my question: is it desirable to teach general computer literacy at the university, and is that what your program represents?

Bork: Depending on your definition of computer literacy, yes, I could regard this as a computer literacy curriculum. But it could need to become increasingly specialized as you go upward, relating more closely to the needs of the discipline or profession.

three

SCIENTIFIC REASONING

Science Literacy in the Public Library—*Batteries and Bulbs*

ARNOLD ARONS
Department of Physics
University of Washington
Seattle, Washington

ALFRED BORK, STEPHEN FRANKLIN, BARRY L. KURTZ
Educational Technology Center
University of California
Irvine, California

FRANCIS COLLEA
Department of Science Education
California State University
Fullerton, California

The Educational Technology Center at the University of California, Irvine, conducted a project in science literacy for public environments by focusing on the public library. These computer-based modules run on personal computers, intended for a wide variety of environments and a wide audience. These modules attempt to tackle deep problems with regard to what science is all about, what a scientific theory is, how theories are developed, how theories are verified, how theories are modified, and the role of measurement. Although public environments are the initial focus, we believe that the materials will be very useful in school programs at a wide variety of levels and eventually can be distributed for the home personal computer market.

This paper reports in detail on one of the programs developed for this project.

BATTERIES AND BULBS

A number of programs at levels varying from primary school through university have used a simple physical situation, the lighting of a flashlight bulb using batteries and wires, to introduce to students the notion of a model. The Elementary Science Study (ESS) material is an example.[1] It has also been used, as indicated, in other programs.

This material is based on guided discovery. The student is not *told* the necessary information, as in typical lectures or textbooks. Rather, with a good teacher in the classroom, the student works by discovering, while guided and moderated by the teacher. One doesn't simply turn the student loose with the apparatus and expect major laws of science to be developed (this is clearly impractical). The teacher acts as a guide, a facilitator, and a helper.

The *Batteries and Bulbs* material does not intend to teach people simple information about batteries and bulbs or information about the behavior of electrical circuits. The aim is *not* to introduce the important terminology in the area, although such vocabulary does eventually get introduced. Rather, the module tries to develop the notion of a *scientific model* as the way of dealing with a range of phenomena. When used correctly, the existing material emphasizes the role of experimentation, the necessity of forming hypotheses and building models, the central role of using models to make predictions, and the attempts to verify predictions through experimentation, modifying the models or constructing new ones.

The difficulty with discovery or inquiry-mode materials of this kind is that they often require a teacher who understands the processes of science and is willing (and able) to let each student progress at individual rates towards these ideas. The sad fact is, however, that not all teachers can proceed in such a fashion.

Implementing many of the new and excellent science curricula at levels from kindergarten through the university is difficult for traditional teachers. Changing the behavior of an entire group of science teachers is extremely difficult, and teacher training has been one of the major problems with the new curriculum projects. These new materials, often excellent, do not reach their objectives in

many classrooms. Although these objectives are clearly explained in teacher materials, many teachers simply do not sufficiently understand the processes of science to use the materials effectively. In addition, to devote enough time to *each* student is often difficult or impossible. Further, teachers are reluctant to follow an approach that appears to mean additional work on their part.

Furthermore, if many people who are already through the school system are to be brought to a better understanding of the nature of science, they must have other educational strategies available to them. The problems of adult education are very much on our minds in the present project. We believe it wise to build on existing experiences. We chose batteries and bulbs because there has been so much thought put into the development of these materials. But we believe that we can bring these materials to a much wider audience, and we can successfully solve the problem of teachers who are not trained for the necessary approaches.

FUNDAMENTAL IDEAS DEVELOPED

The materials do *not* have as their primary purpose the development of terminology or concepts. Nevertheless, the notion of *how* concepts are developed within science is an important issue in scientific literacy, and so is given attention.

In the *Batteries and Bulbs* module, *current* and *resistance* are major concepts.

In following recent strategies at the Educational Technology Center, we do not introduce these terms immediately. We avoid the use of vocabulary, contrary to much of the teaching of science in American schools, until a sound and demonstrated *need* for the terminology has been established in the student's mind. That is, the concept should not appear until the notions underlying it have already been developed and shown to lead to useful consequences.

In introducing the concepts of current and resistance, we therefore proceed very slowly with the student, interacting in an experience-gathering environment. These concepts themselves are introduced only in a qualitative situation and are never assigned any numerical value within this program. Thus, such issues as units never play a role. The currents are compared; students are brought to the point where they can empirically say that the current in one situation is greater than the current in another situation. This comparison is based on the brightness of light bulbs. Four levels of brightness are sufficient—full, medium, low, and off.

Resistance is also developed in the same qualitative manner, without numbers. Students do learn that the resistance of two bulbs in a series will be greater than the resistance of a single bulb. Furthermore, they see several different types of wires, such as copper wire and nichrome wire, and study them from the standpoint of resistance.

The model of an electrical circuit is gradually introduced, although again with little emphasis on terminology. We believe, as already indicated, that one of the major problems with learning about science is the extensive dependence on vocabulary.

"REAL" VERSUS "SIMULATED" EQUIPMENT

One of the interesting issues considered in developing this material is whether the student should have the actual equipment—batteries, bulbs, and wires—available or whether equipment should be simulated within the computer program. We have used a variety of tactics in different modules developed recently in the Educational Technology Center. One tactic is to use equipment along with computer material. Another module under development for junior high science employs a Whirlybird out of the Science Curriculum Improvement Studies material.

However, with batteries and bulbs the decision was that we would *not* use the physical apparatus, although we would mention it within the program and suggest users experiment on their own. Several members of the development team were somewhat apprehensive about this choice. We see both advantages and disadvantages in our approach. Many science teachers consider it important to use the actual equipment to deal as closely as possible with the phenomena. On the other hand, for the purposes of this particular module, the somewhat idealized equipment that we supply within the program had some advantages. Thus, we did not need to deal with the problem that not all batteries are the same, not all bulbs are the same, etc. Occasionally when the actual equipment is used with students, one has to put in spurious discussions explaining away some of the things that happen. With the apparatus we must assure identical bulbs and equally charged batteries.

Although we are not initially conducting an experimental test on actual versus simulated equipment, we hope that the batteries and bulbs unit may allow further research into this problem of equipment in connection with scientific education. We intend to encourage experimental studies comparing computer materials without equipment, computer materials with equipment, and traditional instruction (no computer) with equipment. Many scientists have strong and emotional views on this issue. The research literature seems to have little in the way of careful studies.

STRUCTURE OF THE SEQUENCE

Since this and the other materials in this particular project are designed for public environments in situations in which no assistance is available, we decided that the materials should be broken into a series of quite small modules. The basic notion of these small modules was that students may not have a long attention span for any one use, but that one could expect over a period of time return visits for some students who become interested in the material. Students can work

through as much material as they are comfortable with in a single session. The modularity of the dialogue is an important issue.

The modules are ten or fifteen minutes in length for the average student. However, as with any good computer-based learning material, we expect this time to vary considerably from student to student. The modules in the batteries and bulbs sequence are as follows:

Module 1—Light the Bulb

Module 2—Battery and Bulb
                    Arrangements

Module 3—Other Things
                    in the Circuit

Module 4—A Scientific Model
                    of a Circuit

Module 5—Two Bulbs

Module 6—Obstructing Current

Module 7—Current Paths

Module 8—Multiple Paths

Module 9—Playing with Circuits

The student will initially see the program in what is called the "attract mode." This mode, used in all the materials in this project, lures passersby in the public library into sitting down and trying the program. Because of the general interest people have in computers, we believe that this will be relatively easy. The programs must appear nonthreatening, and they must not have any large number of operating details before getting into the materials. The attract modes in these programs are often made from interesting visual materials within the program.

When the student does sit down and follows the direction (on the screen in the attract mode) to press a key, a map of the modules available appears. The student uses a built-in pointing device to indicate where within the structure he or she would like to start. We would urge beginners to start at the beginning. But, since this is a free environment, there is no assurance that they will do so.

As already indicated, the materials must be entirely self-contained. We do not expect the librarians to spend time aiding students. Furthermore, if the material is used in other environments, there may not even be any knowledgeable people present. So the dialogue must make certain that the students can use the equipment.

A number of strategies are being used. First, we make extensive use of timed "reads." That is, if the student has not replied to a question or a prompt after a given period of time, the program assumes control and gives the student a message. In early parts of the program, these may simply be encouraging input or telling the student what is expected, such as pressing Return when the input is complete. Our input software, developed in our NSF CAUSE project, distinguishes between someone who is not typing at all and someone who has typed something but has not pressed the return key. Furthermore, the student who is actively typing, even though there is a sizable time before typing began, will not be timed out, but will be allowed to continue typing. All of these are simple human engineering strategies used in the Educational Technology Center at Irvine for some time.

There is also a mechanism of assuring that when a student leaves a display, the program will eventually return to the attract mode to await another user. Note that the machine is always on and that no program needs to be loaded by the user.

PRODUCTION PROCESS

These materials were produced by the process which has been used for all recent materials within the Educational Technology Center. One of the major interests in the center has been to develop a reasonable production strategy, one that can be extended eventually to future needs for large-scale production. This process has been described in other papers associated with the Center.[2] The first stage was the pedagogical development stage, the full specification of the script which tells everything about how the program is to behave with the user. The principal pedagogical developers were Arnold Arons, Alfred Bork, and Barry Kurtz. Francis Collea and Stephen Franklin also contributed valuable advice and assistance, particularly in the early stages of the development. Development at this stage ook approximately one week, with the authors developing the material collectively.

As with all of our activities, we concentrate at this stage on the instructional issues; programming issues are rarely considered. The group worked together, rather than fragmenting into several different groups. We argue that we produce much superior material with several people working together than any one person does individually.

The next stage involves the actual development of the running computer materials. With the batteries and bulbs modules, the principal programmers involved were Mark Gugan, Adam Beneschan, James Zarbock, and Michael Potter. We work within the UCSD Pascal system, supplemented with additional software tools developed at the Educational Technology Center. The programmers may discover some difficulties or areas overlooked by the pedagogical developers.

The computer on which the development took place is a Terak 8510/a. We used the Terak for the initial testing phase, but we plan to deliver the materials on a variety of small personal computers. We believe it increasingly important to distinguish between hardware needed for development and hardware needed for delivery. If the material is developed with reasonable strategies, moving it to new delivery machines does not produce any tremendous difficulties.

After the materials are running, much additional examination of them goes on by both the programmers and the authors. Other people at the Educational Technology Center look at these materials and offer advice. Arnold Arons, in a return visit, made a detailed study of the unit with Barry Kurtz and the suggested changes are now being implemented.

At this stage in the process all the testing has been informal internal testing. The next stage is that of moving to the target population.

The follow-up stages involve gathering information during this initial process of testing on the target audience and reworking the dialogues based on this information. Sometimes several cycles are necessary for this.

We can next proceed to larger testing. That step is not planned within the present project. Rather, we believe that it is better for materials to be used for several years and to have reached a stable form before summative evaluation. Our main aim is developing greater scientific literacy in a wide group of people in the general population. Hence, any final testing must look carefully into this particular issue.

January 1981

REFERENCES

1. *Elementary Science Study—Batteries and Bulbs,* Webster Division, McGraw-Hill Book Company; Arons, A., *The Various Languages,* Oxford, 1977, Chapter 9; Arons, A., "Phenomology and Logical Reasoning in Introductory Physics Courses," *American Journal of Physics* (in press).
2. Bork, A., Educational Technology Center at the University of California, Irvine.

A Computer-Based Discovery Module in Optics

ALFRED BORK
Educational Technology Center
University of California
Irvine, California

ARTHUR LUEHRMANN
Computer Literacy
Berkeley, California

BARRY KURTZ
Department of Mathematics
California State University
San Francisco, California

VICTOR JACKSON
Lawrence Hall of Science
University of California
Berkeley, California

Abstract: *This paper describes a computer-based learning module developed for the Educational Technology Center at the University of California, Irvine, and the Lawrence Hall of Science, University of California, Berkeley. The program was supported by a National Science Foundation Development in Science Education grant at the Lawrence Hall of Science and by the Fund for the Improvement of Postsecondary Education, Department of Education, at the Educational Technology Center.*

INTRODUCTION

The optics program described is a discovery module, allowing its users to discover the law of reflection associated with mirrors. It is the product of two projects. One of these projects was a scientific literacy project of the Educational Technology Center at the University of California, Irvine. This project has developed a series of modules to lead a wide range of users to a better understanding of the nature of scientific activities. The initial target environment for these modules is the public library. Additional information about other modules is available on request.[1]

Similarly, a DISE grant to the Lawrence Hall of Science was given to investigate the use of computers within science museum exhibits. A number of projects were undertaken. The Hall of Science already had two exhibits concerning optics. The present material was intended to be used with these exhibits, but to function independently of the other exhibits. The initial intention was to use this program at the Lawrence Hall of Science with a specially designed, touch-sensitive keyboard, with only a few areas to press. This influenced the design of the program, as will be seen. However, the special keyboard was not built, and instead the program now runs on standard personal computers.

The subject area of the program is, as indicated, the law of reflection in optics. The attempt is to have users—either students or visitors to museums and libraries—discover this law in a way resembling that in which a scientist might proceed. Thus, the emphasis is on gathering evidence, developing hypotheses relating to this evidence, making predictions on the basis of these hypotheses, checking these predictions experimentally, and then forming new hypotheses.

OUTLINE OF THE PROGRAM

The program takes about one hour for an average user. However, as with any examples of computer-based learning material, this time can vary greatly.

The program begins with an experiential capability, allowing the student to gather some relevant experience. At first, this capability is used with no theoretical background. The student is supplied with a flashlight, a mirror, and a target. The student cannot shine the flashlight directly on the target, because a wall is in the way. The assigned task is to bounce the light off the mirror and hit the target. The student can turn the flashlight with two keys on the computer keyboard. The student can also press the F key to make the flashlight flash. Since the program is to be used without any human aid, the user is first taught to use these facilities, and then is asked to shine the flashlight on the target.

At first this is done as a game, with no help or theory behind the game. The student builds up some background of experience in this situation. The program gives a variety of feedback, including information about how many times it takes the student to hit the target in various situations.

The student is then encouraged to develop a rule which will tell how to hit the target. At this point, the program to some extent misleads the student. The early cases are picked in such a way that there are some obvious rules that do not work as new cases are tried. The object is to illustrate that a scientist does not necessarily find the correct hypothesis initially, an important lesson in thinking about how the scientist works. We go through several stages of such "bad" rules, in each case showing that when new evidence is gained the rule no longer gives the right result. For each rule developed, the student is led to make predictions on the basis of the rule.

One consideration along the way is an

investigation of which factors appear to affect the hitting of the target. The student is asked to investigate many different possible factors before ending up with a reasonable set of factors.

The student finally attains the law of reflection, and so has a rule which works in all the cases that can be tried. But again the tentative nature of scientific knowledge is stressed.

INPUT FACILITIES

As indicated, it was initially intended that a specially designed touch-sensitive pad would be developed for this keyboard. The technology for such a pad is well known. For example, it is widely used in the computer systems at Sesame Place. However, because of funding and timing problems, such a pad was not built. But because the pad was intended, the program had a special input mode. Each input to the computer is with a single character. Thus, to flash the flashlight, the student presses the button F. Only about eight different commands are used in this one-keystroke fashion.

This is contrasted greatly with other computer-based learning programs at the Educational Technology Center. In all the other programs developed at Irvine, a free-form English is used for input. We pride ourselves in being able to recognize a wide range of input forms from the students, in spite of the fact that the computer techniques used for this recognition are generally not elaborate. But the present program uses only single keystrokes at each input.

Like our other programs developed at Irvine, the inputs are timed. That is, if the student does not respond in a given period of time, he or she will be prompted in ways dependent on the situation involved. Thus, in the early stages when we are training the student to use the facilities, we respond quickly when the student is not doing anything to encourage further use. The general idea is that the student does not necessarily need to be told things, so we use timing to find out when students need additional information.

One aspect of timing in this and other programs developed at Irvine is that after a long delay, with suitable querying of the student, the program will return to the beginning. Thus, when the component is used in a museum environment or in a public library environment (in both cases unattended), the program will return to the beginning when the student leaves the computer to prepare for another student.

DEVELOPMENT

The initial pedagogical specification of the program came in a three-day session in one of the authors' mountain house in Idyllwild, California. Additional pedagogical specification was carried out in both Irvine and Berkeley.

The program was prepared by student programmers in the Educational Technology Center at Irvine, using the

UCSD Pascal system and the various auxiliary software developed at Irvine.[2] Initially the material was developed on the Terak 8510/a system.

We have made commercial arrangements for the availability of this and other material developed at the Educational Technology Center.

January 7, 1982

REFERENCES

1. Newsletter available from the Educational Technology Center.
2. Textport System Description, 1980; The Graphport System, A. Milne, M. Katz, S. Franklin, July 1980.

Computer-Based Learning Units for Science and Math for Secondary Schools

ALFRED BORK, AUGUSTO CHIOCCARIELLO, WERNER FEIBEL, STEPHEN FRANKLIN, BARRY KURTZ, DAVID TROWBRIDGE, RUTH VON BLUM

Educational Technology Center Information and Computer Science, University of California, Irvine, California

This paper describes a development, over approximately five years, of a highly interactive graphic set of computer-based learning materials, primarily focusing on middle school and high school, and concerned with science topics, with a few mathematics issues included. The material was developed in two separate projects, one supported by the National Science Foundation, and one supported by the Fund for the Improvement of Postsecondary Education.

The materials, although probably most useful in secondary schools, have been tested with a wide range of users. Thus we believe that most of these modules will be usable in adult education situations too.

The general focus is on scientific activity, and on placing students in environments in which they must *behave like scientists*. These environments are friendly and helpful and do not allow a student to flounder forever. They offer specific help for students in trouble. The materials generally are in a mode which might be described as a "discovery" approach, but not all sections follow this approach.

While some of these materials have been previously described in papers from the Educational Technology Center at the University of California, Irvine, no complete description is currently in the literature. As the two projects are now complete, and as we are involved in marketing possibilities, it seems desirable to offer such a description.

These interactive units are, as a group, unique. We argue that few other examples of computer-based learning materials demonstrate more fully effective learning use of the computer, particularly the personal computer.

INTENDED ENVIRONMENTS

As already mentioned, these science and mathematics learning aids, while focusing on secondary schools, are intended for a wide range of types of usage. The present section describes some of that usage.

We have also tested the units, particularly in formative evaluation stages followed by improvement, in a number of environments already, including schools, at several levels, and in libraries. Testing in public libraries has been particularly helpful, enabling us to improve motivational aspects of the materials for a very wide audience.

The individual modules are designed to be self-standing. In a sense they are like interactive books for learning, assuming the student has no other learning modes available. They do not require any previous acquaintance with computers, any "computer literacy" background. Thus they will even tell students to press return if necessary, after entering an answer, but *not* repeat this phrase over and over for someone who is already familiar with it, and therefore bored with hearing it.

Because these materials are self-contained, as just indicated, they can be used both in environments where teachers are present, such as the typical school environment, and in environments where there are no teachers, such as public libraries or homes. They are intended to be used without any external "documentation" such as student manuals, books, or teacher guides. All the necessary steps to proceed are contained within the computer dialogues themselves. Students are not assumed to have previous computer experience.

FORMAT

Each of these computer-based learning modules is, for average student use, approximately one to two hours in length. Although some variation occurs, many of the modules will take most students about one and one-half hours. Individual students, because of their own different rate of progress, will move faster or slower through the material. The approach individualizes learning for each student.

The major learning units are broken up into smaller submodules, usually lasting about 10–15 minutes. The programs totally contain about 20 hours of highly interactive graphic computer-based learning material. As indicated several projects were involved, funded by the National Science Foundation and by the Fund for the Improvement of Postsecondary Education. Total funding was about $400,000. Some of this funding was, however, involved in building up the necessary underlying software, and so should not be attributed directly to the development of the dialogues themselves.

The materials are coded in UCDS Pascal, using underlying software and screen design principles developed at the Educational Technology Center. This software is used in all of our materials. In a typical two-hour module approximately 10,000 to 15,000 lines of Pascal code are involved. This figure is somewhat misleading as compared with ordinary code figures, as computer-based learning programs contain a relatively high proportion of textual material. Strategies used for this and other products from the Educational Technology Center are described in our literature. Full references are available upon request.

The remainder of this paper consists of brief descriptions of each of the modules involved. These modules are all available for inspection. We stress that we are not describing hypothetical material here, but we are describing developed and tested modules.

DESCRIPTION OF MODULES

Batteries and Bulbs

The student conducts an empirical investigation of electric circuits using batteries, bulbs, and wires simulated on the computer. Concepts of current, circuit, resistance, and parallel and series arrangements are developed in a qualitative fashion. Technical terminology is not introduced until after the student has developed some intuition into the behavior of current electricity.

Patterns

Based on Conway's game of Life, this module emphasizes the development of rules from experimental data. The student is the chief scientist on a space expedition and observes changing patterns on the surface of a strange planet. The goal is to develop rules for the appearance and disappearance of the patterns based on careful observations of evolving patterns.

Families

In this module, the student, behaving like a scientist, performs experiments, collecting evidence and building a simple (Mendelian) model of genetic

inheritance. The extraterrestrial creatures are studied to determine their attributes, how to predict whether they will mate with each other, and what rules govern the characteristics of their offspring.

Distance

The module emphasizes the role of measurement in science. The initial activity involves simple measurements of distances by students. Concepts of experimental error, averages, scaling, and measurement spread are developed from the data obtained by measurements. Alternative methods for measuring distance, such as timing the sound of voices or thunder, are illustrated using simulations.

Speed

A rich environment, containing balls projected from spring launchers, tunnels to partially hide the motions, scales of position, and digital clocks, is used to develop conceptual understanding of velocity in both physical and mathematical terms. Students observe, compare, and predict the motion of objects. The first three activities are qualitative, focusing on discrimination among the variables of position, distance, time, duration, and speed. The next two activities involve quantitative measurements, and calculation of the ratio distance/time.

Crystals

This module provides a "laboratory" for measuring properties such as mass, volume, and density of some mysterious crystals obtained during a space mission. The student performs simulated experiments to obtain data on the crystals. The goal is to identify three crystals which consist of the same material. A major objective is to develop an understanding of the ratio mass/volume. A second objective is to develop the ability to discriminate between observations and inferences.

Graphs

The *Graphs* module introduces elementary concepts of drawing and reading graphs with one and two coordinate axes. The programs provide highly interactive tools for constructing graphs. Students use arrow keys on the keyboard to point to objects on the screen, and move them to appropriate points on axes of histograms and graphs. All activities begin with concrete activities and then develop more abstract notions of graphic representation. The concept of slope for straight line graphs is introduced and properties of non-linear graphs are touched upon.

Shapes

This module begins with classification of objects according to their attributes. The next activities introduce properties of triangles and lead students to a definition of a triangle as a closed figure having exactly three straight sides. Later activities allow students to explore the relationships between sides and angles in triangles using simple animation. The

terms right, acute, obtuse, scalene, isosceles, and equilateral are introduced.

Whirlybird

The *Whirlybird* program is designed to be used along with a piece of physical equipment, the Whirlybird of the SCIS elementary school science curriculum. The student is required to put together the devices, perform some experiments, and enter data into the computer. The program conducts a dialogue with students, encouraging them to develop skills of identifying and controlling variables, and to construct a model system to meet a given specification.

Area

The student moves from an intuitive notion of area to a precise operational definition, the number of squares which cover a given figure. Extensive practice is available for those students having trouble applying the concept; students who grasp the idea more quickly go through the material more directly. Later activities connect the idea of counting squares with the common formulae for parallelograms and triangles.

Heat

The student is engaged in a number of thought experiments about familiar experiences with heat (reading thermometers, observing temperature changes, mixing hot and cold water, melting ice, and boiling water). These exercises guide the student towards an understanding of the difference between the concepts of heat and temperature. The program has a conversational tone and allows free and unconstrained input.

Reflections

Simple animation provides the student with a moveable flashlight, a plane mirror, an obstructing wall, and a target. The task is to strike the target with a beam of light by bouncing it off a mirror. The program guides the student step by step through acquiring evidence, considering alternative explanations, and constructing and refining hypotheses to explain the observations. Data obtained from variants of this task are used to either support or refute various models of reflection which are proposed.

July 30, 1984

Observation and Inference: A Computer-Based Learning Module

ALFRED BORK, DAVID TROWBRIDGE
Educational Technology Center, University of California, Irvine

ARNOLD ARONS
Department of Physics, University of Washington, Seattle

Abstract: *This paper reviews a computer dialogue to teach the distinction between observation and inference. It is a self-contained program designed to work with a wide range of students.*

An important distinction in undertaking the nature of scientific knowledge is that between what is observed, seen directly, and that which is inferred from the observed evidence. While this distinction is, like all human distinctions, not absolute, it is nevertheless extremely useful in understanding the nature of scientific information. It might also be considered an important intellectual tool, one we want to bring to students at as young an age as possible in order to enhance intellectual development.

Experience shows, however, that many students at all levels have difficulties making the distinction between what is seen, and what is reasoned. Even at the college level many students do poorly on examples of this type. Some of the creationist literature furnishes striking examples of fuzzy distinctions, exhibiting a failure to distinguish observation from inference.

The same kind of distinction arises in other disciplines. In studying history, for example, it is necessary to distinguish between primary information or evidence on the one hand, and interpretations or inferences drawn from such material by the historian on the other.

The program to be described here is a computer-based learning module, intended for students from about 12 years of age or over, concerning the distinction between observation and inference. It involves a variety of situations to illustrate and establish the distinction. This project was funded by the National Science Foundation, through the Development in Science Education Program. It is primarily concerned with aiding students in early adolescence, about the age of 12, to develop intellectual skills which are important for later life. Although initially the primary focus was on various standard Piagetian tasks, we have also considered other exercises in abstract logical reasoning such as the one presented in the present paper. This program has been tested with a very wide range of students, in several different environments, as will be discussed.

ENVIRONMENT

This module is about 15 to 20 minutes long for the average student. It is embedded in a longer program called *Crystals.* The longer program presents a fantasy about space travel in which the student is the captain of a starship which comes across another, derelict, starship carrying some supposed "energy crystals." Measurements of mass, volume, and other properties are made on these energy crystals to try to decide which ones might be a possible source of energy (Figure 1). Students are introduced to the concept of density and use this idea to search for crystals consisting of the same material. From the standpoint of Piagetian taks, the exercise is principally

concerned with ratio reasoning, involving the ratio mass/volume, but an opportunity arises to lead the student into making the distinction between what is observed and what is reasoned.

The observation-inference module comes as the last sequence in Spacelab, but it can also be used independently of the larger program in which it is embedded. In fact, we have two versions of the module, one in which there are references to the "parent" *Crystals* program and one in which there are no such references, so that the module can be used alone.

PROGRAM OUTLINE

The program begins with a sequence from a Sherlock Holmes novel, *The Greek Interpreter,* by Arthur Conan Doyle. There are many passages in the Sherlock Holmes novel in which Holmes, or in this case, his brother Mycroft, makes a series of startling deductions about a person or situation based on

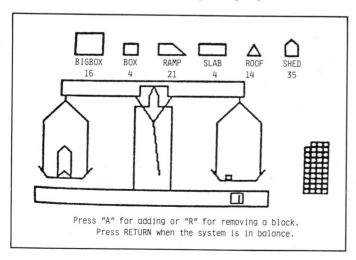

Figure 1 A weighing experiment in the Spacelab dialogue.

what appear to be relatively few, apparently insignificant, observations. We have picked one of these passages to begin the current program (Figure 2). The entire passage is first presented to the student in an attractive way and with some associated visual information. Then the program analyzes the passage, classifying for the student several examples of what is *seen directly* and what is *reasoned out*. In each case, this is done by using a blinking box surrounding a phrase or sentence of text, and then classifying what is in the blinking box. At this point the computer is being used in an expository manner, but this is only a short episode. Note that we are *not* using the "technical" terms, observation and inference, as yet.

The second activity in the Sherlock Holmes sequence requires students to make their own classification of items still remaining in the passage. The blinking box is still used to set off a phrase or sentence, but now the student must decide, on the basis of the earlier examples, whether each item refers to something that Mycroft sees or to something that Mycroft reasons out. If mistakes are made, they are corrected.

When the examples in the passage are exhausted, we finally introduce the words "observation and inference" (Figure 3). In much of our materials at Irvine we have taken care to avoid using a technical term until the idea it denotes has been established operationally through specific examples and shared experience.

The next sequence in the program concerns counting the elapsed time interval between lightning and thunder and calculating the distance between the observer and the lightning strike, the student having to answer questions about observation and inference in this connection. This sequence, however, is not needed by all users. If someone

```
                        ...Of course,
                his complete mourning shows
            that he has lost someone very dear.
        The fact that he is doing his own shopping
              looks as though it were his wife.
         He has been buying things for children....


                       ...There is a rattle,
           which shows that one of them is very young.
             The wife probably died in childbirth.
         The fact that he has a picture book under his arm
         shows that there is another child to be thought of.
```

Please press space bar:

Figure 2 Excerpt from a Sherlock Holmes story.

```
           SEES                              REASONS

   Man is wearing black                  lost someone dear
      carries packages                   doing own shopping
   one package is a rattle                  lost his wife
one package is a picture book           one child very young
                                        wife died in childbirth
                                           has another child


All the things in the first column   All the items in the second column
        are seen directly.                  are "figured out."
                                      They are arrived at by reasoning
                                         from the observations.
         We call them                         We call them

       OBSERVATIONS.                         INFERENCES.



Please press space bar:
```

Figure 3 Introduction of terms *observation* and *inference.*

shows no difficulty going through the first Sherlock Holmes sequence, then the lightning and thunder activities are bypassed.

The next component of the program involves statistical inference. The student is presented with a large field containing many jumping grasshoppers (Figures 4 and 5). The student is told that it is impossible to count all the grasshoppers directly, and is invited to suggest alternate strategies for getting some idea

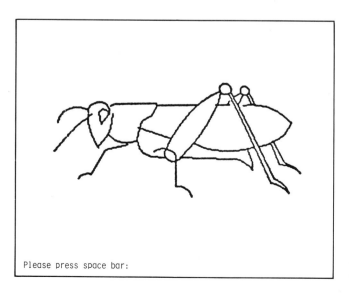

```
Please press space bar:
```

Figure 4 Graphics for activity on counting grasshoppers.

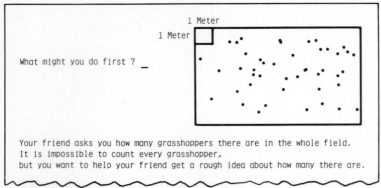

Figure 5   Opening question for grasshopper problem.

of how many grasshoppers there are in the field. Thus approximation and sampling come into this activity. The student is led, through a series of questions, to the idea of counting the grasshoppers in a one meter square. The students then count directly, watching the one meter square with the jumping grasshoppers (Figure 6). The number of grasshoppers in the square fluctuates

slightly. The program checks their value and gets them to count again if they are far off. Students then determine the total area of the field, and obtain an estimate of the number of grasshoppers in the entire field. Again, questions are asked about what is an observation and what is an inference in this sequence.

There is a final sequence providing further exercises in discriminating

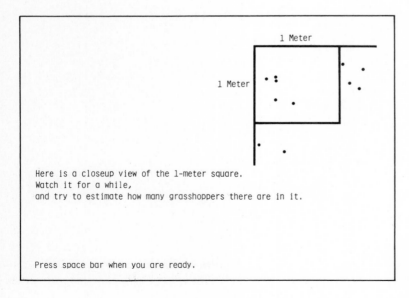

Figure 6   Exercise on counting a fluctuating number of grasshoppers.

between observation and inference. We also show the student that not everything we do can be classified as either an observation or inference. For example, defining a concept or inventing a name do not fall in either category.

OBSERVATIONS OF USAGE

The modules developed under this grant, and under a FIPSE grant concerned with public understanding of science, have all been tested in a variety of environments. The principal testing environment has been public libraries. We have found this to be a very useful environment not only to identify conceptual weakness in the programs, but also to be sure the programs are motivationally strong, holding viewers even in a library environment where there is no pressure to stay at the display.

This program has gone through a number of revision stages after such testing. It now works well with a wide group of individuals. We also used it as one of the programs in another research program involving the behavior of groups in using computer-based learning material. In this case we videotape groups employing the material, capturing their conversation, emotions, and key pushes at the computer. This, too, has been useful in understanding how the program works and in leading to additional revisions.

June 1983

A Computer-Based Dialogue For Developing Mathematical Reasoning of Young Adolescents

DAVID TROWBRIDGE, ALFRED BORK
Educational Technology Center
University of California
Irvine, California

INTRODUCTION

A project is being conducted by the Educational Technology Center at the University of California, Irvine to develop computer-based materials for junior high school students. The materials are in the form of modules dealing with topics in science and mathematics which run on personal computers. They emphasize skills of reasoning (i.e., formal reasoning in the Piagetian sense) such as reasoning with hypotheses, making observations and inferences, isolating and controlling variables, and reasoning with ratio and proportion.

Each module is devoted to a single topic and takes 1-2 hours to run in its entirety. The module consists of 5-10 separate activities, each of which may be entered and exited independently.

The format of the learning modules is the Socratic dialogue. They have been written by teams of teachers who have considerable experience in working with students one-on-one. The modules provide a way of conducting an individualized tutorial with students who otherwise may not have the opportunity to work with a tutor due to limited staff or classroom time.

The topics of the modules include area, density, functions, graphing, speed, triangles, and *Whirlybird*. This paper describes in detail the module concerning the concept of area to illustrate the pedagogical approach we have taken.

EDUCATIONAL BASIS FOR THE PROJECT

A considerable body of knowledge generated by the work of Piaget and others suggests that the development of formal reasoning skills becomes possible around the age of 12 to 15. An equally substantive body of evidence suggests that formal reasoning skills are not developed automatically; in fact, they are strikingly absent in about 50% of college-age students.[1] Educators are generally in agreement that our educational system, all the way from middle school through college, is an appropriate place for teaching formal reasoning skills, and most would agree that the earlier the assistance is provided, the better.

Many educational programs claim to be based on theories of intellectual development. We believe that present research in learning theory does not fully support any single approach to the development of materials to assist learning. However, two factors are favored by many different learning theories: (1) the need for an active learning environment, and (2) the need for individualized material allowing for greater diversity in student background.

The approach we have taken to meet these two needs in computer-assisted learning are based on the Mastery Learning Cycle.[2] Somewhat akin to Karplus's learning cycle, it has a few additional components.[3] Briefly, the Mastery Learning Cycle has elements of experience gathering or other motivational activity, instruction, application, and competency testing with feedback. The process is cyclical so that the results of competency testing can be used to route the learner back to one of the earlier elements for help if necessary.

DESCRIPTION OF ONE MODULE

As an illustration of how the Mastery Learning Cycle can be incorporated into computer-based learning materials, a module is described concerning the concept of area. This module consists of nine separate activities. The first three activities emphasize experience gathering; the next three provide instruction in certain key concepts; the next two activities involve applying these concepts; and the final activity is primarily a self-test for competency. The

activities in each of these groups are titled:

Experience Gathering:

1. Buying a Lot
2. Measuring Area
3. Practice in Measuring Area

Instruction:

4. Area with Two Different Unit Squares
5. Standard Units of Area
6. Recipe for Area

Application:

7. Area of a Parallelogram
8. Area of a Triangle

Competency Testing:

9. Practice Finding Areas of Figures

The groups are not mutually exclusive. For instance, the activities of 4, 5, and 6, which have an emphasis on instruction, also contain elements of experience gathering, application, and testing. Indeed, a single group will often contain all the elements of the Mastery Learning Cycle. The following four sections describe the contents of each activity.

Experience Gathering—Activities 1, 2, and 3

The first activity, Buying a Lot, presents a familiar situation for thinking about area. A map is drawn of a residential subdivision, along with a square figure of variable size. The student is asked to adjust the size of the square until it appears to have the same area as a particular lot. This is an attempt to invoke whatever intuitive concept the student may already have about area in a friendly, informal way.

In the second activity, several aids necessary for measuring area by the method of counting squares are introduced. These are a grid of identical squares, an algorithm accounting for squares on the boundary of the figure (i.e., count them only if they lie more than half inside the boundary), and the notion of uncertainty in measurement. Help measuring the area of an irregular figure is provided along the way.

The third activity provides three examples of irregular figures: a pentagon, a lake, and a map of California. Abundant aid is available for those students having trouble applying the method of counting squares to any one of the examples.

This is a rather atypical approach to introducing the concept of area. Indeed, it is our experience that many students at the college level have never measured area by counting squares. Most have learned some rote procedure such as multiplying length times width to find the area of a rectangle, but when confronted with finding the area of an irregular figure they are at a complete loss. The module concerning area begins with irregular figures and the method of counting area begins with irregular figures and the method of counting squares. Later, it introduces rules for shortcut methods of counting squares when the figure is a rectangle, parallelogram, or triangle.

Instruction—Activities 4, 5, and 6

The next three activities treat some formal aspects of the concept of area: the consequences of changing the unit by which the area of a particular figure is measured, the relationship between standards of length and standards of area, and the operational definition of area.

In Activity 4, the area of a figure is first measured using a unit square specified by the program (Figure 1). Then students are asked to select their own unit square, either larger or smaller than the original unit square, and to make a prediction as to whether the number for the area will turn out to be larger or smaller than before. After

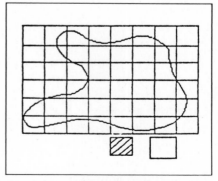

Figure 1 Measurement of area using arbitrary unit squares.

making a prediction, the measurement is carried out to confirm or reject it.

In the fifth activity, an attempt is made to draw from any familiarity students may have with terms for standard units of area. A rather sophisticated analysis of the students' responses is made to determine whether they have included both "square" and "inch" or only "inch," or have given a common misspelling of an otherwise correct standard unit. The activity concludes with instruction about the number of square feet in a square yard using diagrams.

Activity 6, Recipe for Area, has a somewhat different format. It draws from all of the earlier material, attempting to review and summarize the steps that were required to obtain a numerical result for the area of irregular figures. Reflecting on one's thinking like this is a formal reasoning skill. The program suggests several plausible alternatives for the first step, second step, etc., in the process of measuring area and asks students to select the most appropriate sequence. The series of steps representing the operational definition of area are:

1. Choose a unit square that is much smaller than the figure;
2. Cover the figure with a grid of unit squares.
3. Count all squares entirely inside the figure;
4. Estimate a number to account for the parts of squares along the boundary lying inside the figure; and

5. Add together the two numbers you have obtained and call this the area.

Application—Activities 7 and 8

Activity 7 begins with a review of the rule for finding the area of a rectangle. A parallelogram is sketched, and by using a simple process that involves cutting off an "ear" of the parallelogram and transposing it to the opposite side, shows how the problem can be reduced to finding the area of an equivalent rectangle (Figure 2). Identifying what dimensions of the parallelogram may be called its base and height is somewhat subtle, so considerable help is provided at this point.

A second application of the concept of area is in Activity 8, Area of a Triangle. By construction it is shown that a triangle constitutes one half of a parallelogram. Again, the issue of just

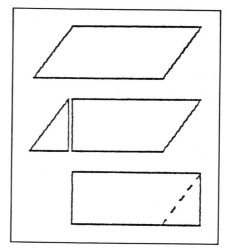

Figure 2 Construction of a rectangle from a parallelogram.

what constitutes base and height is treated not ex cathedra, but by discovery.

Competency Testing—Activity 9

The final activity provides students with an opportunity to test themselves on measuring the areas of several different figures: irregular figures, rectangles, parallelograms, and triangles. At each point of trouble, they are either given some immediate help (in case of initial or minor errors), or directed to an earlier activity in the module (in case of repeated or major errors).

STATUS OF THE PROJECT

Altogether, seven dialogues were written this past summer. First drafts, including all pedagogical specifications, were completed by writing groups which included at least one middle school teacher, an expert on intellectual development, and a staff member of the Educational Technology Center familiar with the technical details of computer-based materials.

Participation of junior high school teachers in each group was invaluable. They could easily identify vocabulary which would be too difficult for 7th and 8th graders and suggest alternative wording. Their experience was helpful in pointing out common conceptual and reasoning difficulties among their students, and they had a sense for the kinds of contexts students would find attractive or interesting. They had no difficulties interfacing with the authoring capabilities provided.

The scripts produced by the summer writing teams were reviewed in detail. Comments by reviewers have been very valuable in making revisions, rewriting sections of dialogue, and filling in gaps that were overlooked in the first draft.

Coding for four of the original seven modules (on area, density, speed, and triangles) has been completed. The remaining three modules (graphs, functions, *Whirlybird*) are in the process of being revised and coded.

A group of a dozen or so student programmers write the programs in Pascal. Development is taking place on Terak 8510 microcomputers. With slight modifications in graphics routines, the programs will run on a variety of inexpensive personal computers.

After the student modules have been completely coded, we will begin development of corresponding teacher modules that will serve as a kind of computer-based teacher's guide for improving the effectiveness of the materials. The teacher modules will provide an outline of the overall structure of the module, a description of available help sequences, comments on the pedagogical purpose of each activity, and suggestions for incorporation of the computer materials into regular classtime activities.

The materials are aimed at developing formal reasoning skills that have wide applicability in science and mathematics instruction. We expect them to be useful for some high school and college students as well. We would expect college students who are weak in mathematics and elementary education majors who will teach these ideas in the schools to benefit from these materials. We would encourage others to use these learning modules and give us comments as to suggestions for improvements or indications of their effectiveness.

ACKNOWLEDGMENTS

We would like to acknowledge the contributions of Arnold Arons, Barry Kurtz, and John Pitre as authors of the Area module, and the efforts of those who have coded the various activities: Danielle Bernstein, Steve Bartlett, Elinor Coleman, Jeff Oswald, John Pitre, Naomi Salvador, Scott Tanner, and Jim Zarbock.

June 19, 1981

REFERENCES

1. Arons, A., and Karplus, R. "Implications of Accumulating Data on Levels of Intellectual Development," *American Journal of Physics,* 44(4):396, 1976.
2. Karplus, R., et al., *SCIS Teacher's Handbook,* Berkeley: University of California, 1974.
3. Kurtz, B., and Bork, A. "The Mastery Learning Cycle in Computer-Based Education," *Proceedings* of the Psychology of Mathematics Education conference, Grenoble, July 1981.

Computer-Based Learning Modules for Early Adolescence

DAVID TROWBRIDGE, ALFRED BORK

Educational Technology Center
University of California
Irvine, California

This paper describes a project for developing computer-based materials designed to assist early adolescent students to develop abstract reasoning skills. Interactive computer programs are being produced dealing with scientific and mathematical subjects which engage students in dialogues emphasizing formal thought. Examples will be presented which demonstrate how carefully designed help sequences can be used to address common problems of students. The learning modules make extensive use of graphics and emphasize active participation by the student. They run on inexpensive, standalone microcomputers.

INTRODUCTION

Applications of computer-assisted learning in our schools seem to have potentially great educational value. Here we will concentrate on one aspect of computer-based learning: interactive dialogues for science and mathematics instruction. We will discuss a project being carried out by the Educational Technology Center at the University of California, Irvine, under the direction of Alfred Bork. We are developing computer-based materials for junior high school students (12–14 year olds). Emphasis is placed on the formal reasoning skills which are necessary in typical high school science and mathematics curricula. In this paper we will use examples from two of the dialogues to illustrate the kinds of materials being prepared.

FEASIBILITY OF COMPUTER-BASED TUTORIALS

Evidence from both education and computer technology suggests that the implementation of effective tutorial dialogues is now feasible on small standalone machines. We note first of all that students display great commonality in the processes whereby they learn new material. Often they go through the same steps and encounter the same pitfalls along the way. Experienced teachers in every field share the observation that students repeatedly misunderstood important concepts in the same way, and predictably display certain preconceptions which are impediments to learning the crucial ideas of that field.[1-6] In developing educational materials we must both capitalize on the similarities and provide for the individual differences among students. Computer-based materials provide a way to do this.

Suitably programmed, microcomputers can mimic the alertness of a skilled tutor. They are uniquely capable of analyzing student input and branching accordingly. They can provide reinforcement, carefully phrased questions or extensive help sequences. Microcomputer graphics is now reaching a stage where high-quality drawings and animation are possible.

EXAMPLES OF DIALOGUES INVOLVING RATIO REASONING

Density

The concept of density involves reasoning with the ratio of mass to volume. Ratio reasoning is widely recognized as one component of formal thought. It is a skill which is prerequisite to understanding many of the concepts which are part of the middle school science and mathematics curriculum.

Let us describe briefly a computer dialogue that deals with this concept. The dialogue has three parts, emphasizing, respectively, the concepts of mass, volume, and density. To give continuity and motivation to junior high school students, the dialogue is embedded in a fanciful story line involving a search for "energy-producing crystals." The energy-producing crystals are characterized as consisting of some unique material. The key to the solution of the puzzle lies in the fact that among several candidates, three particular

crystals have the same density. When the inference is made that the ones with the same density consist of the same material, a test is performed to determine whether indeed they produce energy when placed together.

The exercise involves a variety of experimental investigations conducted by students as if they were actually in a laboratory provided with a balance, a graduated cylinder, and a number of other devices for measuring the physical properties of crystals.

For instance, in the first activity students are presented with pictures of a magnet and a collection of crystals. Using directional arrow keys on the keyboard, they move the magnet near the crystals to find out whether each crystal is attracted to it. They are provided with a picture of an equal arm balance and a set of standard weights which they use to determine the mass of each crystal. Using very simple animation, we simulate the operations of placing the object to be weighed on one pan of the balance and placing a number of standard masses on the other pan until a pointer indicates that the pans are in balance (Figure 1).

In the investigations of both magnetic attraction and mass, the student is actually performing experiments to obtain data. At the end of the first activity, the student is introduced to the distinction between intensive and extrinsic properties. Magnetism is characteristic of material composition, and independent of the size of the sample; hence, magnetism is called an intrinsic property. Mass, on the other

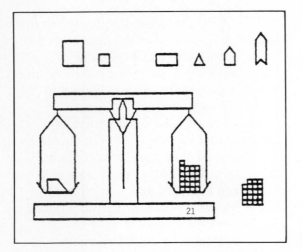

Figure 1 Simulated measurement of mass.

hand, depends on the size of the sample and is called extrinsic.

The second activity involves investigations of shape and volume, carried out in the same manner. Two approaches to the concept of volume are taken. The first involves building a stack of unit cubes which approximates in size and shape the crystal to be measured, and then counting the cubes in the stack (Figure 2). The second involves a graduated cylinder with water (Figure 3). Initially, the cylinder is calibrated by placing unit cubes in the water and recording the water level after each addition. Then, the volume of each crystal is measured by water displacement.

The objective of the third activity is for the student to be able to calculate density from mass and volume numbers, and to interpret the result of dividing mass by volume as the number of kilograms contained in each one liter of the material. There are a number of branch points at various places in the

activity on density, and each branch has subsequent remedial activities for the student.

As teachers, we frequently encounter students who have learned rules of division and are able to divide one integer into another, but in real world problems involving division are often either unable to set up the problem correctly, or unable to interpret their result. Our goal in teaching the concept of density goes beyond having students memorize the formula $D = M/V$. We want the student to be able to interpret the result of dividing mass by volume as well. That is, the student should understand density as the mass contained in each one unit of volume in the object.

The computer dialogue on density contains several branch points at which the student's understanding is assessed. If necessary, the program routes the student through a brief tutorial sequence. One such sequence involves a hypothetical instrument called a "laser knife."

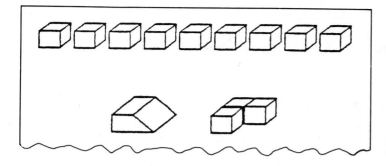

Figure 2 Measurement of volume by counting cubes.

The function of the laser knife is to extract a unit cube of material from a selected crystal. The unit cube is then weighed on a balance to determine the density number directly. This demonstrates one of the great strengths of experiments using computer graphics: the experimental tools can be designed for optimal pedagogical impact without regard to any of the "messy" effects inherent in an actual laboratory experiment. The laser knife extracts a precise unit cube quickly, cleanly, and effortlessly.

The help sequence establishes a connection between the equivalent processes of obtaining density directly by weighing a unit cube, and computing density by dividing total mass by total volume. This step too is facilitated by graphics in which the crystal is broken into several unit cubes and then units of mass are evenly distributed to each of the unit cubes. Thus the mathematical process of dividing by a volume number is presented as a physical process of breaking up an object into a number of pieces of unit volume.

We believe that development of the formal skill of reasoning with ratios in the context of density is encouraged by concrete experiences in the same context. Thus, while the goal of this dialogue is to develop the student's facility with mass/volume ratios, the approach to that goal involves a manipulative task requiring only concrete reasoning.

Speed

Another dialogue we are developing in this same group concerns the concept of speed. Once again, this concept involves a ratio; fostering understanding of this ratio is the goal of this dialogue.

Without formal reasoning skills a child

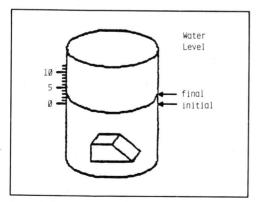

Figure 3 Measurement of volume by water displacement.

is generally capable of judging (using concrete reasoning) which of two objects is faster when the motions are at least partly simultaneous.[7] That is, when two objects traveling along parallel paths start and stop at the same instant, the child has no difficulty comparing speeds on the basis of the distances traveled by the objects. Similarly, when the distances traveled are the same but either the starting times or ending times are nonsimultaneous, then the child may compare speeds on the basis of the time required to traverse equal distances.

However, when both displacements and time intervals differ, or when the motions are entirely nonsimultaneous, concrete reasoning is no longer satisfactory for comparing speeds. Instead, the child must construct some kind of ratio (either distance traveled for each unit of time, or time required for each unit of distance) to make a successful comparison. According to Piaget, this is a component of formal thought.

In the computer dialogue on speed, the student is provided with an experimental setup which simulates the rectilinear motions of two balls traveling along parallel paths. Some of the motions are under user control, while

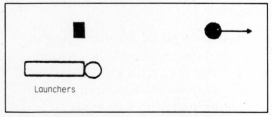

Figure 4 Animation for comparison of uniform motions.

others are demonstrated by the program for the purpose of asking the student to compare two motions. In the beginning exploratory activity, a black ball is controlled by the program and a white ball is controlled by the student. A device resembling the launcher on a pinball machine has a "spring" which can be "stretched" using simple key press commands (Figure 4). Upon a launch command, a ball moves across the screen at a constant speed which depends upon the initial extension of the spring launcher. Tasks are presented to the student such as, "make the white ball go faster than the black ball and pass it," or "make the white ball start behind, stay behind, but travel with a speed greater than the black ball."

The next two activities involve demonstrations of two balls which travel equal distances in unequal times or take equal times to travel unequal distances. Students are asked, "Was the speed of the white ball greater than, less than, or the same as the speed of the black ball?" Each example provides a situation in which the concepts of position and speed must be discriminated (e.g., the distinction between being ahead and traveling faster).

Sometimes, the motion of the balls is hidden under two tunnels except at the endpoints so that comparisons of speed must be made in terms of the variables of distance and time rather than on the visual phenomena of catching up, overtaking or falling behind (Figure 5).

In the fourth activity, the ratio concept is introduced. If the student has any difficulty making comparisons of small whole-number ratios, help sequences are provided. In one case, the student is provided with the option of analyzing the motion of each ball by measuring directly how far it moves in one second. That is, by repeatedly launching a ball at the same speed each time (from a spring of constant extension), the student may choose to view the path of the ball executed during a unit time interval. In this way a connection is established between the mathematical operation of dividing a distance by a time interval and the operation of measuring the path directly which corresponds to a unit time. Computer animation provides a simple way of performing these experiments and leaving a visual record of the motion.

Additional help sequences are provided for students who still have difficulty with the idea of dividing. For example, an analogy is presented between dividing a line segment into a number of equal pieces and dividing a quantity of money equally among friends.

OTHER DIALOGUES INVOLVING FORMAL REASONING

Other dialogues currently under development to aid formal reasoning treat some other topics which are relevant to middle school science and mathematics programs:[4] classification of triangles, the concept of area, mathematical estimation, number relations, and graphing. Each emphasizes one or more reasoning skills which are characteristic of formal thought. In addition to the dialogues involving reasoning with ratio and proportion, we are developing materials for control of variables, hypothetical reasoning, and inductive reasoning.

Each dialogue is written as a "module" composed of from 3 to 6 separate activities. Each activity takes the student between 5 and 15 minutes to complete. Students may perform the activities on different days if they choose. The activities build on one another, beginning with exploratory exercises, continuing with sections that introduce key concepts, and concluding with an activity requiring application of the concepts to some slightly new situation.

The materials were written by small groups of authors, including university faculty with expertise in the theory of intellectual development, exceptional middle school teachers, and staff familiar with microcomputer implementation. They were coded by skilled student

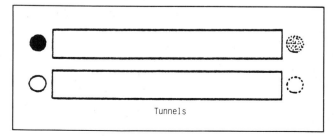

Tunnels

Figure 5 Comparison of motions using tunnels.

programmers. The programs are written in Pascal and run on the Terak 8510 microcomputer. With minor modifications of certain graphics routines, the programs will run on other inexpensive personal computers.

At present, the programs are being tested with small numbers of young adolescent students. We are using the materials in both public library environments and in our own institution with children recruited from the local school system. After revision and recoding, the materials will be placed in regular school classrooms for further testing.

We have not as yet undertaken a program for evaluation of the effectiveness of these materials. However, informal experience suggests that these interactive dialogues do serve the function of engaging students in interesting, thought-provoking experiments from which they gain valuable practice in scientific reasoning.

The dialogues are first and foremost interactive in nature, requiring frequent input from the student and diverse branching opportunities for guidance through appropriate help sequences. The modules will be available for use in middle school classrooms to serve functions of both enrichment and remedial help. The interactive nature of the dialogues makes them ideal for individualized instruction.

SUMMARY

We have attempted to demonstrate that computer-based educational materials can provide useful tutorial assistance to young adolescent students. An examination of the common conceptual problems and troubles with scientific reasoning of students at this age suggests that automated dialogues may help to overcome these difficulties. We have described two examples of programs which attempt to do this. Both have been concerned with the reasoning which underlies the understanding of two important physical concepts: density and speed. We encourage others to use these materials and suggest changes for improvements.

July 1981

REFERENCES

1. di Sessa, A. A., "Unlearning Aristotelian Physics: A Study of Knowledge Based Learning," Unpublished manuscript, Division for Study and Research in Education, Massachusetts Institute of Technology (September 1980).
2. Hawkins, D., "Critical Barriers to Science Learning," *Outlook,* 29 (1978), Mountain View Center for Environmental Education, University of Colorado, Boulder.
3. McCloskey, M., Carramazza, A., and Green, B., "Culvilinear Motion in the Absence of External Forces: Naive Beliefs about the Motion of Objects," *Science,* 210(5):1139–41 (1980).
4. Trowbridge, D. E., and Bork, A., "A Computer-Based Dialogue for Developing Mathematical Reasoning of Young Adolescents," *Proceedings of the National Educational Computing Conference,* Denton, Texas (June 1981).
5. Trowbridge, D. E., and McDermott, L. C.,

"Investigation of Student Understanding of the Concept of Velocity in One Dimension," *American Journal of Physics,* 48(12):1020–28 (1980).

6. Trowbridge, D. E., and McDermott, L. C., "Investigation of Student Understanding of the Concept of Acceleration in One Dimension,"*American Journal of Physics,* 49(3):242–53 (1981).

7. Piaget, J., *The Child's Conception of Movement and Speed* (New York: Ballantine Books, 1970).

four
PHYSICS

Computer-Based Instruction in Physics

ALFRED BORK

Until now, the computer has played only a minor role in the teaching of physics and other subjects. In the next few years we can expect this to change dramatically because of the development and profusion of relatively inexpensive personal computers and because of the growing pressure to streamline the educational system. In the future, computer-based instruction may make practical the organization of colleges in which almost all funds are used for the development of curriculum material and relatively little is spent per student for delivery.

The instructional capabilities of the computer give it several great advantages over many of the other educational media currently in use. A computer with a good instructional program in physics, for example, allows the student to engage in Socratic dialogue about the details of the subject, to display the laws of physics graphically, and to see the results of varying not only the initial conditions but even the laws themselves. Computers can let students cover course material at their own pace and can administer examinations, giving the student feedback after each test item. The advantages of computer-based instruction are particularly appropriate for dealing with a severe problem in education: teaching an increasingly hetrogeneous

group of students. We must create a learning environment in which a greater number of students, with a more pronounced mixture of backgrounds, can succeed. Our current physics classes fail many students.

In the past the teacher has almost always viewed this lack of success as a problem of the student. There is an increasing feeling in society, however, that students are not entirely to blame for their failures; our schools and our teachers are frequently called upon to bear a portion of the responsibility. There is a growing consensus in society that the schools need to be improved.

The first advantage of the computer is interaction. The computer allows every student to play an active role in the learning process, in contrast to the passive role that is characteristic (for most students) of lecture and textbook formats, particularly in large classes. It is difficult for one to appreciate just how interactive the computer can be without spending some time running good computer-based learning material. The student in such a situation is no longer a spectator, but is an active participant.

A second advantage of the computer is the possibility of giving the student individual attention. As soon as the student types a response to a question asked by the computer, the reply is analyzed by the program. The program makes many decisions, which are based not just on the student's last input, but on previous responses as well.

It is common knowledge among educators that students are different; not all students have the same backgrounds and not all students learn in the same way. But many of our conventional approaches to education use a lock-step procedure for all students and do not allow us to take these differences into account. An advantage of the computer is that with good material we can individualize instruction. This can also be achieved if a single extremely good tutor works with a very small group of students, say no more than four. The classical model for such a tutor is Socrates. But this second way, although superior to anything we can attain with the computer, is impractical in our society, except in advanced graduate education. We have too many people to educate, not enough teachers, and not enough money to proceed in this fashion. The computer can give us some of the advantages of Socratic dialogue, in an affordable manner.

A third advantage is also related to individual differences among students. As all students do not learn at the same rate, it is important to give different students different amounts of time to go through the learning material. Computer-based instruction allows the student to control the pace of the individual learning sequence or unit and, in a "Keller plan" or other self-paced situation, to control the overall pace of the course. Another student choice that

the computer can provide is a choice of content, even within a single course.

COMPUTER-BASED LEARNING

In the following examples we discuss four of the many ways we can use the computer to aid the physics student: the computer as an intellectual tool, the computer-controllable world, the computer as a testing and diagnostic aid, and the Socratic dialogue on computers.

Intellectual Tool

In this context the computer is used to expand the user's mental capabilities and understanding. It often allows us different approaches to the content of physics. We consider the computer to be an intellectual tool when the student is a programmer. But the aim of the programming activity is to learn physics. Our students use a common standard programming language, usually APL or Pascal for beginning students.

The most well-developed example within physics of the intellectual tool use is in beginning mechanics. Here, students use the computer to study the laws of motion in a new way, differing significantly from the typical approach in the standard texts. Two physics texts, *Basic Concepts of Physics*[1] by Chalmers Sherwin, and the *Feynman Lectures on Physics,*[2] pioneered the notion, but without using computers. The basic concept is to approach problems involving $F = ma$ through numerical techniques for solving the differential equations, using simple methods that are easily understandable even at the high school level.

The most widely used physics material of this kind, *Introductory Computer Based Mechanics,* is available through CONDUIT at the Computer Center, University of Iowa. This material is in the form of two units or modules, and is designed for "supplemental" use in physics classes. The first module[3] considers only one-dimensional systems. The second module[4] extends the notion to two-dimensional systems and considers auxiliary concepts such as energy. CONDUIT will soon issue a new version using the graphic capabilities of personal computers.

The basic ideas can be introduced in several ways. Richard Feynman approximates the derivatives of position and velocity as ratios of finite differences. In any approach the student is led to the following equations as the basis of the numerical method:

$$X_{new} = X_{old} + V\Delta t$$
$$a = F/m$$
$$V_{new} = V_{old} + a\Delta t$$

A significant aspect of this approach is that it can lead to a quite different beginning quarter or semester in physics. Even the problems that students study are different. The traditional course tends to offer problems that can be solved by handling $F = ma$ algebraically. This restricts the user to a narrow range of problems: projectile motion, "block sliding down inclined plane," "rope over pulley."

To give some idea of the flavor of the intellectual tool approach to beginning mechanics, here are several of the problems from module two of *Introductory Computer Based Mechanics.*

Starting at (3,0) and moving initially upward, investigate the motion of a satellite for initial speeds between 0.4 and 0.8. Comment on the curves obtained.

Suppose the gravitational force law was $F(r) = -1/r^{1.8}$

(a) Run your program for a circular orbit.

(b) Run your program for initial conditions which would provide an elliptical orbit for the inverse square law. In which direction is the precession of the orbit?

(c) By using several exponents between 1.8 and 2.2 relate the precession of the orbit to the deviation of the power away from 2.

Elliptical motion is still possible with two fixed force centers! Speculate as to how this could happen, and then experiment at the computer to verify or refute your speculation.

Controllable Worlds

The second type of computer use in physics courses is directed toward building up a student's insight or intuition. This important goal is difficult to accomplish in traditional courses. Again, I will use an example from beginning mechanics. The basic notion is that we can help the student achieve better insight into physical problems by allowing the computer to simulate a great range of experiences and make them available to the student.

As an example, let us examine a unit that we developed, called *Newton,* on planetary motion in the ordinary inverse-square case. The student is allowed not only to examine in a free and easy fashion the usual spatial orbits, but is introduced, even at the beginning physics level, to various abstract spaces.

Consider a planet moving around a fixed sun. This system is always discussed in physics classes, but no one has ever seen a planet move around the sun! Direct experience is not available. Hence, there is a certain abstraction to the results that are presented to the student; a student may not necessarily

build up a feeling for the situation. In a program such as Newton, we can let the student in an easy and natural fashion begin by looking at several planetary orbits, simply picking slightly different initial velocities, as in Figure 1.

The figure does not show an important aspect of the display seen by the student—that the orbit develops in time. Thus, the type of motion that Kepler's second law tells us must happen is something the student experiences as an actual fact, not simply an abstract idea. The student "sees" phenomena not ordinarily seen.

But the user does not need to stay in *x-y* space. The student might be asked to look at what happens for the same orbits, with the same initial conditions, but in velocity space, where the *x*

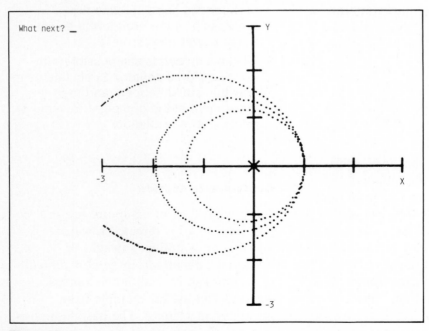

Figure 1

component of velocity is plotted against the *y* component of velocity. Figure 2 shows the results. Looking at the figure, we see that the "orbits" in velocity space are circles, something not known to a great many physicists. This leads to some interesting views of what is happening; an approach to mechanics developed by Andrea di Sessa and others at MIT uses this as a way of attacking gravitational problems.[5]

The student can also easily view other aspects of gravitational motion. *Newton* allows us to plot any mechanical variable against any other mechanical variable and allows complete student control of initial conditions, constants in the equations, scaling details, and other factors of the motion. In order to reach all students in a large class, auxiliary workbook material is needed: we are preparing such material.

Testing and Diagnostic Aid

A third kind of computer usage, the testing of students, is something we are giving increasing attention to at the Educational Technology Center at Irvine.

The main advantage of testing via the computer is that we can give the student immediate feedback and aid. This stands out in contrast to normal testing, where often it is days or even weeks before the student receives any information on the

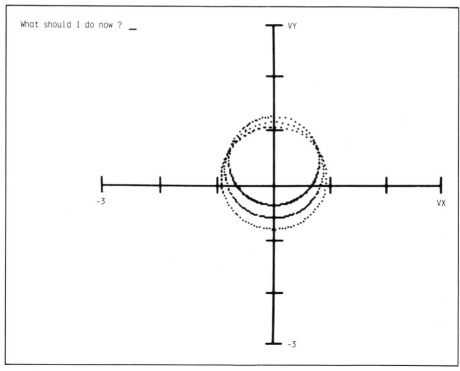

Figure 2

difficulties encountered. From an instructional point of view such a delay is unfortunate because feedback is most effective at exactly the time the student is taking the test. It is then that students are most amenable to learning, particularly from material that points out just what kinds of difficulties occurred. Often it is possible to be very precise in this regard; good instructors know the typical errors made by students and write programs that check for such errors. On other occasions the aid will be more general, reviewing the student's problems.

As an example, consider one of the early quizzes used in our beginning course, a course we will describe later in the article. The quiz is concerned with geometrical calculus as used in physics. Can a student seeing a position–time curve, for example, recognize the correct corresponding velocity–time curve?

The quiz starts by checking to see if the student has adequate background to read a graph and to place a point on the graph. While most of the students in the

University of California can read graphs, a few cannot. Hence, it is reasonable to find out early in the course that a student needs help in this regard. Figure 3 shows a situation in which a student correctly reads a point from the graph. The graph is different each time the quiz is given, as is the particular time the student is asked about. So we examine the students on their understanding of concepts, not their knowledge of particular examples of concepts.

In the next part of the quiz the student is asked where the velocity is zero, given a position–time curve. The student answers using the video display terminal's built-in pointer. Again, the curve will be different each time the program is run. Figure 4 shows a situation in which a student has pointed to a place where the position, rather than the velocity, is zero. Most of the feedback is self-explanatory. What is not shown is that the student has pointed several times and has received a number of different replies. The program was quite responsive in pointing out a likely

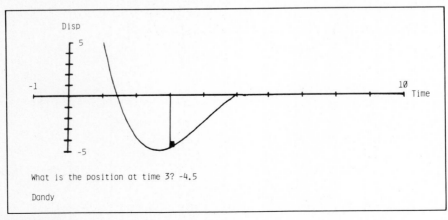

Figure 3

student error, confusing the zero of position on the curve with zero velocity.

The next sequence of the quiz, one of the two main sequences, offers the student a position–time curve and velocity–time curve and asks whether they are a good pair or a bad pair. The position–time curve stays the same as various velocity–time curves are presented, but only one at a time. The student may see a matched pair right away or may go through five or so possibilities before that. Likely wrong answers are presented. Figure 5 shows a problem presented to the student. Again, the curves are different each time the program is run. Similar sequences of questions ask the student to match acceleration–time curves with velocity–time curves or present the student with a velocity–time curve and ask about position.

Unlike ordinary multiple-choice questions, this variant does not show the student all the possible responses, but makes the student accept or decline each possible answer. A large number of possible answers are available in the program, and these are picked at random for each student taking the quiz. This technique, developed by Stephen Franklin,[6] is widely used in our quizzes. Thus, we avoid one of the major disadvantages of ordinary multiple-choice questions: allowing the student to guess from a series of possibilities. We very seldom find it necessary or desirable to use the standard multiple-choice format

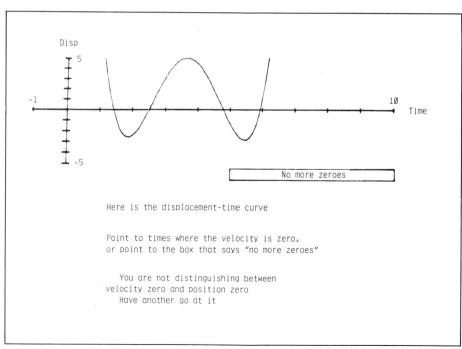

Figure 4

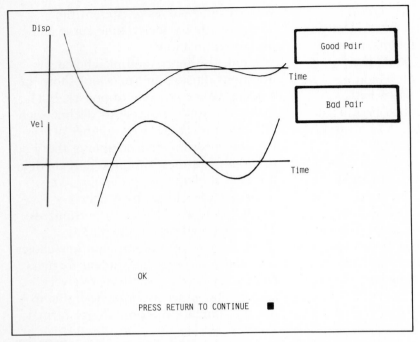

Disp

Good Pair

Time

Bad Pair

Vel

Time

OK

PRESS RETURN TO CONTINUE ■

Figure 5

in our computer-generated quizzes. If the student chooses an incorrect answer, the correct answer is displayed immediately.

Socratic Dialogue

The last type of computer usage that we will discuss is one in which the computer plays the role of an excellent tutor. The notion of Socrates teaching through a series of carefully chosen questions, responsive to the student's answers, has been well known for 2500 years. This procedure is very different from the typical lecture–textbook system of education, where the student is constantly being *told* things. Socrates very seldom gave any information to the student but tried to lead the student's

thinking toward the critical ideas, through question after question.

We will look at an example that was developed by Arnold Arons, Barry Kurtz, Stephen Franklin, and myself, with aid from Francis Collea. It is based on curriculum material first developed in the Elementary Science Study units. The immediate situation involves the use of batteries, bulbs, and wires, but the emphasis in the material is not to teach the simple information involved, but rather to lead the student, through questioning and empirical investigations, to a satisfactory model of what happens in electrical circuits. Thus, the question of how we know what we know is very important.

This material was prepared for use in

public libraries. The general subject of the modules is scientific literacy, bringing a wide variety of individuals to a better understanding of what science is all about. Figures 6 and 7 show stages along the way. One can get some flavor of what is happening by looking at the questions the users are being asked.

The reader is reminded that the four computer uses we have discussed are illustrative rather than exhaustive. A full program can occupy several hours of student time.

AN EXAMPLE AT IRVINE

I will now describe computer-aided physics instruction from a different point of view, that of a particular course. Physics 5A at the University of California, Irvine, is the first quarter of a calculus-based course taught primarily to science and engineering freshmen.

On the first day of Physics 5A students are told that they have a choice among three different courses, all carrying the same credit. Course 1 is conventionally taught and graded; the computer plays no role except as a possible optional learning device. The second and third choices both heavily involve the computer and are based on the "Keller" or "Personalized System of Instruction" strategy.

Students move through courses 2 or 3 at their own pace. Before proceeding, they must demonstrate knowledge of a unit by passing a test or tests at essentially the 100% level. The personalized system of instruction has been well described in the literature, and has been shown to be an effective way of learning. What makes this particular course interesting is that the testing is all done directly on-line at the computer except for the final exam.

The two computer courses differ in content. Course 2 has the same content as course 1 and uses the same standard beginning textbook. Course 3 is based on a set of notes developed at Irvine. It makes use of the intellectual tool aspect

From BULB BASE
To   RIGHT BATTERY TERMINAL

Point where you want to connect one end.
Now place the other end.
Please connect your second wire. ▮

Use Arrows to move pointer. Press Return when done.

gure 6

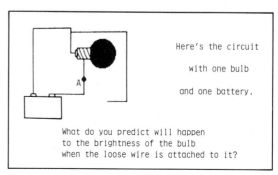

Here's the circuit

with one bulb

and one battery.

What do you predict will happen
to the brightness of the bulb
when the loose wire is attached to it?

Figure 7

of computers, presenting a quite different approach to $F = ma$, as discussed earlier. Courses 2 and 3 are quite different in content, as demonstrated by the fact that there is very little overlap in their quizzes.

In the winter 1981 quarter approximately 450 students enrolled in Physics 5A. About three-quarters of these students chose the two computer tracks, a dramatic increase from the initial offering of the course, indicating a favorable reputation among the students. Students spend about three hours per week at the computer display screens. Each student takes about fifteen different quizzes, often taking a quiz several times until he or she demonstrates mastery of the material covered. We gave about 15,000 computer quizzes during the ten weeks of the quarter, providing immediate assistance when needed.

A full course management system on the computer backs up the course. As the students take quizzes, pass/fail information is recorded. The course management system also controls access to the quizzes. Students are not allowed to take quizzes in a unit until they have completed in all the previous units. If a quiz is not passed, twelve hours must elapse before the computer will allow the student to take the quiz again, emphasizing the need for additional study. If a student does not pass a quiz after four attempts, he or she must come in and see the instructor before being allowed to take the quiz again. Thus, the instructor sees each student in trouble individually, and the system assures that

this will be the case for every student continuing in the course.[7]

This is only one of many different courses that could be put together with the computer. Other uses in physics courses are described in the literature.

WRITING COMPUTER-BASED TEXT

So far we have been looking at existing courses and material. But very little in the way of good computer-based learning material exists at the present time. The past twenty years have been a period of experiment, where much of the effort (sometimes unknown to the developers) has gone into understanding the capabilities of the computer as a medium of instruction. Now we have a reasonable, but not perfect, understanding of these capabilities. The hardware has continued to decline in cost during this period, so that now, with the advent of the new personal computers (see Figure 1) based on microcomputer chips, it is reasonable to plan large-scale production and use of computer-based learning material.

Earlier attempts at producing computer-based learning material tended to follow what might be described as the "coursewriter" strategy. The notion of this strategy was that each author would develop a unique set of programming commands and use this as the basis for producing material; one person would do all the work. This is somewhat like requiring that an instructor who wants to write a textbook learn how to run a typesetting machine and a printing press.

At the Educational Technology Center at Irvine the process of producing computer-based course material begins with specification of the teaching strategies to be used for each concept. This requires extremely good teachers, who work in small groups with those who have knowledge of the computer's capability. The teachers do not need to know anything about computer programming, and most of those who work with us do not. They have complete freedom to make the best choices possible from an instructional point of view; they need not be concerned with the associated programming problems.

The second stage is that of visual and temporal design of material on the screen. Earlier computer material often paid no attention to screen layout, implicitly using the same strategies that are used in books. But more recently teachers have realized that the screen is a very different medium from the book with many different nuances. For example, diagrams and even text can be made to appear on the screen slowly in order to show a sequence of development; the screen can be cleared at will, without regard to conservation of paper as with the pages of a book.

A third stage is the actual programming. At Irvine the programming work is typically carried out by undergraduate students using powerful higher-level languages. Our recent activities employ Pascal, with various auxiliary software to aid the process.

A series of testing and revision stages follow. One of the advantages of computer-based teaching is that the instructional material itself can collect very detailed feedback on what happens when it is used. Then the material can and should be rewritten, perhaps several times, based on the information so obtained. The information received can be much more microscopic in detail than that concerned with students learning in lectures or from textbooks.

At each stage we can record student responses to computer questions, and these answers can be analyzed to improve the program.

FUTURE

The development of new computer-based instructional material, and the associated research, will have one interesting effect not directly associated with the material itself. We can expect to learn more about the way people learn. The computer is a unique tool for learning about learning, and has only recently become available for research in this area.

A second factor that is very important to remember is the continual evolution of computers themselves. Chip technology is still young and vigorous and is leading to better and less expensive machines. All indications are that this process will continue for a considerable period of time. New developments are continually extending the possibilities. Costs for equivalent computing power have gone down about 25% per year in recent years, and it looks as if this striking reduction will continue. The net effect is that we can expect more and more computers to be available for use in education. Economic factors are on the side of the computer.

Computers will also become better from an educational standpoint. We will have more memory, both fast memory and slower backup memory, at less cost. We will have faster and more sophisticated central processing units, a development already reflected in the newer chips such as the Intel 8086 or 432 and the Motorola 68 000. Graphic capabilities will improve considerably over what they are today, allowing better color, resolution, shading, and even full animation with much better treatment of three-dimensional aspects. Voice output is already practical, and there is the increasing possibility that within a decade we will see unconstrained voice input. So our capabilities will continue to grow.

Another continuing development with computers is the availability not only of better software, but of more powerful programming tools with which to develop software. Newer languages such as Pascal and most recently Ada, were developed to meet the need for better programming techniques. With regard to the preparation of computer-based learning material, this gives us the ability to produce programs that will be easier to modify and use.

From the instructional point of view, however, the main interest will be the effects on courses and curricula. The computer will allow much more self-pacing, along the example of the course just described. For such courses the computer will present learning material, give unit tests with not only diagnostic value but with instructional value as well, and manage the entire process. We will be able to break away from the notion that courses always have to begin and end at a certain time, or the notion that courses must have the same duration for all students, independent of the needs of the students.

But the greatest change will probably be in the quality of the courses. As courses are rethought, with the possibility of using an interactive and individualized learning medium, we can produce curriculum materials far superior to those currently in use. How this process will take place is not certain. One possibility is the formation of an American Open University, with the associated curriculum development activities.

Finally, we may see considerable changes in our institutions. Some of these changes will be made practical by the computer. The enrollment problems of the next fifteen years, universally predicted, may be a major stimulus. Although figures differ, in most parts of the country enrollments in universities can be expected to decline between 10% and 25%. The situation is much worse in the northeast and north central areas of the country than elsewhere. This demographic factor, combined with increasing public resistance to funding education, will increase greatly the external pressures for budget and personnel cuts in our institutions. Computers are one good possibility for accommodating these new and increasing outside pressures on education.

One interesting recent trend is the formation of a variety of nontraditional universities, universities which depart from the pervasive pattern of universities in the United States. Some nontraditional universities emphasize the notion that one can avoid constructing buildings. For example, Coastline College in Southern California is a community college that did not build a campus, but uses community buildings, television courses, and other nontraditional techniques.

Another interesting new type of university is that connected with an industrial or commercial firm. Perhaps the most interesting recent example is the graduate school in computer science formed by Wang, a computer manufacturer.

Another new type of institution is exemplified by the Open University in England and to some extent by the University of Mid-America in this country. The notion is similar to that suggested by Coastline College, but in a direction that completely abandons the traditional campus. Almost all The Open University students work in their homes, coming only in a summer session to any central location. These summer sessions are held at universities all over the country, which are not in use then.

The most interesting aspect of The Open University from the standpoint of our current discussion is that it represents a very different balance of funding. The Open University puts almost all of its funds into *development* of curriculum material, using relatively little per student for *delivery.* Our

traditional universities are based on almost the opposite balance. The Open University has proved successful, in terms of the quality of its students and in terms of its costs per student, a significant factor for us to consider for the future. The Open University does not use much computer material at the present time, but as the technology becomes more sophisticated, they and others will move further in this direction. If such universities develop in this country, there will be important consequences for both teaching and research.

The computer materials described in this paper were developed with support from the National Science Foundation and the Fund for the Improvement of Postsecondary Education.

September 1981

REFERENCES

1. C. Sherwin, *Basic Concepts of Physics,* Holt, Rinehart and Winston, New York (1961).
2. R. P. Feynman, R. B. Leighton, M. L. Sands, *The Feynman Lectures on Physics,* vol. 1, Addison-Wesley, Reading, Mass. (1963–65), chapter 9.
3. A. Bork, A. Luehrmann, J. W. Robson, *Introductory Computer Based Mechanics I,* CONDUIT, University of Iowa, Iowa City 52242.
4. A. Bork, D. Merrill, H. Peckham, W. Lang, *Introductory Computer Based Mechanics II,* CONDUIT, University of Iowa, Iowa City 52242.
5. A. Bork, *Learning with Computers,* Digital Press, Bedford, Mass. (1981), pages 83–97.

6. S. Franklin, J. Marasco, *Journal of College Science Teaching* 7, September 1977, page 15.

7. *Physics in the Irvine Educational Technology Center, in Computers and Education, An International Journal,* 4, D. F. Rogers, P. R. Smith, eds., Alfred Bork, guest editor, Pergamon, New York (1980).

Newton—A Mechanical World

ALFRED BORK, STEPHAN FRANKLIN, MARTIN KATZ,
JOHN McNELLY
Educational Technology Center
University of California
Irvine, California

This paper reports on an aid for learning classical mechanics developed at the Educational Technology Center at the University of California, Irvine. The simulation, the type we call a controllable world, has gone through a number of stages and variations. Its primary role is to improve intuition of students in the beginning quarter or semester of a physics class. Although our use of programs such as this has been at the beginning college level, the program is suitable for high school use.

CONTROLLABLE WORLDS

A *controllable world* is a computer program providing a world in which the student can move around freely, exploring at will. The idea is related to play activity as seen with young children. A rich collection of facilities is provided, and the learner has freedom in using these. A key to the success of such a controllable world is to make its use as easy and as obvious as possible.

We do not provide structured learning in such an activity. Rather, we are concerned with the experiential phase which might precede a more formal learning approach, as described in the learning cycle of Robert Karplus.[1] The ease of use cannot be overstressed. If the student is to be encouraged to experiment, to try many things, it must be easy to do so. Thus, controllable worlds should incorporate a wide variety of vocabulary rather than restrict the learner to a very specialized menu of choices. They should forgive typing errors as far as possible. They should let the student know what is happening at each stage. They should be visual, because the visual world is for many students a more interesting, exciting, and intuitive world than the world of numbers and words.

The main role of the controllable worlds as developed in the Educational Technology Center over the past dozen years is to increase student intuition and insight into the phenomena. Courses often put too much stress on formal manipulation, the skills that are needed to solve particular classes of problems. But often students do not develop an intuitive background that leads to imaginative solutions of new types of problems. The controllable world can provide a rich collection of experience which can lead to such intuition. But it does not necessarily do so,[2, 3] as we will comment later.

NEWTON

The controllable world discussed is based on Newton's laws of motion. The computer "knows" that $F = ma$, and furthermore knows the mathematical tools necessary to turn this into visual information about how bodies move. The student is given plotting capability. After the force is chosen, the learner can plot various physical variables against each other, alter initial conditions and constants in equations, and move freely through the program. Newton is self-explanatory, not dependent on print material. But certain types of print material will typically be used by students with the program.

HISTORY

A program of this type was described in the initial proposal from the University of California, Irvine (to the National Science Foundation) for developing graphic computer-based learning material. Shortly after the grant, Richard Ballard joined Alfred Bork on the project. They developed the initial version of a controllable world called Motion. This program, in a timesharing environment, is still used with beginning physics students at Irvine. Motion went through a number of variations, as we experimented with how it could be used most effectively.[4]

Several years ago the focus of development at Irvine began to move from timesharing to the newer personal computer environment. At that time we also abandoned earlier software

approaches, as they were no longer in keeping with what was known about the art of complex programming. Our new developmental language is Pascal, under the UCSD Pascal system.

Martin Katz, then an undergraduate student working with the Educational Technology Center, developed a Pascal version of Motion soon after we began to use Pascal. This version was not completely equivalent to Motion; it omitted some facilities but had some additional ones. This program eventually evolved into Newton.

The current version of the program was developed by Alfred Bork, Stephen Franklin, and John McNelly. It does not follow all the details of Motion. Rather, we tried to use what we had learned in the many years of using Motion with sizable numbers of students to guide the development of the new program. Motion ran on Tektronix displays. Newton was developed on the Terak 8510a. By and large, we found that the advantages of the personal computer far outweighed the disadvantages; that is, the switch from timesharing to the personal computer was primarily a gain. We gained selective erase capabilities and better control over timing issues at the expense of poorer resolution.

As of this writing, the latest version of Newton runs only on the Terak. However, earlier versions were successfully moved to the Apple, and we expect to eventually run on a variety of other personal computers. As with other recent developments at the Educational Technology Center, we find it convenient to develop materials on a more powerful machine than the eventual delivery machines.

CAPABILITIES OF NEWTON

As already suggested, Newton is primarily a plotting program. After the mechanical system has been picked, the student can ask to plot any two or three mechanical variables. Time in each case is the independent variable, as is generally the case with mechanical systems, but time does not need to be one of the variables plotted. The user can change the force, change the constants in the force law, change the initial conditions, choose what to plot (including functions of the variables), and query the system for various information. Control over scaling is also available. These capabilities will now be described in more detail.

1. Choosing the Force. When the program is initially entered, the learner must choose a force. At any time during the program, a NEW FORCE can be requested, and the choice will be offered again.

Two basic options in choosing a force are available. First, built-in forces can be picked. Currently the built-in forces are gravitational motion with one force center, gravitational motion with two force centers, simple harmonic motion, and force-driven harmonic motion. New built-in forces are being added. Built-in forces can be selected from a menu.

The user can also choose to enter almost any force whatsoever. These are accepted in a typical linear computer

algebra form with some flexibility. The computer queries for each component of the force. In specifying the force, if constants are used that are not known to the system, the system will query the user as to what initial value should be assigned to these constants. The program can handle almost any force within the limitations of typing.

2. Plotting Capability. After a force has been chosen, either initially or at some later time in the program, the machine is prepared to plot something. That is, if the user simply types PLOT, a curve will appear. The curve is dependent on the force law chosen. We have chosen in advance an interesting case with all the initial conditions already chosen.

Many computer simulations query students for everything necessary to plot. Beginners seldom understand what things are necessary or what values to assign to them, so such querying should be delayed until the learner has attained better understanding. Our notion is to provide an interesting case to begin with and allow the student complete control over changing each of the variables involved.

If the student wants to plot two different variables, then the command is

    PLOT X,T

or

    GRAPH X VS T

Other forms are also possible. Newton is flexible about what terminology is needed, often providing alternates. One function of the variables can be plotted against another.

The typical way to stop plotting is by pressing the space bar. One can continue plotting by typing CONTINUE PLOT after such a stop. There are certain circumstances where plotting may stop on its own, such as when the body crashes into a sun, or the values calculated become abnormally large.

A number of other capabilities are associated with plotting. One that is frequently useful is OVERPLOT, which allows learners to keep a previous curve while seeing a new one. If parameters change, it is convenient to see the curves before and after the change.

The current values of variables plotted can be determined at any time by typing a question mark. This is often convenient when you need numerical values in addition to the curve.

3. Querying for Information. The user can ask for information about current values of variables, either before or after a plot. Thus, you can ask for INITIAL CONDITIONS and Newton will give you these values. Or if you want to see all the variables associated with a particular case, you can simply type ALL to see them.

Such information is often more detailed than necessary. Usually learners need to know only certain variables, either the initial conditions or some of the constants in the equations representing the force law. The student can ask directly for these in one of the following fashions:

a. WHAT IS X?
b. X = ?
c. X ?

Newton will regard any of these commands as equivalent.

4. Changing Variables. A user can not only query variables; variables can be altered. This is done by entering small assignment statements:

a. X = 3
b. FRED = 2
c. DT = DT/2

In the second case it is assumed that a user-specified force was used and that the variable FRED was picked by whoever entered the force. When a variable is changed, Newton verifies what the user has done by showing the value of the variable as changed. This is often not necessary, but it is a reasonable precaution to overcome typing errors.

5. Changing the Scale. Often it is necessary to modify the scale of the plotting to see a convenient picture on the screen. This must be done by the user, as Newton cannot know what details the user expects to see.

The overall changes of scaling are indicated by the commands MOVE BACK and MOVE CLOSER. Both of these produce a scale factor change of 2 on both axes.

Direct scaling is possible by plotting variables in the following way:

PLOT .5 * X*X, 3 * VX

The net effect will be that the scales of both variables change independently. Axes will be labeled appropriately, reminding the user of this change.

USES OF NEWTON

We have implied that the development of materials and their effective use in class or learning environments are two quite separate issues. In this section we discuss this situation and clarify the use of Newton and similar programs.

The primary use of such a program is to build intuition, to allow learners to gain a range of experiences that are not present in everyday life, and so have a feel for mechanical systems that goes beyond the ability to manipulate mathematical details to obtain solutions. Simulations, such as the present one, often have an immediate appeal to scientists. They are closest to the directions scientists follow in their professional activities using the computer. Most scientists are stimulated by running such simulations. Indeed, in our early days with Motion, scientists could hardly keep themselves away once they became exposed. We would have visitors spend large amounts of time running it. Motion would also draw very large crowds when presented at professional meetings.

We began to understand the distinction between the program itself and the program operating in a classroom when we began running Motion with sizable groups of students. Here the excitement of the scientists was often not present. Only a small percent of the students would become excited while using the program. The rest would use it a brief time and then stop unless forced to continue. While we thought the program exciting, the bulk of students in any large class did not appear excited.

This situation puzzled us until we began thinking about incorporating the material in the classroom. Our first step was to develop computer exercises that assured each student would see at least the most important experiences. These computer exercises are still in use in the timesharing environment, about six years after their initial development. Here is a sample of one exercise concerned with gravitational motion:

Now you are to see what would happen if gravitational force were *not quite* inverse square. Ask for the EQUATION again; the power is N. Set

N = −1.9

Return to plotting the X–Y space, investigating a range of values around −2. You may want to continue plotting each orbit. What can you say about the results? What happens for values less than 2? Greater than 2?

What happens if we examine behavior in velocity space?

Now consider the case of *two* gravitational force centers, as if you had two *fixed* suns. Request

2 FORCE CENTERS

at any input. The initial conditions will be reset. Determine them by typing

X,Y,VX,VY = ?

PLOT the orbit. Discuss the possibility of life on a planet with such an orbit.

See if you can find velocities that give closed (repeated) orbits. What velocities do this? Sketch the orbits.

We want to make certain that the student has some structured experiences that aid *learning* about how mechanical systems work.

This second round, using Motion with computer exercises, was not entirely successful either. In the evaluation of the course made by Michael Scriven and his colleagues, this was one of the most criticized activities. At this time we made it a required part of the course. We found that students did not see its connection to other material within the course. Now the material is explained better and used as an option with much greater success; it is used by a sizable number of students.

But we do not regard this approach as entirely satisfactory either, because we believe the experiences should be for *all* students. In another controllable world dealing with field lines, we have greater success with a different tactic. We built an on-line quiz around the simulation. The quiz notes if students have developed the insights we expect about the way field lines behave. As yet, we have not followed this same tactic with mechanics but probably will do so.

The computer experiences for Motion only cover some of the areas of beginning mechanics. We could increase the viability of this program by making it

a constant component of the beginning course, making every unit depend on it to some entent. We are working with CONDUIT (specifically Arthur Luehrmann, Herbert Peckham, Harold Peters, and Alfred Bork) to develop a more extensive set of computer exercises for Newton. These are intended for use in high school and beginning college physics courses and will cover areas not [covered] by the present exercises. For example, we consider motion with no forces acting and motion with constant forces. We plan to have these new exercises available at the conference.

This project is supported by the National Science Foundation through a CAUSE grant. The project manager for the grant is Stephen Franklin. Other members of the Educational Technology Center, Barry Kurtz and David Trowbridge, have offered helpful suggestions for developing Newton and the associated exercises.

June 17–19, 1981

REFERENCES

1. Karplus, Robert, "The Psychology of Teaching and Thinking for Creativity," Anton Lawson, ed., 1980.
2. Bork, A., "Computers as an Aid to Increasing Physical Intuition," *American Journal of Physics,* 46 (8), August 1978.
3. Bork, A., "Learning with Computer Simulations," *Computer,* October 1979.
4. Bork, A., "The Physics Computer Development Project," *EDUCOM,* 10, 4, Winter 1975.

five

PRODUCTION AND DESIGN

Production Systems for Computer-Based Learning

ALFRED BORK

INTRODUCTION

This paper is concerned with the variety of possible production systems for generating computer-based and related learning material. A *production system* is the set of activities beginning with vague ideas about the concepts to be taught and ending with finished materials in the hands of users. These materials may include computer programs of various types, written material, visual material, and other pedagogical aids. They may also involve a variety of machinery for delivery—computers, videodisc players, slide projectors, [and] print material.

The need to seriously consider production systems for computer-based learning development is a result of many initial "cottage industry" efforts. In the early days of developing computer-based learning material, little was known about how such material worked with students, and little was known about the production process. Not too surprisingly, beginners in this new experimental medium began to produce material with a variety of strategies. At this early stage projects did not produce sizable amounts of material, because we still had much to learn about the capabilities of the new medium.

As we have moved toward the era of very inexpensive personal computers, the possibility of large-scale production and distribution has become more and more viable. Little large-scale production and distribution is currently going on, but the prospects look very promising for the immediate future. Many companies are now considering the marketing of computer-based learning material.

Hence, it is important at this stage to explore possible production systems. Without this step, sizable sums of money may be devoted to inappropriate approaches generating poor material.

The production ideas which form the basis of this discussion were developed over a 13-year period at the Educational Technology Center. Thus, it is rooted in the experience of producing a sizable body of curriculum material. I begin by formulating criteria for production systems and by reviewing some of the strategies that have been commonly used.

CRITERIA FOR PRODUCTION SYSTEMS

It is reasonable, before discussing particular ways of organizing the production process for computer-based learning material or intelligent videodisk learning material, to develop a set of criteria and emphases for such systems. That is, we need to ask what *should* be the properties of such systems before we begin to develop the systems directly. This section outlines such criteria.

109

1. **Major Focus on Pedagogical Issues.** As the material developed is to be learning material, the focus must be on the learning or pedagogical issues. This would seem to be almost a truism. Yet it can be argued that many of the production systems in existence dilute this focus and, in fact, tend to place the major emphasis on the technology itself. The overriding considerations should be pedagogical, and these factors should drive the development.

2. **The Best Possible Material.** The system should produce the best possible material for aiding learners. Systems which can produce material of limited capability should be avoided.

3. **Reasonable Costs.** The costs associated with the full production process should be reasonable. The implication is that the material developed is to be marketed, either commercially or noncommercially, and that the costs must be in the range that can attract users.

4. **Estimatable Costs.** In addition to having a reasonable cost, it is important that a developer be able to estimate costs in advance, within reasonable accuracy. A product will be usable in the market only if this is possible; an extensive product will be developed only if costs can be estimated. In the early days of working in an area, it was difficult to estimate costs. One must work toward systems that produce reliable cost estimates.

5. **Involve a Wide Range of Good Teachers.** The development of learning materials is still partially a science and partially an art. There is no substitute at the present time for very experienced, good teachers, familiar with the way students will react and learn. This is particularly important in computer-based learning, as the materials are usually designed to work with a wide variety of students. Hence, strategies which allow many excellent teachers to participate in ways that the *teachers* find congenial are highly desirable. One cannot expect to work with only a few teachers, if one is to produce sizable amounts of material, just because of the volume of material involved.

6. **Easily Revisable Units.** One of the advantages of computer-based learning material is that it can gather very detailed feedback on a moment-by-moment basis of the responses given by users. Hence, it is potentially very easy to revise, to make the material better and better. This means that whatever is written must be constructed to facilitate easy revision, often many times. Revisions may stretch over a period of years, and so many different people may be involved. Thought must be given in the production process to how revision is to take place and how it can be as simple and as economical as possible. Maintenance of instructional materials, regardless of the media involved, is an important component of their life cycle.

7. **Encourage Interaction.** A major advantage of computer-based

learning material is that it can create an *active* learning environment for each student. This is unattainable with most of the mass learning techniques currently in use, primarily "spectator" techniques. The computer allows us to achieve some of the aspects, although not all, of a Socratic dialogue.

As our capabilities for developing more and more intelligent computer materials improve, we may be able to approach closer to the Socratic tutor. But even at the present time, we can develop highly interactive units for large groups of students, and we can compete extremely well with books and lectures in this regard. Nevertheless, not all computer material achieves this goal of interaction. In some cases this is the result of the production systems employed; some systems tend to cut down on the amount and level of interaction that takes place.

8. **Encourage Individualization.** A computer dialogue can offer specific aid to a wide range of students. The notion that different students learn in different ways is widely believed. But many learning strategies find it difficult to provide for this range. We can do so with the computer. But again, computer material does not *necessarily* do this. Rather, individualization and adaptability must be encouraged within the production system.

9. **Maximize Motivation.** Computer material should be attractive to the users. That is, it should explicitly consider motivational issues. An important goal of instruction and instructional materials is to increase student time on task, and thus to increase learning. One important way to accomplish this is by making the material more interesting.

There are many facets to motivation. For example, one important set of motivational factors is screen design—how the material is arranged on the screen both temporally and spatially. An issue that needs more consideration is that of which factors should be turned over to the "reader." The reader can potentially control many aspects of the screen which are fixed in book or lecture environments.

10. **Minimize Transferability Problems.** In the foreseeable future we can expect a continual procession of new, small, personal computers. These machines will reflect some combination of increased capability and reduced cost, depending on the marketing choices of the vendors. Hence, material developed in an effective production process must be economically transferable to these new student delivery machines as they become available.

Many issues are associated with transferability. The first consideration is what might be called technical transferability, the taking of materials written for one machine in one programming language and moving them to another machine with different hardware capabilities and possibly with different programming languages. This is often the *only* aspect considered. The production system can ease this process or can make it very difficult.

Another consideration is the scale of the entire project. Transferability becomes more practical when there will be sizable use of the material on the new machine, because the unit cost is less.

Another issue in transportability is that of visual appearance on the screen. When one moves from a display with 80 characters on a line to one with 40 characters, material must be rearranged, usually both text and visuals, on the screen. Different graphic facilities also may be available— such factors as resolution and intensity control may be different on the systems considered. The production approach must be set up in such a way as to ease the rearrangement of such screen factors during the transfer process.

A final issue in transferability is the use of extensive new capabilities not available on the original delivery machines. It must be possible to redesign the material relatively easily to allow for new capabilities as they become available.

In all these issues of transferability, it should be kept in mind that we will be talking about an increasingly large body of computer-based learning material as we move more and more into the future. Hence, the transferability process must be applicable to many different units of learning material, developed over a wide span of time.

11. **Adaptability to Large-Scale Production.** While currently computer-based learning materials are being produced on a small scale, we need to look forward to the time in the not very distant future when sizable amounts of material will be produced. Strategies which may work for small amounts of production may be quite inadequate for large-scale production.

COMPONENTS OF A PRODUCTION SYSTEM

Various production systems may all have the same fundamental components. These components may be arranged in different ways; some may be omitted. Furthermore, the choice of who carries out each activity and how the developers of the components interface with each other will differ from system to system. In some systems a particular component may be repeated at several stages. We will give further details later.

Although we are grouping the components roughly in the order in which they would normally follow, there are many exceptions to this. As indicated, some might be omitted. Some might be repeated in different ways at various stages in the process. A few refer to activities that are typically carried on through much of the process.

The present section should not be taken as a description of any particular production system, but rather only as an overview, delineating components common to *all* production systems.

I assume that the computer learning material may be part of a larger activity, which may involve some print material and possibly other kinds of visual aid. Thus, with the process described, we might be producing intelligent videodisc material, combining the computer and the videodisc.

1. **Preplanning Activities.** As with any sizable project, a number of activities must take place before the project begins. For example, it will be necessary to secure the initial funding, arrange for personnel, establish the production mechanism, and generally oversee the beginning of the operation. Development of the proposal, either to a governmental agency or to a company, will be necessary in this stage of the operation. Preliminary consideration of objectives may also take place at this stage.

2. **Production Management.** The production process may in some systems be a complex activity. So it is necessary to consider how this activity is to be managed. While we list this second, because it must be set up at an early stage of the process, it is an activity that will continue for the entire project.

3. **Objectives and Specifications.** For detailed work to proceed, a detailed overview must be available of what is to be produced. This overview can be developed in a variety of ways. As a minimum it would describe the modules to be produced in terms of the objectives each is trying to attain. It might provide fairly detailed outlines also as to how these objectives are to be attained.

4. **Training Activities.** Training activities for the personnel involved might be important in a number of the following stages. Hence, this might be not a single activity but a series of different activities. The people involved in the different stages of producing materials may not know initially how to do the assigned tasks. Even if they are trained in some aspects, they may need special assistance. So several training programs, formal or informal, may be required.

5. **Pedagogical Design.** This critical stage in the process involves the full pedagogical specification of the material. It goes far beyond the third step, the statement of objectives and specifications. The "script" which is the product of this stage contains *all* the decisions of an instructional nature, at least in their initial form.

6. **Visual Design.** Another component is designing the material—placement of graphical information and textual information on the screen both spatially and temporally. Temporal considerations would also include delays. There might also be some user control as to how the material is to be displayed on the screen. Decisions must be made concerning the details of such user control.

7. **Technical Development.** This is

the stage in which the actual materials are initially produced. These materials may include computer programs, videodiscs, print material (typeset and printed), and other associated materials.

8. **Editing.** Editing is another process which is likely to occur at several stages. For example, it might well occur between stage 5 (pedagogical design) and stage 6 (visual design), as well as after technical development.

9. **Evaluation.** Evaluation of computer-based learning materials is important in improving their capability (formative evaluation) and in demonstrating their effectiveness (summative evaluation). Hence, because of these different roles, evaluation will probably occur at several stages in the production process.

10. **Revision.** Formative evaluation implies that there will be a revision cycle or cycles. Revisions can lead to significant improvement of computer-based learning material. Several evaluation-revision loops may take place.

11. **Marketing.** After material is in release form, the issue then becomes how to market it. Marketing includes awareness, making potential users aware that the product is there, and includes providing opportunities for them to "see" and try the materials.

12. **Distribution.** The aim of the production process is to place the material in the hands of users, teachers, or students. Distribution may be through commercial or noncommercial channels.

I stress again that this outline of production components does not attempt to describe any *particular* production system. A particular system may leave out some of these components, may combine some, may alter the order, and will have its own particular strategies for executing them. Different systems make different choices in determining what person or persons carry out one component and how the products of the different stages or components interface with each other.

The reader may have noticed that these components are *not* peculiar to computer-based learning material. Rather, they are stages that one might see in a process for producing any type of learning material—print, film, videodisc, or intelligent videodisc. A corollary to this is that the production process is not necessarily different for computer material than for other material. In many multimedia developments, a range of material, computer and others, may be produced.

PRODUCTION SYSTEMS WITHOUT COMPUTERS

In looking at specific production systems for generating computer-based learning material, it is reasonable to view systems for producing high-quality educational material that have already been developed. Thus, we can hope to profit from the types of strategies already in existence. Development of learning materials has many common factors regardless of the media and the subject area, particularly if these materials are to be of the highest quality.

Books

The production of textbooks is an interesting example for us because it represents a mature production system also based on technological development. The printing press, invented in about 1450, is the basis for the modern book industry. Later developments, such as the invention of efficient typesetting machines, also played a critical role. So we may learn something about how to use a new technological development, the computer, to aid in the educational process by looking at this older process, printing.

It is worth noting that several hundred years elapsed between the invention of the printing press and the widespread use of textbooks in schools and universities. It is no accident that such a time span is necessary. Initially people do not understand how to use a newer medium for learning, and so much experimental trial work is necessary. Practically everything that has gone on so far with using the computer in education should be viewed as fitting into this early experimental period. We are now beginning to see a variety of modes in which the computer is effective, so we are approaching the end of this experimental stage.

Many variant systems have been employed for producing books. But a typical process might go something like

this. Let us consider, for example, a new calculus book to be produced by one of the major publishers. In the preplanning stage the company may decide first that it needs such a book to supplement its product line. Or the idea may have come from an author or group of authors. In modern publishing this decision is likely to be followed by extensive market survey activities, going out to current teachers of calculus courses. This market research and discussions with possible authors, including eventually those for whom a contract is signed to write the book, determine the objectives and specifications for the book. The specifications may be reviewed by sending them out to outside consultants for suggested modifications.

The book industry has moved from a loose structure, where almost all the decisions about objectives were made by the individual authors, to one in which the publishers, following market research, now play a considerable role in the process. Often detailed outlines, including how much material is to go into each section, are specified before any actual writing is done.

The pedagogical component in writing the book is a well-known activity. Several authors may be involved. They produce a manuscript, one that will typically go through a number of editorial stages, with again outside reviewers playing a role in the process. Some publishers work now with authors putting the "manuscript" directly into a word processor, so it is available in computer-readable form for later stages of the process. But this is still rare. Mostly, manuscripts are done on local typewriters and are not in machine-storable form, but this situation is likely to change.

When the manuscript of the book goes to the publisher, several activities take place. First, artists will be employed to create necessary illustrations. The author has sketched these in the manuscript, and the artist may talk to the author in the process of doing the design of these pictures. Graphic designers are employed to determine an overall structure to the book. This includes many decisions, such as typefaces, use of blank space, the size of the type, the placement of the diagrams, the size of the page, the page layout, the paper to be used, and other factors of this kind. The publisher may bring in outside graphic designers for this process or may work in-house.

The typesetting activities may or may not occur within the company. Many publishers will "farm out" such technical tasks as setting the type. If the manuscript is developed on a word processor, typesetting is done directly from the floppy disks. After the type is set, many publishers go through a two-stage process of looking for errors in typesetting, first in galleys and then in pages. Both the authors and internal proofreaders may be involved. Publishers strive to keep changes at a minimum in page proofs, because changes become increasingly expensive. However, as printers have moved to more automated equipment, perhaps coming out of word-processed manuscripts, the changes at this stage become less expensive.

Printing with most contemporary publishers is not done within the publisher's own organization but in a specialty house. Marketing and distribution are well-known activities, so they will not be described further.

We can see a number of important points in book production. First, it took hundreds of years for the production system to become established. Second, it involves many different people. Third, each person is involved in an activity that that person does effectively. That is, the teachers teach and the printers print. Finally, the production system is still evolving, under the impact of technological changes.

Although we have described this process for books, it is not too different if one looks, for example, at the production of films for instructional use. The technical development aspects vary because the medium is different, but many of the other details are quite similar.

The Open University

As a second example of production of course materials, I describe briefly the system used at the Open University in England.[1] This system is producing perhaps more curriculum material than any other group in the world. The computer so far has played a minor role in the activity, although some courses developed at the Open University have computer components.

First, it should be emphasized that the Open University offers far more than a production system. In a new and interesting way it combines both the production and delivery of learning materials in an overall process that is economical. Great attention is given to production issues. The Open University represents a financial balance different from the typical conventional university system anywhere in the world. Far more money is spent on the production of learning material and far less money on delivery. The overall results are encouraging both in terms of the effectiveness of the learning process and in terms of the relatively low cost per student involved.

The Open University system begins with putting together a course team. This will be a group of individuals who, typically for an 18-month period, will be concerned with the planning, pedagogical design, and some phases of the production of the overall materials. Technical production will still take place elsewhere. The course team will have a variety of individuals on it, since an Open University course will involve a number of media. Thus, it will have television specialists who will advise on how television could be used, and then later will be involved in designing the actual television material.

The team may begin by reviewing existing similar courses, including the common textbooks. Occasionally the material from existing sources will be found to be useful in the new course, but this is seldom the case. The members of the course team may not all be Open University faculty members. Some people are brought in for a particular development, even from abroad, some for the entire length of the project and some for shorter times.

To some extent the strategies used in the Open University are also employed in commercial and military development of training material, particularly by the various commercial concerns that seek participation in that market. The details will not be discussed. An interesting thing to note is that in all these cases a team effort is involved.

PRODUCTION SYSTEMS FOR COMPUTER MATERIAL

Single-Individual Systems

In looking at production systems for computer material, I make a major distinction. First, I will look at systems which were designed for single individuals, usually individual teachers, to be concerned with all the stages of the production process. I will argue that these systems, although widely developed and widely advertised, are quite inadequate for the problem at hand.

These systems date from the earliest times of development of computer-based learning material. In their most simple form they combine pedagogical design (component 5) and technical development (component 7) into a single process. They then either downplay or ignore most of the other components associated with production.

The fundamental notions of these single-person systems are appealing, but naive. They are appealing in the sense that it is nice to think of a single individual having complete control of the process and being able to produce a wide range of flexible material. But severe limitations exist, enough to rule out this method from serious consideration for large-scale effective production.

We can distinguish several variants in approaches. One of these might be described as the "CAI language" approach, although computer-assisted instruction (CAI) languages, as we will see, can also be used in other ways. In some cases the language involved is a general purpose language. The second approach is the interactive user approach.

The first approach involving one person began with the development of the Coursewriter system within IBM. Its strategy was to develop a computer-based instructional language that would be taught to the prospective user, the writer of materials. The writer would then proceed to write materials using this language. The languages developed for this purpose have always been advertised as easy to use.

In the interactive approach, the second variant of the single person approach, the developer of the materials sits down directly at a computer display and furnishes information, sometimes in the form of queries from the program, sometimes in other ways more determined by the user. Fixed logic structures, templates, are built into the program by the designers of the program. Both these types of single-person system

may have some type of training phase to acquaint authors with the capabilities.

Both approaches are represented by many different reincarnations. Thus, if one looks at "CAI languages," one might estimate that there have been as many as fifty of these developed. Most, indeed almost all, of the CAI languages and interactive systems have had very little material written in them. Examples of the first approach are Coursewriter and Pilot (widely touted on small machines), and examples of the second approach are Ditran, IDF, and the Utah system. New systems of both types continue to be developed.

What are the difficulties with the single-individual approaches to production? First, and perhaps foremost, they assume that many good teachers either are or can become good programmers. But this is seldom the case. Figure 1 indicates a more realistic situation. It might be better to label the *potentially* good programmers. If someone can teach, it is not necessarily the case that that person can become a competent programmer or, perhaps even more important, will want to become a competent programmer. The notion that one should persuade teachers to

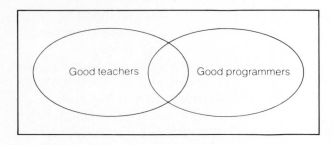

Figure 1

program, even in "simplified" languages, is similar to saying that someone who is going to publish a book must learn how to typeset and how to operate a printing press.

A second problem is that these systems restrict what the user can do. Even the most complex CAI languages around still provide limited capabilities, not the full range of what is possible with the computer. So the creativity of the good teacher is restricted. Furthermore, good teachers may resent these restrictions, as they cannot do what they think is pedagogically best. This violates step 5 above for a production system.

Furthermore, judged as programming languages according to current standards, almost all the CAI languages are quite primitive. They do not provide the features which encourage good structured programming. Perhaps the only exception to this is a programming language developed particularly for this application, Natal74. Thus, they do not conform to the best present practice for modern programming.

Even if the language has a full set of capabilities, the typical *strategy*—involving people without programming experience and pushing them quickly to writing material—is almost bound to lead to a limited use of the language, and therefore simple material. They write limited material because they only know a small subset of the possible capabilities.

The great bulk of the material done with single-individual strategies is pedagogically uninteresting, reflecting the limitations of the strategy. This is not to say that some very shining exceptions to this rule cannot be found. In a number of cases individuals worked for years in this format and became very experienced programmers. Furthermore, extremely good pedagogical ideas will serve to overcome a variety of difficulties. But the evidence indicates that this family of approaches has not been a useful way to produce materials. There are simply too few Renaissance men and women available. In many cases little exists beyond the CAI language itself; it has been employed relatively little for any actual development of material.

The two problems with single-individual systems are closely tied together in an unfortunate fashion. If the "CAI language" is extremely simple, then it can be, as advertised, quickly learned by some teachers. But it can only write very simple-minded material. As the language becomes more complex, increasing the range of computer-based learning material possible, it becomes less and less usable by naive individuals.

Another difficulty with production strategies of this type comes in connection with revision activities. As programs are revised a number of times and become more complex, they become more difficult to revise. The authoring languages, as indicated, do not satisfy the best modern standards of structured languages, and therefore the programs produced are not easy to modify. With some approaches modification becomes almost an impossibility, done only by essentially redoing an entire segment of the material. So the many detailed revisions necessary after evaluation stages become very impractical.

Finally it should be clear from the arguments already stated that the single-individual strategies will not lead to large-scale production. Any one individual can produce only a small amount, because that individual must do a variety of tasks. Strategies which allow the individual to concentrate on particular tasks, such as the pedagogical design task, are likely to lead to increased production. Furthermore, as indicated by the fact that most good teachers will not become good programmers, the supply of people who can write decent material with such systems will always be small.

Team Systems

The other set of possibilities for production activities is that a *group* of individuals will be involved in the process, not a single individual. Sizable production in the future must be done in this vein for the reasons just stated. But saying that the production system should be a team system still leaves many choices to be determined.

Perhaps the first category of team production systems that occurs are those which represent the extensions of the single-individual systems when serious production is considered. The single-individual systems begin to get into difficulty for the reasons described. Then the developers of these systems begin to see that it is *not* necessary to have things done entirely by one individual. So they begin to split the tasks, but maintaining essentially the *same framework*—

languages and facilities—indicated above. The major change is to split the pedagogical design stage and the technical development stage; but for each the developers follow similar strategies as they did in single-user systems. Thus, the "CAI language," or interactive capability, becomes used by a person other than the teacher. The teacher is then constrained to step 5 in the process.

An example of this modification of a single-user system was the development of the Control Data Plato authoring system after Control Data became itself heavily involved in Plato. While the system was at the University of Illinois, at least in the early stages, it was typically a single-individual system, with one person doing everything. But when Control Data took it over, it became a team system. The strategies for step 7, technical development, were essentially the same strategies that had been developed initially. In this case the Tutor language, initially developed with a single-individual strategy in mind, was extended to a more elaborate production system which in most cases separated off the pedagogical design from the technical development. The programmers in step 7 used Tutor, although it had initially been developed with teachers as the prospective users.

As the single-individual strategies have begun to move toward larger-scale production, they often attempt to preserve some features of their older system, such as the languages, but try at the same time to move toward a team involved in the developmental process. But the difficulty with this approach has already been mentioned. The languages developed were really developed with the novice coder in mind, *not* the professional coder or other special individual who is likely to be involved when the stages are separated. All the problems mentioned above that deal with languages are still problems in the present strategy. In particular, few of the CAI languages satisfy minimum criteria for good programming languages.

A few such groups were willing to recognize this problem with CAI languages, and so completely discarded older software when they moved away from the single-individual strategy. But this is a difficult thing to do, given the emotional involvement in the previous software.

Beyond this extension of the one-user system, many variants are possible in a team production system. Each of the components already discussed allows a number of possibilities. The criteria stated earlier in this paper give a way of looking at any one such system that has been developed.

Much of the remainder of this paper will be devoted to explicating one particular production system, that developed in the Educational Technology Center at the University of California, Irvine. In the course of this exposition I will discuss some of the design considerations that led to the choice of strategies with each component of the production system.

THE IRVINE PRODUCTION SYSTEM

The Irvine production system has been under development in the Educational Technology Center during the past 13 years. It has produced a very sizable amount of material, ranging from elementary school through university material and in a variety of modes. This approach has been well described in the literature, as have the resulting modules.[2]

We will discuss the system in terms of the way we work at Irvine with regard to each of the components of production mentioned. Like the production of books and like The Open University process, a variety of people are involved, so it is a team process. I will describe the system in terms of how it typically operates and how we would like it to operate if the resources were sufficient.

1. Preplanning. There is little to say that is unique about preplanning. In our case, since we are primarily dependent on grant support, the preplanning consists primarily of negotiations with the granting agency, either a federal granting agency or a commercial source interested in producing materials.

Preliminary planning of other stages must go on here. As these may not be funded as yet, this activity can present problems.

2. Production Management. The process is complex, so management is an important issue. Each of the projects in the Educational Technology Center has a program manager associated with it, a person who is responsible for managing the entire operation.

The management procedure we have followed is one based on the structured analysis and design technique, commonly referred to as SADT.[3] This technique (developed by SofTech), coming out of modern software engineering, is both a way of describing our activities (to be indicated later) and a mechanism for managing the projects. Since it shows the stages of activity, we can identify the status of each module in a project, within the developmental cycle, at a given time.

3. Objectives and Specifications.   A principal mechanism for developing objectives and specifications is a preliminary meeting. At the beginning of this meeting brainstorming is the principal technique. We bring a variety of people, including many teachers who typically deal with the students we are attempting to reach. The purpose of such a meeting is to develop the objectives and outline each of the sequences of modules contributing to these objectives. Overall decisions about the modular structure are also made at this time. The attempt is to produce a specification for each of the pedagogical writing groups to be formed in stage 5.

In some cases it is not possible to proceed this way because of budgetary limitations. Then the objectives and specifications are done primarily by the internal staff at the Educational Technology Center, perhaps working with outside consultants.

In this stage, as in all the components of our production system, we often bring in outside aid. We do not believe that it is either desirable or necessary to work entirely with people at a particular location. Rather, we seek specialists from everywhere who can contribute to our activities. So it is necessary to budget expenses and honoraria for such specialists from outside our campus.

4. Training Activities.   We conduct, at least for some projects, three types of training, corresponding to each of the next three components of the production process.

In connection with pedagogical design, component 5, we want to acquaint the teachers and others who write with us with the learning capabilities of the computer. In one-half-day training sessions we put particular stress on how these capabilities differ from more familiar educational media such as lectures and textbooks. A major technique followed is to sit down with the relatively small group involved and show them many examples of different types of material, pointing out in each case the pedagogical factors involved. An important issue is pointing out possible pitfalls for the novice developer, pitfalls often identified from previous experience with other media.

Along the same line, we have also been responsible for running many workshops at university campuses and elsewhere that are particularly concerned with training novice faculty in the preparation of materials. These workshops are more formalized than the half-day sessions we typically run for our own work and usually involve groups of about twenty or twenty-five faculty members. The center of these activities is the group production of the pedagogical design of some computer-based learning material, usually followed by supervised small group design experience.

A second type of training, one that we still understand poorly, concerns the training of artists for the development of the visual design material in stage 6. The artists must learn to use the interactive design facilities, to be described later. We also convey to the artists at this time our general design standards for the visual and temporal appearance of material.

Finally, since we work with student coders and since students graduate, we are constantly in the position of training new student coders. Such training would also be necessary in a commercial environment. We do this training primarily by examples, starting with simple material, a pedagogical design, and tracing through all the coding procedures necessary to get this material running. We have written material to support this activity. After the initial activity we assign a programming task, usually in groups of three beginning programmers, giving the coders a simple bit of script (see stage 5). An important component of this training is the emphasis on the need for adequate documentation.

At the present time the training activities we are undertaking are restricted to the Irvine campus or to specially run workshops in other locations. These activities are dependent on the individuals who have the experience. But it would be possible to make the training materials transportable, so that authors in a wide variety of locations could be taught to use them without individuals from the Educational Technology Center presenting the materials. Much of the training could be done using on-line computer materials particularly developed for this application.

5. Pedagogical Design. We regard the pedagogical design stage, the stage in which the instructional materials are fully specified from an instructional point of view, to be the most critical of all the stages in the production process. Material that is to work well with students must depend heavily on the experiences of extremely good teachers and specialists in the areas involved.

One important issue is whether the pedagogical design is to be done by a single individual or by a group of individuals. Most materials in most of the computer-based production systems followed so far have been developed by single individuals, ignoring the experience of such group design of curriculum material in such institutions as the Open University. But we have long argued, based on experience at the Educational Technology Center, that one obtains much superior material if a *group* works together in the instructional development of learning material.[4] The implication is that the group stays together during the entire developmental stage. We have found that groups of from three to five are the most effective in this process. Smaller groups often do not do a competent job of accounting for all the variants of student input. Larger groups engage in endless pedagogical debates and get little done.

The composition of the groups is very important. We try to pick people because of their experiences, particularly in interactive teaching. At least some of the people must be familiar with the intended target audience. Others may bring in special backgrounds, perhaps from learning theory or instructional design, visual design, or various media. At least one person in the group should already have had experience in developing computer-based learning materials. But it is not at all necessary for the other people in the group to have had previous computer experience. Indeed, our feeling is that usually it is better *not* to have had such experience. What is needed is an understanding of the medium as a learning medium, rather than any view of how to program. People with some programming experience often have a very limited view of the capabilities of the computer in aiding learning.

Another important issue is the environment. We believe that since the task is a difficult one, requiring concentration, it should be done in an environment where there are no interruptions, except those planned by the group itself. Thus, we do not find it conducive to work in the typical office. Rather we tend to work in pleasant environments away from the office. In our case, California provides many such environments.

The question of how long the group should work does not have a clear answer. Many of our recent materials have been developed by groups that stayed together for a week or two. Often in a particular week we will have two or three groups working at the same time, and they may interact over lunch or dinner. In some projects it is desirable to have the group together for longer periods. But because of the exacting nature of the tasks, it may be tiring for the same group to work together for very long periods of time. Our typical experience is that, for average material, a group working for a week will produce between $1\frac{1}{2}$ and 2 hours of material, as viewed in terms of usage by the average student.

The group, working together, must produce a complete pedagogical specification, one that moves into the other stages of the production process and gives all the necessary information for those stages. Hence, it must show the text to be displayed, the pictures to be displayed, the analyses of student inputs, and all the logic decisions.

Since we want the members of the pedagogical design team to have the greatest possible freedom, the method of displaying this information should not restrict them to any fashion. Thus, we do not employ any templated (fixed) logic structures, limited structures in which it is assumed that everybody will work. Rather, groups are encouraged to make their choices entirely on pedagogical grounds and to be as free as possible about these choices. The training session which preceded this work emphasizes the capabilities of the media and tries to tell of common pitfalls by those first beginning to write materials.

The form we have found most convenient for authors is one that might be described as an informal or loose script. We make no attempt whatsoever to teach formal techniques. Indeed, the procedure, mostly learned by watching one member of the group who is already experienced, is presented as a way of specifying the pedagogical situation. The pictures are sketched. Additional information about pictures or other details may be offered to the programmer, as notes on the script. The group may make sketches of the screen as to how material is to be displayed and may indicate delays or other timing considerations. The tests to be made on student input are shown sequentially, indicating (by lines flowing out of the boxes) what to do with success on a particular test, either the first time through that box or at some later time.

The exact form of the structure is not too important, provided the conventions that the individual groups use are made clear in the material. We have usually found it convenient to work on large sheets of paper, since there is less referencing of other sheets. We also encourage developers to make copious comments, notes to the programmer or designer, about what is to happen and for future reference when new media capabilities are available.

6. Visual Design. It is in visual design that actual practice at the Educational Technology Center often departs from what I view as the most desirable strategy. This departure is because of limited resources, and because we have not yet completed all the software to make the most desirable approach feasible.

Ideally visual design should be done by a competent graphic designer who does magazine layout or develops brochures advertising products. The person needs some special training, as indicated, mostly in understanding how appearance on the screen may impact learning capabilities. The person also needs to be trained in the use of special on-line capabilities that allow the design to take place directly on the screen. Thus, we do not regard it desirable for the screen to be designed on paper, although in the pedagogical stage the authors may offer many suggestions in this direction. Rather, the visual designer should be working directly at the screen. This strategy is not unique with our project, although we have worked in this direction for many years. For example, the Canadian Telidon system has put considerable energy into developing screen design capabilities.

In practice, the visual design aspects at Irvine are often handled by a combination of the pedagogical authors and the coders involved in the technical development stage. In the timesharing environment we had developed software to work with graphic designers, and this proved to be useful. But the software and the environment we have developed so far on the small machines are not yet fully capable of performing all the necessary tasks. Furthermore, our resources for employing artists are often limited.

7. Technical Development. The next stage is coding computer-based learning materials. The coders work from the dialogues produced in the pedagogical design stage, a script arrangement, and from the products of the visual design stage.

The question of how the coders should work is the most important issue. That is, what is the programming environment in which the activities are to be carried out? This not only includes the programming language itself and the various auxiliary software for supporting it, but also involves issues of supervision, working conditions, and quality control.

In structuring our approach to the coding task, modern software engineering practices are of considerable aid. Following the practices there, for example, we insist on structure charts before any actual coding takes place. The program manager or supervising programmer will inspect these charts. We also have very high standards for code, insisting that it be "good" code with the highest standards of modern structured programming. It is only by maintaining such high standards for code that we will be able to satisfy several of the criteria mentioned at the beginning of this paper: the material should be easy to revise, and we should minimize transferability problems.

A critical factor is the choice of a language, to satisfy the two criteria mentioned and to make the coding process efficient. We believe that the only reasonable choices are the best languages that have come out of contemporary language design, the languages that allow all the features of structured programming. Our own choice has been to work within Pascal. In particular, we use University of California, San Diego Pascal. The fact that the UCSD Pascal

system, including the compiler as well as all the other features of the system, is easily transferable onto a new small machine means that we have assisted our transferability problems. Pascal at this stage is also more standardized than many other languages that could be used, although the Pascal standards committee in the United States has not yet finished its deliberations. Ada presents interesting possibilities for the future.

Various auxiliary software is also necessary to ease the programming task. Since our coders are typically undergraduate students (or in some cases professional coders), this software is designed with them in mind. An extremely important component of this additional software is a completely new input-output package, including both text and graphic capabilities. The graphic details follow those in the core graphics SIGGRAPH recommendations. The textual details have a similar philosophy in that they too put text on the screen through individual viewports. This software allows much more flexible control over input and output than is possible within the relatively crude capabilities native to the language. This approach is also designed in such a way that the details of differences in screen capabilities can easily be taken care of when one is transferring from one machine to another. The text itself may be part of the program, or it may be kept in separate files called by the program. Full information is available.[5]

In addition, a library of procedures for the commonly carried out functions is also necessary and useful. This library, however, is difficult to maintain in a personal computer environment in which each programmer is using his or her own floppy disks. We hope to move soon to a local network, with a storage machine that will keep all the common library capabilities of this kind. This will assure that all programs have the latest version available at the time they are developed.

Other specialized tools may be developed for particular purposes. Thus, at Irvine we have developed an elaborate quiz driver to assist in giving on-line quizzes. The point of this quiz driver is to allow the individual teacher to make many individual changes in the way the quiz is presented to students.[6] In other situations similar tools might prove useful.

An important issue is that of the hardware, the computer system including associated devices, to be used in this phase of production. The naive assumption is that one would use the same hardware that is intended for delivery. But we have come to believe that this is seldom the correct choice. Because the delivery hardware is evolving rapidly, one needs to develop not for a single delivery machine but for a whole range of delivery machines, many of which do not exist at the time the development is going forward.

The hardware requirements and capabilities needed for development far surpass those needed for delivery of material. Much of the materials we have developed at Irvine recently could not have been developed on some of the delivery systems that these same materials now run on.

The specification of full developmental hardware needs additional attention. In most cases the hardware used for the developmental activities for computer-based learning has been inadequate for aspects of the task.

8. Editing. Editing can and should take place at several stages. The first stage for editing at Irvine is directly after pedagogical design, between steps 5 and 6. A second stage of editing takes place after initial coding, as indicated by the ordering in our listing of the components.

After the pedagogical design stage, the editor is playing a role similar to that the book manuscript editor plays. Nothing has been cast in concrete at this point, everything can still be changed. We have experimented with a variety of styles.

The typical approach is to give the script, produced in the pedagogical design stage, to someone who is already experienced in reading such charts. This individual makes recommendations for changes, and then the original authors decide which changes should be carried out. Some of the changes may be editorial, changing the vocabulary, while others may reflect pedagogical issues.

But we are worried that this process may be very dependent on who the individual is who does it. Unlike book editing, relatively little experience in the process exists, and so different individuals may look for quite different things. We have also experimented lately with some strategies which have involved "dry runs" with actual students before any coding is done. The person doing this works with predesigned sheets of paper, playing the role of the computer. But it is not yet clear whether this tactic is useful.

The second stage of editing comes after the material is first coded. Then the authors, the visual designers, and the technical developers, or some subset of these, sit down and run the program many times. We find that at this stage many changes are suggested, and so extensive rewriting will typically take place. Material is different in the interactive environment, not like the paper version. This stage of revision emphasizes the need for a system which allows easy revision.

In a sense this process is like editing a book after all the typesetting has taken place, and the book is in page proofs. With books this is an expensive process, at least with most modern production methods. But with computers, particularly if an effective language has been used in stage 7, such editing is not only feasible but relatively easy to do. It is, however, somewhat boring for the competent programmer, particularly when he or she goes through many cycles of such changes.

Stages 9 to 12.   Stages 9 to 12, evaluating, revising, marketing, and distributing, the last stages in development, will be considered as a group. The activities do not differ too widely from those involved in any good development of educational material, and so follow the general principles of instructional design.

It does need to be said, however, that the computer is capable of gathering very detailed feedback as to what happens when it is used with students. So formative evaluation is much more easily carried out; we can make many more significant changes in the material than is typical in instructional development employing other media. Again, the choice of an effective programming language will ease this stage. We believe that one of the real strengths of the computer material is that it can be revised many times, based on evaluations. But unfortunately not too many materials currently in existence have gone through many cycles. Expense becomes an issue, because each evaluation and revision adds cost.

I do not discuss in this paper issues of how the material is to be marketed and distributed. Extremely little marketing experience is available for computer-based learning material. There are clearly problems which need to be overcome, such as the problem of possible pirating of material. Technical solutions are available for some of these problems.

Overview of the Irvine Production System

In the preceding section of this paper, I described the choices made at Irvine as they have evolved over the past 13 years in producing computer-based learning material. The present section is designed to give a visual summary of the approach. The approach used, already mentioned, is the structured analysis and design technique (SADT).

The SADT description of the Irvine production system was developed by

Barry Kurtz. A number of diagrams are involved. First, as with other SADT charts, the top-level diagram shows the overall details of the process, but without specifics. The charts that we are drawing are concerned with the processes, not the data. Lines coming into the side of a box indicate products entering that process, while lines coming out to the side indicate things produced at that stage. Lines coming into the top represent controls on the process. . . . The overall chart is presented in Figure 2.

The reader will have no difficulty picking out the various features of the production system as we have outlined

them already. This chart provides simply an outline, but it does show how the major stages are related to each other.

The next two charts presented [Figures 3 and 4] show the expansion of the first box on the left, "write dialogues," and the second box on the left, graphic and structural design. It is as if we are looking inside each of these boxes and seeing the details of the process. Again, these details can be related to the discussions that we have already had. We will not present SADT charts corresponding to the other components of the main box; they are available on request.

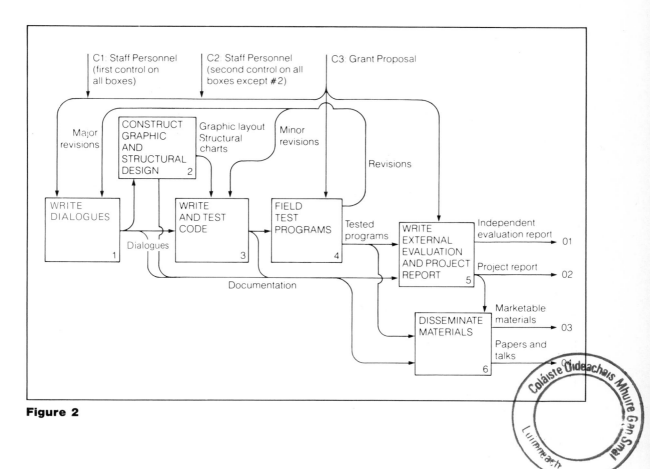

Figure 2

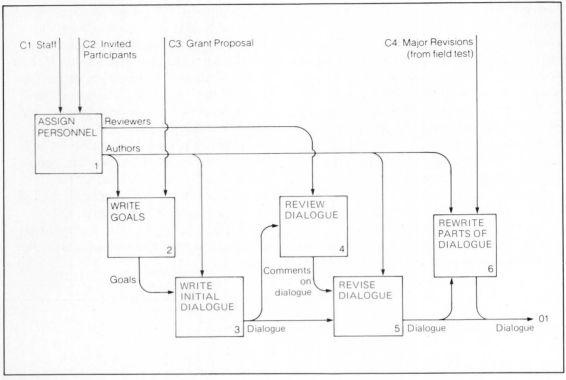

Figure 3

RESEARCH NEEDED

The production system just described, which developed at Irvine, is only one of many possibilities that involve many people.

At the present time developers of computer-based learning material have extremely limited experience with full-scale production systems. We do *not* have the vast amount of experience that has gone into books, and even there many different variants of strategies have evolved. Hence, it is not too surprising that we have much to learn in this area and that research is badly needed about many of the details. Careful research in

this area is critical for future progress in developing computer-based learning material. I mention a few of the areas particularly in need of additional research aid.

1. Underlying Learning Capabilities. In development of learning material we need to understand the process of learning better than we now do. The computer introduces many new variants into this process, ones that were not present in older media, so it is particularly in need of study. For example, at this stage we do not really have a detailed view of what goes on in

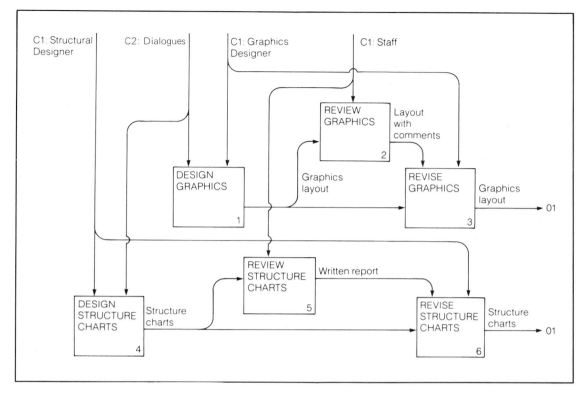

Figure 4

students' minds when they run computer-based learning materials. We are beginning to get some appreciation of motivational issues in game materials,[7] but even in this area information is limited.

To give one example where additional information is certainly needed, I discuss an interest of the Irvine group, the use of the materials by groups. We have always urged that two or three people work together at a computer display, except in situations in which the student is taking an on-line test. Our casual observations have been that the student interactions in such groups are an important component of the learning process. But we have little empirical information, because we have not made careful studies of the situation. Nor have we particularly tried to design material with groups in mind. Hence, much additional research is needed in understanding the learning process when groups are involved. We remain convinced that students do an excellent job of teaching each other. But it would be desirable to have some evidence for this, particularly in the computer-based learning environment. Furthermore, we need to understand how the materials can encourage group cooperation. This is by no means the only type of learning theory research that would be useful, but is given merely as an example. This example is one of applied research, but fundamental research is also necessary.

2. Graphic Design. We have already stressed the importance of the spatial and temporal design of the material on the screen. Such design can have a considerable effect on how the material works with students. We find that much computer-based learning material does not allow for this component. In fact, much of the material seen on the screen is very much like material in books, in spite of the very different parameters in the computer situation.

One would like to run experimental studies of the various features of graphic design and experimental studies on several different types of capability provided to those who are designing the screen. We suspect that these capabilities might be sensitive to the users. Thus, a capability that might be satisfactory for a coder might be very poor for a graphic designer or a novice user.

3. Editorial Control. We have mentioned several possible stages for an editorial role in the process. In recent book production the commercial companies have moved toward greater and greater editorial control. While it is not clear whether this is desirable in all cases, it probably will be an important factor in commercial production of computer material, simply because the book publishers becoming involved with computer material are already familiar with the process.

One approach would be to design training material for people who are going to be involved in editorial control at several stages. As mentioned, we feel that at the present time the editorial comments that we receive on computer-based material tend to be very subjective, different for each individual. While this is true to some extent in dealing with books, there seems to be somewhat more consensus there, perhaps because of greater experience. Training sequences might furnish an answer. But again experimental work is needed to compare different ways of training editors for computer-based learning materials. Research can help us to a better understanding of the editorial process.

4. Pretesting Before Coding. Modern programming environment studies have often recommended a process called "rapid prototyping" of complex programs in the early stages of development. The notion is to bring up a quick "mock" version of the full program. Such a program does not do what the full one does, but it does give some experience with actual users.

It has puzzled us for some time that rapid prototyping seems to be possible only in limited ways with most computer-based learning materials, because of the way such materials are typically organized. Some of the goals accomplished by rapid prototyping would be extremely important in developing computer dialogues.

One possibility is that already suggested, pretesting paper and pencil materials with actual students before the coding activity. Although we have begun to carry out some preliminary efforts in this direction, far more work is necessary. The aim of this new activity is to avoid a long series of very expensive design and coding activities for material that does not turn out to be usable in the form considered by the original designers.

5. Variants of Production System. As yet, we have little experimental evidence about how varying the production system affects the materials produced, the costs, or other parameters involved. Experimental studies which produce material with a variety of strategies would be extremely useful. Although many of the components of the production system can be argued on rational, pedagogical, or economical grounds, it will be desirable to have more than arguments available.

6. Intelligent Videodisc Production. As we have stressed, many of the techniques discussed apply to developing curriculum materials involving a full range of media, even though we have emphasized primarily the computer material. A new and very interesting possibility is the development of material that uses one intelligent videodisc, a full combination of the computer and optical videodisc using the capabilities of both media.

Although there have been a number of projects, very limited experience exists in developing intelligent videodisc materials, far more limited than our meager background with the production of computer-based learning material. Since

this technology looks as if it may be very important for the future, it seems extremely important to gather such experience and to study variants in the production system. Furthermore, we have almost zero experience in using such material with students.

7. Rapid Coding Techniques. One of the most expensive and time-consuming of the stages we have examined is that of technical development, stage 7. The development of ways to speed up this stage would, therefore, be an important contribution to the overall production system.

Although we have already commented that development of computer-based learning languages in interactive systems has so far not proved to be a viable approach, there are still possibilities in this direction. We have developed in the Educational Technology Center an interactive code-writing program, one that queries the user and then writes Pascal code. The program is then modifiable easily, just as with any good structured program. This technique still has limited applicability, however, because it allows only a limited range of capabilities, similar to those in many of the interactive systems developed. But this approach could be explored further. Another approach, tried elsewhere on a small scale, is to develop an interactive capability where one places on the screen essentially the same script that was developed by the authors, by a series of interactive techniques. A third possibility is the use of intelligent editors such as that developed by Teitelbaum and Reps[8] at Cornell for students learning PL/CS and more recently Pascal. Techniques could be developed with modern programming approaches in mind, taking into account the criteria mentioned at the beginning of this paper.

8. Readability Aids. Students are notoriously poor readers. They tend to read in a careless fashion, stimulated (and often approved) by everyday reading experiences. So a student's reading capabilities are often inadequate for the careful reading needed in most study. Since textual material is in most cases to be part of what is displayed on the computer screen, it is important to consider the questions of readability on the screen.

As indicated, computer learning material has many aspects that differ from print material. Some of these differences, such as very poor type quality on the screen, may be hindrances to reading. But others, such as the fact that blank space is free and that we can use timing as a positive aid to reading, if used wisely, are likely to lead to increased comprehension and retention capabilities.

Until recently, very little study of screen readability has taken place. There is literature of variable quality on print readability. But it is not clear which of these print readability factors can be easily extended to the screen. Furthermore, print readability studies do not take into account things which are possible only on the screen, such as control by the reader.[9]

9. Visual Design. The process of designing the screen is one that still needs additional attention. As indicated, our work at Irvine has assumed an interactive design process, one in which the designer is working directly at one or several screens for the creation of the pictorial and textual information. Just what capabilities should be provided to the designer and just how the designer should work are considerations which need to be explored further with detailed empirical research. Furthermore, the question of how to train the designer is one that needs additional consideration.

This examination of needed areas of research is not complete. But it does give some flavor of some of the problems which need to be examined.

February 1982

NOTES

1. Walter Perry, *The Open University* (Jossey-Bass, San Francisco, 1977).
2. Alfred Bork, *Learning with Computers* (Digital Press, Bedford, Mass., 1981), Chapter 6.
3. Barry L. Kurtz and Alfred Bork, "An SADT® Model for the Production of Computer Based Learning Material." In *Computers in Education*, R. Lewis and D. Tagg, Editors (North-Holland Publishing Co., New York, 1981).
4. Alfred Bork, *Learning with Computers* (Digital Press, Bedford, Mass., 1981), Chapter 6.
5. Description available from the Educational Technology Center, University of California, Irvine.
6. Description available from the

Educational Technology Center, University of California, Irvine.

7. Thomas W. Malone, *What Makes Things Fun to Learn?* (Xerox Palo Alto Research Center, 1980).

8. Tim Teitelbaum and Thomas Reps, "The Cornell Program Synthesizer: A Syntax-Directed Programming Environment," *Communications of the ACM*, vol. 24, September 1981, pp. 563–573.

9. Alfred Bork, "Textual Taxonomy," Technical paper, Educational Technology Center, University of California, Irvine, January 1981.

Interaction in Learning

ALFRED BORK

The notion of *interactive learning* is one that is receiving considerable prominence these days, particularly in the development of either computer-based learning material or intelligent videodisc learning material. The idea that learning can and should be an interactive process, one in which the learner is a full-time participant rather than a spectator, is an old one in education, going back at least as far as Socrates.

The learning environment today, for almost all students, is *not* an interactive environment. The vast majority of learning is now done in lectures or with books. While a few good students can make the use of these media interactive, this is rare; for almost all students these methods are passive, a spectator activity rather than a participant activity.

No single view of the nature of learning has general acceptance. On the contrary, very divergent views are vigorously supported. But most learning theories suggest that it is better for students to play active roles in the learning process. In spite of this it has been difficult, given the number of students to educate, to provide such an active learning environment. For example, in the typical sixth grade class, likely to be a group of about twenty-five students, it is clear that each student cannot receive much individual attention from the teacher. The possibility of each student learning in a Socratic fashion,

through interaction with the teacher, is simply out of the question, given typical class size and typical teachers. Rather, passive learning modes dominate. The situation is even worse in the large classes which are necessary in most universities. Indeed, when class size gets above about ten, few teachers can maintain an interactive environment. So even in schools that pride themselves on being small, the learning situation is seldom interactive.

COMPUTERS

Modern technology applied to the learning process, particularly the use of computers, either alone or in combination with optical videodiscs, allows the possibility of an interactive learning environment for all students. The developer of materials in this area is often thrilled with these interactive possibilities, since no interaction has been possible in the use of many of the older media in which they worked. An unfortunate tendency exists to view *any* interaction as marvelous! The major purpose of this paper is to try to point out that there are *levels* at which interactions can occur, various degrees of interaction, and that it is likely that the levels of greater interaction are ones which will have the more profound effects eventually in the creation of learning materials. Not all interactions are equal!

FACTORS DETERMINING INTERACTION LEVEL

Two aspects concerning interaction in computer-based learning material will be considered in this paper. First, we will look at the quality of *each* interaction. Three factors are considered here: the type of input required of the student during the interaction, the method of analysis of this input, and the action taken in the program after the input. The second aspect might be termed the overall level of interaction.

Although we will discuss a possible *increase* of interaction, this measure is by itself not the focus of this paper. Rather, we want to show developers the range of possibilities in the hope that they will move to more sophisticated levels of interaction.

USER INPUT FORMS

We can distinguish a variety of ways in which a student can interact with a computer-based learning program. We will consider first the types of inputs which are possible. These types are listed roughly in order of increasing level of interaction, starting with very simple types of user interactions with the program and ending with very complicated types.

The program preceding such an interaction may have done a variety of things. It may have shown some material to the student and asked a question. It may have allowed the student to ask certain types of questions. In any case we would expect that there would be many such interactions within the program if the program is to be considered interactive; we will later discuss the number of interactions.

The following list shows types of user input forms which can be considered. As indicated, we have tried to rank them from less sophisticated interactions to more sophisticated interactions. It would be difficult to defend the exact ordering in this regard, but the overall ordering is, I believe, clear.

1. Multiple choice
2. Multiple choices
3. Yes/no
4. Concealed multiple choice
5. Fill in the blank in a sentence
6. Pointing input to identify a feature
7. Numerical input
8. Natural language input

It is actually hard to distinguish between yes/no and multiple choice, since yes/no is a form of multiple choice. However, in spite of this, our experience is that yes/no in general is a much more pleasant form of interaction than is multiple choice. For reasons that will not be fully discussed, our group at Irvine almost never uses multiple choice in any of its programs, whether quizzes or any other type. We regard multiple choice as a particularly inhumane form of input, leading to guessing activities having nothing to do with purposes of learning.

The term "multiple choices" implies the possibility of having several right answers. The situation is slightly better than for multiple choice, but this is still a form which the Educational Technology Center considers to be a weak form of interaction. There is not quite as much guessing involved in the process, but still a considerable level. One need only investigate briefly the literature available for students about how to take tests (mostly meaning how to take tests with either multiple choice or multiple choices) to see how many factors are involved in taking such tests that are completely independent of knowing the material.

We have found the *concealed* multiple-choice strategy to be very useful. This strategy was first developed many years ago by one of my colleagues, Stephen Franklin, in connection with on-line quizzes in the precalculus mathematics class. It is used extensively in our physics quizzes. The basic notion is that the computer has stored, or can generate, a large number of both right and wrong answers to a question. These are presented to the student in a random order. The student sees only one possible answer at a time and must make a decision about the correctness of each answer before seeing the next possible answer. The process can be stopped in at least two different ways. One is to give some fixed number of possible answers; the other is to continue until either the student correctly identifies a correct answer or makes a mistake. This form of input overcomes many of the difficulties of multiple choice. It is particularly useful in quizzes.

While we would not want to use the "fill in the blank" approach in all or most inputs, it is often a convenient strategy with students. It has the advantage that almost all students are familiar with it from workbooks and other precomputer materials. Furthermore, it is a "comfortable" form of input in some situations, with the student having a pretty good idea of what is demanded. When fill in the blank is used on the computer, it can be used in a very natural form, with an underlined blank at the right location and with the input cursor moved to this blank.

Numerical inputs are frequent in mathematical and scientific contexts. Often with a numerical input, one is asking for the solution to a problem.

The most sophisticated form of input listed is natural language input. Here, however, we must be cautious. Natural language input in this context means natural language *as seen by the student*. What techniques are used internally in the program to analyze, for example, an English sentence typed in by the user, are an entirely different issue. In most of our computer displays we have not found it necessary to parse English in the sense that is possible in modern artificial intelligence. Rather, simple string matching, with some logic, is often sufficient in identifying correctly what appears to the student to be a very free-form input. We will discuss this further later in the paper.

Pointing input may be simply another variant of some of the other forms, such as multiple choice. But it can also be used in ways that are difficult to use in verbal input at all. Thus, if we are trying to get a student to see a key feature of a graph—for example, a place where the graph has a maximum or a minimum—pointing input may be the best way to do this. The type of pointing input will vary with the computing system, but fundamentally from the student point of view, the input is the same whether touch input is used, a mouse, a joystick, paddle wheels, or other devices.

ANALYSIS OF USER INPUT

The next stage in determining how interactive a program is is to ask what analysis is conducted internally in the program each time the user inputs something. We have already touched slightly on some of these factors in the last section on forms of student input. The following possibilities for analysis might be considered. Again, we are to some extent lising them in terms of increasingly sophisticated interaction, although again the exact difference between neighboring items is vague.

1. None
2. Exact string match
3. Exact match of substring
4. Partial match
5. String matches with logic
6. Possible processing of string
7. Parsing of natural language

The listing of "no analysis" may be surprising to some readers. But with an actual computer-based learning program, this is sometimes a useful way to proceed. We may ask a question of a

student with no intent of analyzing the student response. For example, early in a program, one might want students to simply spend some time *thinking* about a critical issue. One way to obtain such thinking is to ask the right question and then let the student type in a response. At this stage one may not try to analyze this response at all because it was the student process of *attempting* to answer it that was really the important thing, not the answer itself.

The second type of analysis is an *exact* string match; we look for a match with the student input and a predetermined string. This is seldom used in our programs, since it assumes that students will be extremely disciplined in exactly what they will enter to the computer. A more common strategy would be to match only a substring, but even this is a rather simple-minded matching technique. Usually many such matches will be necessary to each input.

Some projects have used partial matches; that is, they have a facility which says "accept that if it occurs in the student input with only one letter off or two letters off." The attempt in such a case is to overcome possible spelling or typing problems. We have found that we can obtain quite good success by a simpler procedure, never testing on whole words but only on characteristic pieces of words.

The most common matches used in much contemporary computer-based learning material are a series of string matches with some logic. That is, one asks, "Does the string contain this string and that string but not some third string?" Or one asks, "Does it have this string followed by this string?" One can make quite sophisticated analyses of student input, fully adequate in most circumstances, by relatively simple use of such logic.

In all these cases the developers may want to precede the matching with some processing of the string. Thus if one is looking for both a number and some units attached to the number, the processing might consist of first separating off these two pieces and proceeding to analyze each independently. Or it may be desirable to remove certain material in the student input string, perhaps after it has been recognized, and work only with the rest of the string. Or it may be desirable to split a string at a certain symbol, word, or number and analyze the parts separately.

We have little new to say about analysis of numerical input, most common in programs in the sciences and mathematics. In checking such an input, the designers of the program should allow a reasonable possible range for the answer, as an exact match will often be unlikely.

We have already commented that in most computer-based learning material full parsing, both syntactically and semantically, of natural language is usually not possible. In most cases in our work we have found it unnecessary. However, as our techniques in this direction improve and we understand more about how to build intelligence within even small programs, it may be

that this type of interaction will become more important.

ACTION AFTER INPUT

We have a variety of possible actions that can be taken in the program after the input. Here the listing becomes somewhat more uncertain as to how to classify these, although some are more desirable than others. Here is the list.

1. None
2. Right/wrong reply
3. Right/wrong reply with additional information
4. Aid sequences
5. Linear action
6. Nonlinear action

Again, the possibility that there may be no action after input, with or without analysis of the student response, may be strange to many. However if one considers conversations between human beings, one will note that this is often the case. A human being does not constantly say, in conversing with another human being, "Right!" Rather, you may often simply go ahead to another question, with no immediate feedback. Sometimes the nature of the student input will be noted within the program, and so can affect either future statements by the program or even the entire flow of action in the program. The goal is a quality of interaction which resembles that between a highly trained, interactive teacher and one or a few students.

Undoubtedly the most common interaction found in computer-based learning material is a right-wrong response. In fact, one sees many programs in which in *every* response the student is told immediately whether the answer is right or wrong. Some schools of psychology may even favor such an approach.

But our group at Irvine does not believe that it is necessary. A right/wrong reply is often not very helpful and may, in fact, discourage the student in some circumstances. If a right/wrong reply is used frequently, we consider it desirable to change the vocabulary. For example, one can have a series of different "good" messages available in the program, perhaps at different levels of praise. This is particularly useful in areas of the program where much repetition occurs, because the code is used over and over. It also has the advantage that the developer of the material does not need to spend large amounts of time at each action after input deciding what type of good message to give to the student.

A right/wrong message will usually be of more help if it comes with additional information. Again the model of a human teacher should be followed. When we read the Socratic dialogues, Socrates's reply to a student answer to one of his questions was often long and often proceeded eventually to a different question.

The possibility of extensive aid to the student is one that certainly needs to be considered frequently in developing computer-based learning material. Sometimes this aid may be remedial in

nature. Thus, in physics material, one may discover that a student lacks some critical mathematical background. It is possible to have a sequence at this point in the program that develops that mathematical background, and thus assure that the student can proceed with full understanding.

The distinction between linear and nonlinear approaches is an important one. In the linear approach, each student passes through the same material; that is, after a given question the next question will be the same for all students. In a highly nonlinear environment, the student inputs may alter the flow of the material and so different students may find themselves in different tracks, with different approaches. Undoubtedly some nonlinearity is desirable to take into account individual differences. But most existing computer-based learning material is not highly nonlinear, simply because we have little experience so far in creating such highly nonlinear material.

MEASURING THE NUMBER OF INTERACTIONS

So far we have considered only a single interaction and talked about a number of ways in which that interaction could be classified. Based on these classifications, some interactions will represent, therefore, a high degree of interaction and others a very low level of interaction. Thus, a typical low-level interaction would be a multiple-choice question with only a right/wrong response.

However, a program does not contain a single student input. Rather, a full program has many different student inputs, and therefore many different interaction points. Hence, in developing a scale for measuring interaction, it is important to ask not only about the quality of each interaction, but to get some overall information about the number of interactions. A program which has ten minutes of no interaction with the student, and then has one extremely good interaction and then ten additional minutes of no interaction, is not an interactive program.

In developing a total measure for interaction then, we need to have some measure for each interaction or perhaps for an average interaction in a program and some measure of the number of interactions. It is the question of the number of interactions that we consider in this section.

There are at least two ways of measuring the number of interactions. One is to ask: What is the *time between two interactions* on the average for an average student? This number could actually be determined empirically, simply by observing students using the program. Undoubtedly existing material will differ greatly in this interaction time factor. This is probably the most reliable way of measuring the number of interactions within a program.

Another possibility, with some difficulties, is to ask how many interactions occur on a single screen. This mode of working was satisfactory in an environment where the whole screen had to be erased at a single time, such as with direct view storage tubes. But with more modern raster-based displays, often portions of a screen are erased, so there is not an entirely clear view of what constitutes "a screen." Hence, it seems more difficult to measure interactions in this fashion.

A TENTATIVE NUMBER OF INTERACTIONS

Based on these considerations we now can offer a tentative measure for the quality of interaction in a program. The factors involved have already been discussed, and I will not try to pin them down further numerically. The time between interactions must be taken into account reciprocally, since the smaller the time between interactions that occurs, the greater the interaction of the program. Hence, one possible measure is as follows:

$$\frac{\text{Quality of the Average Interaction}}{\text{Time Between Interactions on the Average}}$$

Perhaps the time should be given additional weight.

I stress that the exact numerical details are not as important as is the qualitative difference. We do not need to assign a measure to interaction correct to three or four decimal places! Rather, we need to understand that some programs *are* more interactive than others, and that interaction is in general a desirable feature for learning materials.

The author welcomes further discussion on this issue.

June 1982

Right Justification and Word Processing

ALFRED BORK

Justification refers to various mechanisms to "line up" either the left side of a printed document (left justification) or the right side of a printed document (right justification). Almost all books, with a few exceptions to be mentioned later, use both left and right justification.

Print technology typically secures right and left justification in two ways. The first way is increasing the amount of space between words. Occasionally letter space will also be varied. The second way is by using hyphenation. If hyphenation is used on certain lines, the space between words can be reduced. Typically in print technology, for any given line the space between any two words is kept constant.

One of the major future uses of the computer is for word processing. New personal computers are now routinely introduced with word processing software. Such software is likely to be common on home personal computers. Word processing technology, as commonly seen today, is not print technology. Nevertheless, it has, in many ways, strived to imitate the print medium. This is not so unusual. A new technology often unconsciously carries over many of the assumptions of an older technology.

The output device in word processing is usually similar to an electric typewriter. The most common technology used is the daisy wheel, although there are others; high-density dot matrix printers are also used. In the vast majority of current word processors, each character in hardcopy output, *including space,* is of the same length. Proportional spacing typewriters, allowing different spaces for different letters, exist; but even in word processing, where it is easier to use such typewriters, they are still relatively rare. Contrast this with print technology, where it is almost universally the case that every character occupies a different amount of space and where spaces between words can be varied by very small amounts.

Most of us are beginning to send and receive letters, papers, and many other kinds of documents produced by word processing systems. The vast majority of the documents that I receive, even though done on typewriter-like devices without proportional spacing, use both right and left justification. Word processing has increased the use of right justification in typewriterlike output. The purpose of this column is to claim that this is a mistake. We should *not* right-justify with most word processing systems.

A RULE

There is a very odd "rule" in new technologies, which is strange but nevertheless true. *There is a tendency to believe that if something can be done, it should be done.*

This rule is almost a naive assumption. I suspect that the vast majority of users of word processing systems who are sending out right-justified material have never stopped to think about whether it is a good idea or a bad idea! They do it because it *can* be done. Indeed, some word processing and computer editing software makes it difficult or even impossible to avoid right justification. This particular "rule" is not unique to word processing, but rather is often a problem with the use of a new technology.

IS RIGHT JUSTIFICATION DESIRABLE?

I want to raise the seldom asked question as to whether, in the word processing context, it is desirable to use right and left justification, or whether one should use the older typewriter format of only left justification. Other possibilities exist, such as right justification *without* left justification, which is rarely used. I stress that I am still talking about *paper* output, not about information displayed on the screen. The factors involved in screen displays are not the same as those in paper output.

What are the sources of information concerning the desirability or undesirability of right justification? I shall refer to two different sources of information, almost completely independent sources. One place to gather information about whether right justification is desirable is to look at the practices of the best graphic designers, built on years of experience and design intuition. A second source is to look at print readability studies. In one case we are appealing to the professional's intuition, and in the other case we are appealing to research results.

GRAPHIC DESIGNERS

When we consider the attitudes of graphic designers toward right justification, we want to look at the *best* graphic designers. Unfortunately, because of economics, the best graphic designers have seldom been involved in book production. Rather, they tend to work in different print environments of exhibits and ads in expensive magazines or fancy product brochures for major companies. Such a designer might work for a company such as IBM (which has always had very high design standards both in its products and its graphic material). Over the years IBM has employed such major designers as Elliot Noyes and Charles and Ray Eames and a host of other extremely competent graphic designers.

When we look at these brochures and ads, we see immediately considerable use of what the designer calls "ragged right." This means that the right margin is *not* justified! This practice is not universal among all excellent designers—some justification is used, but ragged right is certainly common. The fancier the brochure, the likelier it is that one will see ragged right. For example, most of the recent IBM promotional literature for the personal computer uses ragged right.

Occasionally a very good designer does work on a book too. One can, for example, note the books that come from such major bastions of design as the Museum of Modern Art in New York. Here again we see the use of much more ragged right than is typical, say, in textbooks, where it almost never appears. In the ads, brochures, and books from good designers, one also sees relatively little use of hyphenation, much less than in normal usage.

It is probably worth noting that the evidence quoted, the use of considerable amounts of ragged right by outstanding designers, is really referring to the fancier print medium rather than to the typical word processing medium. So we are, as we will be in the next case to be considered, extending slightly beyond the actual evidence. But this extension would appear to be justified (no pun intended).

PRINT READABILITY STUDIES

It often comes as a surprise that a considerable body of research literature of variable quality is concerned with issues of print readability. It is even more surprising to find that even in textbooks, where one would think that readability should be given a very high value, this literature is almost entirely

ignored! The glowing exception to this is in the print material produced at the Open University in the United Kingdom. The Open University made a detailed study of the print readability research and gleaned what it could out of that literature to use in its own products.

The reader will probably not be surprised to learn, given the tenor of this [paper] so far, that print readability studies suggest that ragged right is an aid to readability, particularly when coupled with shorter lines. Furthermore, these same studies show that hyphenation is a definite detriment to readability.

HYPHENATION

In several places in this report I have mentioned hyphenation, which often accompanies right-justified word processing material. At the present time, even in word processing systems, hyphenation is mostly a hand operation, with some systems making it easier to do it and some systems making it more difficult. On more elaborate word processing systems, justification software is already in use with more or less control from the user. I am already getting documents which clearly use this software. It is usually spotted by the huge amount of hyphenation which is occurring in the material, often almost every line! It is another case of the rule above: Because it can be done, it will be done.

The evidence does not favor such extensive hyphenation, to say the least. Unfortunately, more and more word processing systems are likely to have such software and so the situation will probably deteriorate.

CONCLUSION

In using current word processing systems with typewriter-like output devices, avoid the use of right-justified text and avoid hyphenation.

More and more we can expect that personal computers, particularly in the home environment, will be used for word processing. Indeed, word processing is likely to be one of the four or five activities of the personal computer which will make it most desirable for the home. So these issues, while applying to a wide range of machines, have particular future emphasis to personal computers.

April 20, 1982

Books Versus Computers: Learning Media

ALFRED BORK

Abstract: *The most widely used learning media of the past century is the book. But the digital computer is now challenging that position. The relative advantages of books and computers is compared, particularly with regard to the future of education.*

The topic for this discussion is learning as it occurs in today's society. I will be particularly interested in problems (and solutions to these problems) that arise because of two major factors which affect the learning process. The first factor is that very large numbers of people have a *need* to learn, probably a larger number than we are adequately serving at the present time. The second factor is that these people are by no means similar. Not only do they differ in age, but they differ in almost every other conceivable measure that we can think of. They differ too in many ways that we still do not understand as far as learning is concerned. These two problems guide the present discussion.

I emphasize that I am speaking of learning in the broadest sense. That is, I include not only the types of learning activities that occur in the school environment, but also adult and continuing learning, including the many forms of self-study. It is these latter learners, according to recent studies, which represent the bulk of the learning taking place.

The theories of learning, or any practical details, are not the focus in this discussion. Rather I concentrate on two learning media, an older dominant medium, the book, and a newer medium, the computer, and its associated technology.

The book is the dominant delivery mechanism for learning today without question. Even where other modes such as lectures are important, in schools and universities, the book is still the most important learning mode. If we leave these formal institutions and look at how most students learn, books constitute the major tool available. Remember that the book is a relatively recent learning device, considered against man's history; it is only within the past 500 years that books were possible and only in about half that time that books were widely used in the learning process. A technological development, the printing press, made the book possible.

But now there is a challenger, the computer. The computer, while very little used in learning environments at the present time, shows great potential, particularly in dealing with just the two problems raised. The contention of this paper is that we are on the verge of a major change in the way people learn, the change that Eric Ashby has already designated as the fourth revolution. I intend to present the evidence that such a change is about to occur.

In the next two sections I will present two examples showing the computer in use as a learning device. One of these is an example that has been underway for a number of years. The other is a currently developing situation. I have chosen these two examples to illustrate a range of possibilities. Both examples represent work done in the Educational Technology Center at the University of California, Irvine.

EXAMPLE: PHYSICS 5A AT IRVINE

The first example is a beginning college physics course, heavily dependent on the computer. More complete descriptions of this course are available from the author.

The course has been offered in several forms during the past five years. The version described is the most recent one, taught for three years for the beginning course for science and engineering students. The course is the first or mechanics quarter of that course.

On the first day the students are offered a choice among three "courses," one taught and graded conventionally (not discussed further) and two based on the computer. Both of these computer-based courses follow the personalized system of instruction (Keller plan) approach. The emphasis is on knowing

the material before going on to another section. Students study a given unit until they feel that the material is understood. Then the student takes on-line tests that cover the details of that unit—usually two tests per unit. If a student does not do perfectly on these tests, further study is advised and the test is tried again. The student stays with given material until that material has been learned.

The on-line tests not only provide immediate interaction as to correct answers, but also provide extensive assistance to the student. Some of this assistance may come in the form of an initial help sequence, offered to the student before the test is taken. In other cases the student may be given aid particularly pertinent to problems that have arisen. The tests, therefore, are a combination of testing and learning. The studies of the class indicate that learning sequences in the tests are considered the most effective learning material available.

A full course management system records the results of the on-line tests and provides control. A student is not allowed to take a test in a unit until previous units have been completed. Furthermore, a student who does not pass a test must wait for 12 hours before the test is taken again. The system also imposes a 40-minute time limit; most of the quizzes should be workable in about 15 or 20 minutes. Finally if a student does not pass a test after four attempts, the management system locks the student out of the test until the student has consulted the instructor.Thus, all students in difficulty must work individually with the instructor.

The computer is used in other learning modes in the course too. Some dialogues offer direct learning aid. Furthermore, some material is particularly oriented toward building student intuition about the behavior of mechanical systems.

The two computer tracks differ from each other in content. The first one uses the same textbook and thus has the same content as the conventional course. In the second computer track a new use of the computer comes in, the computer as an intellectual tool for problem-solving activities. The language we have been using for this activity is APL. Students learn programming in APL as one of the units of the course. Graphic capabilities are introduced immediately.

About 250 students took the computer tracks during the winter quarter of 1979. During this 10-week period, there were 17,000 accesses to dialogues, the majority of them to the on-line quizzes. We used approximately 250,000 terminal minutes of time in the course.

Development of this course and the associated material was made possible by grants from the National Science Foundation and support from the University of California.

EXAMPLE: SCIENTIFIC LITERACY IN PUBLIC ENVIRONMENTS

The other example shows a different use of the computer as a learning medium, a project still underway as of this writing. The notion is to aid a very diverse group to achieve greater understanding of what science is all about. The emphasis is on the nature of scientific theories, how these theories are connected with experience, the nature of observation and experimentation, the criteria for good and bad theories, and the problems of discovering theories. Scientific content is used only as far as it elucidates these general issues about the nature of science.

The initial environment addressed by the project is the public library. Small, stand-alone personal computers will be available in public libraries where they will compete with books to aid students learning. Some associated displays will lure users into using the materials. The materials thus must be completely self-sustaining—there will be no one around to assist the student with them, just as there is little assistance to help the student in browsing through books in a library. Later we hope to use the materials in other public environments, such as shopping centers, museums, and airport lounges, etc.

As indicated, this project is currently underway. Most of the material has been designed in the pedagogical sense, and a few running modules are already available in early form. The initial trial use of some materials in public libraries will take place in the summer of 1980. The project is funded by the Fund for the Improvement of Postsecondary Education.

BOOK ADVANTAGES

In the next two sections I review the strengths of each of the two learning media, books and computers. It is not too surprising that some of the factors I consider are *time dependent*. That is, some of these issues will be different five years from now than they are at the present time.

One of the major advantages of the book is *familiarity*. Almost all learners at all ages are familiar with books, while the computer is still unknown to the overwhelming majority of learners. The notion of a learning device already well known to almost everyone is certainly a powerful one. The situation of familiarity can change quickly, however. During the first year we offered a choice between computer and noncomputer approaches to the beginning physics quarter, about three-quarters of the students picked the noncomputer approach. This number has changed in each of the years we have offered it. Now three years later the percentages have reversed, with three-fourths of the people picking the computer approach. The individuals picking it do not have familiarity, but more and more people in the environment are and can presumably offer advice to the incoming freshmen. Nevertheless, the fact that the book is now a much more familiar device is important.

Another advantage of the book is portability. At the present time even the home computers can be carried around only with some effort, and there is always the need for a power plug. But the book can be taken anywhere, although it might be subject to damage in some situations. Thus, one can take a book when one goes rowing, but on the other hand, it may get wet! At the

moment no learning computer that I am aware of will work on a rowboat.

Another major current advantage of the book is widespread availability of a tremendous range of learning materials. No matter what one wants to learn, a choice of many different books is available to aid with that area. Books continue to be produced at a large clip, and a considerable backlog is available in libraries and other places.

On the other hand, almost no learning materials are currently available in an "easy to acquire" fashion for the computer. We are the *premarketing* phase with respect to the computer, with the possibility of major marketing just being considered. The few computer learning materials on the market are often done without quality control and without the impetus of competition from other materials. This factor alone makes it almost out of the question to use computers extensively for learning at the present time. Before computers can become a major component of the learning system, a vast amount of curriculum material must be developed.

COMPUTER ADVANTAGES

The computer has two very strong advantages as a learning medium, interactivity and individualization. The computer can make the learning process an active experience for every individual. The computer engages in a conversation with the student, constantly asking the student to respond, to do something, to play an active role in the learning process. This is to be contrasted with books, which, for many readers, are very passive learning devices.While a good reader may be asking questions and trying to answer them as he or she reads a book, this active reading is rare. Today readers are typically not good readers and tend to read not only in a nonactive fashion, but in a way that is almost casual.

The second of these two important advantages for learning with computers is individualization. The book is the same for everyone, making no allowances except in very general ways for different student backgrounds, interests, or other factors. With the computer, however, we can individualize learning so that each student receives information specific to that student's needs. Thus, difficulties in solving a problem can be responded to directly, as indicated in our discussion of the on-line tests.

These two factors do not exhaust the benefits of the computer. The computer offers new and unique control over space and time.The situation with regard to material displayed on the screen and material in books differ in a variety of ways. Thus, we can use blank space freely on the screen, while in a book blank space costs money. Timing is available on the screen, so we can use it to emphasize a particularly important concept or phrase by delaying before and after its presentation. In a book, no such delays are possible—all the text and pictures are there. We can weave back and forth between pictures and text in the time domain, again in a way that

cannot be done in the print medium. Thus, we gain a considerable degree of versatility when we move from books to computers.

COSTS

One factor that I have kept out of the discussion of relative advantages to this point is the cost. Estimating costs presents considerable problems. As indicated, relatively little computer-based learning material is currently available, and the market for it—the number of potential users—is small. In estimating developmental costs, therefore, at the present time the book is a much less expensive medium, since the cost of development can be written off over a great many users. As more computer material is available, we can expect the situation to change drastically.

Another aspect of cost concerns *delivery* costs, the actual cost of getting the material out. In the case of the book, the printing technology and the paper technology are still increasing in cost. On the other hand, computer technology is coming down very rapidly in cost and will continue to do so for a long period in the future. The future is with the computer.

Given this information, it seems clear that the computer will eventually be less expensive than books as an educational delivery system for mass education.

FINAL COMMENTS

The question of books versus computers in learning environments is presented as if it were a contest. But it should be made clear that in many environments, both will continue to be used. A likely scenario for the future is that books and computers will both be used, often together, but it should be clear from my comments that the relative advantages of computers in mass education will become more and more apparent. The problems of mass education and the problems of different backgrounds will be more and more met by the computer rather than by the book. So we will see, over 25 years, a transition from one dominant learning medium to another dominant learning medium, a transition that does not occur often in human history.

October 1980

Graphics and Screen Design for Interactive Learning

ALFRED BORK, STEPHEN D. FRANKLIN,
RUTH VON BLUM, MARTIN KATZ
University of California, Irvine

BARRY L. KURTZ
San Francisco State University

Abstract: *This paper concerns the role of graphics in computer-based learning material. We consider both textual and graphic components of screen design and both spatial and temporal aspects. Informal design standards are developed. Several software approaches are discussed.*

COMPUTERS AND OLDER MEDIA

The computer's use as a learning media is just beginning. It promises major changes in our educational system. Every new learning mode, such as the computer, has unique properties. This paper addresses those aspects of learning via computers that are particularly concerned with spatial and temporal aspects of display on the computer screen.

The computer screen is the arena for spatial and temporal display of information in computer-based learning for both the computer and for the user. (We may also have sound information.) On the display we may find both iconic (pictorial) components and textual components. The way information is placed on the display can have a great effect on learning.

The computer as a learning medium is very different from older media such as books and lectures. Thus, the computer screen is very different from the page of a book. Successful curriculum developers in older media treat the new medium just like the older one, carrying over successful tactics from previous use: the screen is often formatted like the page of a book. It is only by conscious effort that we begin to understand the great differences between the computer display and these older media. Some differences reflect different capabilities. For example, as soon as a reader turns the page of the book, the entire information on the new page appears at once. The computer display is extremely different; information can *develop in time*, under control of the computer and the user.

A second difference concerns cost. Things which are possible in new and older media may be practical in one and impractical in another. Thus, while sophisticated designers understand that blank space in books aids learning, the amount of blank space in books is rigorously controlled for financial reasons. One cannot afford to put only a few words on each page, even if that were the most effective way to promote learning, because the cost of a book increases as the amount of blank space increases. However, with the computer screen no such relationship exists between the amount of blank space and the cost. Hence, blank space, while possible in both, can be used much more freely with the computer.

Even a cursory review of much current computer-based learning material shows that the developers often are blissfully unaware of the differences between books and computer displays. The usual procedure is to start at the top left corner and to put the information densely on the screen at the maximum possible speed. The computer "pages" thus resemble the pages of a book. Few authoring systems give developers any capability for better control of this medium.

Often decisions are made purely on a technological basis. Thus, many developers of computer-based learning material appear to believe that the faster the information appears on the screen, the better. This does not match our experiences at the Educational Technology Center with young novice computer users. We suspect that fast output reflects a desire to use the technology to make the computer presentation look more like a book presentation.

CHANGING CAPABILITIES

In dealing with the computer as a learning medium, we must recognize that its capabilities are improving rapidly with time. Some of this improvement, such as faster and cheaper processors and more memory, simply refers to general computer capabilities. These factors will influence the effectiveness of the computer as a learning medium.

It is a fundamental mistake to consider today's small personal computers—the PET, the Radio Shack, or the Apple—as typical of personal computers in the very near future. Any realistic consideration of screen characteristics must look into the immediate future and must make some reasonable assessments as to what will soon be available.

Developmental strategies must take into account the changing nature of the medium. Thus, the development should be done in such a way that it is reasonably easy to incorporate into new versions of the learning units new capabilities not available at the time of development. The *programming* must ensure that it is relatively easy to modify the code; the question of how to program in a dynamic environment where changes are expected is the major issue. Indeed, in most major applications areas the cost of maintaining and revising programs over their life cycle is likely to be greater than the cost of initial development. The criteria we need to consider are the same criteria used in large-scale complex programming.

We can delineate areas where we can expect screen capabilities to be improving in the near future. Consider first characteristics of screen graphics. Current graphics on inexpensive personal computers are limited by poor resolution, low speed, inadequate numbers and control of color, the lack of shading and intensity control, and the severe limitations on animation. We can expect all these to improve. Several technological factors are important in this improvement. First is the separate processing unit to handle the display. These processing units may be designed for graphic capabilities, such as the recently announced NEC chip. It is reasonable to expect competitors.

Another factor in the rapid improvement of visual quality is the decreasing cost of memory. Screen resolution in a raster system, storing bit maps of the screen, can improve as the cost of memory comes down until the limits of current video tube technology are fully realized. Beyond this point we need inexpensive, higher-resolution monitors. This may be a slower process, because we cannot piggyback on the large TV market.

As increasingly powerful processors stop using low-quality monitors to control the display, the importance of languages which allow multitasking will increase. Many graphic activities could be improved by using separate graphic processors. While some aspects of separate use can be handled without tasking capabilities within the developmental language, to make full use of separate processors it is necessary to start separate processes and have them proceed independently.

Character display capabilities will also improve, although not as quickly as graphics. Currently computer users have mostly an abominable set of characters on the screen, characters which would be considered completely unacceptable in the print medium. The main concern of those designing character sets seems to have been to make certain that an "A" is distinguishable from a "B." Thus, hundreds of years of print character technology has been lost in most computers.

This situation is changing. We now have experimental systems capable of different character fonts, and we also have systems which allow user choice of characters. We are also beginning to see systems that allow choice of size and color of characters and other similar features. The character problem is connected with resolution, already raised with respect to graphics. We may expect major improvements in quality of characters to come from Japan, since Japanese characters require better resolution than those in Western alphabets.

A third area for improvement is the development of new and better forms of input and output. Thus, we are very much looking forward to greater availability of voice output. Voice output, such as that available from Texas Instruments, is rare on personal computers. High-quality music is available but also rare. Several current projects are considering voice input, but none can be expected to reach full fruition for personal computer use for many years.

Personal computers are often weak in pointing devices, and additional work and study in this area is needed. Some widely touted pointing devices, such as the finger, have relatively poor resolution. Others are difficult for the novice to use.

Based on these future considerations, we can ask about reasonable design standards for computer-based learning. Our design standards will include both the spatial and the temporal aspects, since both space and time are controlled by the designer and (possibly) the user.

REASONABLE DESIGN STANDARDS

The design standards specified in this paper are based on extensive experience at the Educational Technology Center in developing a large amount of computer-based learning material, both initially in the timesharing mode and more recently with personal computers. During the fourteen years in which our group has been active, we have considered design issues very seriously. Recently we have been fortunate to have funds for experimental studies from the Research in Science Education program in the National Science Foundation.

The first thing to be said is that *design standards for computer-based learning material should be the standards of good graphic design* in any application. By good graphic design we mean the standards that would be followed, for example, by an excellent designer in producing an ad for a high-quality magazine, but as appropriate to the new medium. The necessity for such standards in computer-based learning is not generally recognized. Nevertheless it is important in effective use. A corollary to this comment is that a professional designer should be employed in the development of the highest-quality computer-based learning material. We consider later the environment in which the designer should work.

We can formulate a basic general design principle, applicable to all the material that follows. Since we are concerned with learners, we want the learners to focus on what is important, whether this information be visual or textual. The implication is that we should *remove unnecessary information from the screen,* and only show at a given time material important for the learner at the time. We do not need to follow this rule slavishly, but it furnishes a good guiding principle for the developers and for the graphic designers.

ICONIC INFORMATION

One aspect of what appears on the screen are the images, the pictures to aid learning. Here too we can state a general principle. We want to *use as much educationally relevant visual information as possible.* Much of the learning experience should be carried by visual information. This message is one that the pedagogical designers as well as the graphic designers must keep in mind. Redundancy—information in both forms—is desirable.

The tendency, unfortunately, is in the other direction. Since many curriculum developers are the successes of our current highly verbal educational system, they tend to be verbally skilled, more skilled than many students. Therefore, they often do not realize the necessity of good pictorial information for the *average* learner. Many people who are "failures" in our current educational system could be successes in a system which paid more attention to the uses of visual information to aid learning.

It is still not easy to satisfy this need for iconic information. We must keep focusing the designers' attentions on pictorial design. Material that is heavily verbal can be sent back to the pedagogical designers, prodding them to give more consideration to visual components to aid learning. On the other hand, *pictures should be relevant to the learning process,* not just pretty pictures.

Several features of the use of pictorial information are unique to the computer, as compared with books. Some are devices which are well-known on the blackboard or on TV.

For example, it is not necessary for pictures to appear instantaneously. *Material can develop in time.* Often the text and pictures can be interwoven with parts of pictures coming on in response to specific references in the text and with suitable delays in between. *Timing can emphasize critical features of the pictures* by delaying before and after those critical visual features. We can also highlight these critical features or make them stand out in other ways such as blinking.

Another factor derived from studies which preceded computer use is that *a picture can have too many details.* That is, details which distract the student from critical features can cause learner problems. In any picture we must identify the critical features and ask how these can best be brought out by the way a picture is presented. We ask if a given detail is really essential, or whether it can be omitted.

TEXTUAL INFORMATION

The pictures and text cannot be considered separately. They both contribute to learning, working together.

Perhaps the major consideration with regard to textual information is that we should *use large amounts of blank space.* A given screen should be relatively sparse, both textually and pictorially, at any one time. Much of the area on the screen should typically be *blank.* As indicated above, one way to achieve this is to *eliminate the information from the display no longer needed by the user.* Often we see screens which contain a large amount of "past history," not relevant to the current situation. This is neither necessary nor desirable.

A second consideration is that text should be placed on the display with the same care that would normally be used in placing a picture on the screen. Text placement should not be a system accident. Software for computer-based learning is poor if the *system* decides where text is to go and how it is to be displayed rather than the pedagogical designer, the graphic designer, or the learner making this decision. *Conscious placement of text,* allocation of display information, should be considered at all stages in development.

Strategies to increase comprehension with print material are known. Although little definite information about these strategies refers specifically to the display, it seems reasonable that previous print readability research will be applicable to screens. Thus, *short lines*, requiring less eye movement in reading a line, are generally desirable. *Avoiding hyphenation* is highly desirable—hyphenation is a barrier to comprehensibility. *Keeping natural phrases together* on a line is also another important consideration; the phrases can be defined syntactically or semantically where the experienced reader will pause. Justification at both ends of the line is also undesirable.

A variety of methods, again both spatial and temporal, are available for stressing material on the screen. Thus, there can be a *pause before and after a critical word or phrase* or the word or phrase can blink or it can appear in bold or in some other way, such as an alternate font or color, that sets it off.

An important consideration, unique to the computer, is the quantity and degree of *viewer control* allowed in the display text. In all of our current programs we allow the user to choose at any time the rate of text output. The decision followed by young students is often different from that provided by most developers of material—the typical person not acquainted with computers prefers a *much slower rate of text output* than is usually seen.

Students can control not only the overall rate of text output, but also the timing between words and other aspects of timing. Furthermore, many of the features stressed in the last paragraphs also can be turned over to the user. The question of which of these is most important for increasing comprehension and motivation needs additional investigation. A current research project at the Educational Technology Center is considering learner control.

To maintain interest, we can *vary the style of display* with size of the type, fonts, and varying alignment or justification procedures so the learner doesn't see the same old thing repeatedly. Varying style has strong motivational components. Our software for text output at the Educational Technology Center supports three justification modes: Left justification (without right justification), right justification (without left justification), and centered text, the text centered on the line within a particular area of the display. We use specified areas, ports or windows, with a strategy similar to that used for display of graphic information.

For student text input, our group borrows from good word processing practice. Text input is always in a "port," an area on the screen as just described in connection with output. The port for input may or may not be the output port. The software handles *wraparound* like word processors; if students type a word too long to fit within the port, they see it on the current line until the edge of the port is encountered. At that point, without any fuss, the partial word is moved to the next line and students can continue typing with no need for any special action.

Timing is also important on input. We want a user to be reminded of what to do in many situations ("Don't forget to press return!") or given other specialized time-dependent aid. On the other hand, the software should not cut off someone currently typing, even if a sizable delay preceded this typing. Again, these factors are in the Educational Technology Center software and so are in all of our programs on the personal computer.

THE DESIGN PROCESS

Several individuals can be involved in design. The visual design components come from at least two groups in the design process. In the pedagogical design component, excellent teachers, curriculum designers, and others work closely together to develop the necessary pedagogical specifications. They must be concerned with any factors which they believe will influence learning. Among these factors are the factors of design in both space and time.

We encourage pedagogical development teams to specify any design details they regard as critical for use. Of particular importance, often determinable only by someone with special expertise, is the question of what needs to be on the screen at a particular time.

The pedagogical design team specifies design details in two ways. First they may draw sketches of the screen, showing approximately where pictorial information and various types of textual information are to appear. In some cases the pedagogical designers will give this information in considerable detail. In addition, visual information, the scripts produced, can also contain extensive verbal instructions for the visual designer or for the coders, timing considerations or information about where and how things are to appear on the screen.

We run a half-day, informal workshop for our authoring groups, before the full pedagogical design process. One of the components stresses the display design details that form the basis of this paper.

The amount of screen design input which comes from the pedagogical designers will be variable. Some individuals are very conscious of these issues and will give them very careful specification. Other groups will almost entirely ignore these issues. So the quality of visual and temporal design at this stage will vary.

The next person who may be involved is the graphic designer, an individual with a good design background in other media. This individual also needs to understand the educational implications of design, implications which often are not part of the standard design curriculum. So it may be necessary to train this person. Unfortunately we are not often in a position to afford a graphic designer. Much of our materials have had to rely only on general design principles as stated, rather than on the insight of a graphic designer. As we move toward more large-scale development of computer-based learning material, graphic design will be a critical feature of the full-blown production system.

DESIGN SOFTWARE

If graphic designers are to function effectively, they should be working on-line, creating in an easy-to-use system the actual displays that the viewers will be seeing insofar as these displays can be determined before user input is known.

If the designer is to work interactively at the screen, special software must be provided. We have developed a variety of such software at Irvine, although we are still not satisfied with it. Several systems developed at the Educational Technology Center will be described briefly.

The first graphic design language was developed for timesharing, initially as a picture editor by student programmers working with a program where many pictures were necessary. It evolved into a general display editor, used extensively for several years.

This facility, a series of APL functions, allows users to create, modify, store, and delete objects, either text or pictures. All objects can be referred to by names.

The user interactively constructs objects needed for a display, placing them in the desired locations. They can be easily moved. When the design is complete, it is "pasted down," just as a graphic artist might do in developing an ad for a magazine. While most objects come through functions, tablet input is available for drawing objects.

The program is a code-generating program, writing commands in the macro capability that we used in our production of computer-based learning units. It stored the full graphic data, since we were working on a timesharing system with adequate file space. It wrote either in-line code or three types of procedure calls, depending on whether the object's position was known at the time that the designer was working or whether the position depended on choices known only when the final dialogue was actually run.

We also developed learning sequences to aid people to become familiar with the facilities. The most successful was in print form.

When we shifted from timesharing systems to personal computers, we created tools to support efforts on these smaller machines. In this area, we initially developed three tools: a text display package, a graphics display package, and a graphic design system. The last was intended for the designer.

The text display and graphic display packages are similar. Both support the goals of effective screen design, transportability, software maintainability, and simplicity of use. The vocabulary and programmer interfaces for the two are consistent, and new programmers are able to use them effectively after a single introductory course in programming. These packages provide a uniform and "friendly" user interface where the display of information and handling of input is controlled in a manner dictated by sound instructional and graphic design. The graphics procedures were motivated by the ACM SIGGRAPH core graphics standard.

The graphic design system allows definitions of the position of ports and objects to be displayed. The design of the system is based on three concepts: the importance of screen layout, the hierarchical design of displayed objects, and a hierarchical display interface.

Most graphic objects have naturally hierarchical composition with "natural" subobjects. Eventually one arrives at primitive constituents, such as points and lines. This hierarchical structure facilitates creating and editing of graphic objects. Pictures can include other objects, which may be selected from libraries of previously defined objects called "sketchbooks."

Users are presented with choices from a tree of menus, graphics-related functions put together. The cost is that one must know something about the overall organization to know where a particular function is located. To alleviate this problem and that of possibly needing the same function at different places, commonly used functions were made available from multiple places.

To protect against mistakes, designers can "back out" or undo most actions. For example, when an object is edited, only a copy of the object is changed until, after viewing the fully edited object, the user requests that the changed version be "saved." The ability to "back out" is implemented at every level. Development is still proceeding.

CONCLUSION

Design is an important component of good computer learning sequences. In this paper we have suggested some design standards.

March 1982

A Preliminary Taxonomy of Ways of Displaying Text on Screens

ALFRED BORK

This paper considers the computer screen as a space-time arena. It develops a taxonomy of the various variables associated with the display of textual material.

INTRODUCTION

More and more people are seeing text material displayed on screens through both video and computers. For example, text-based displays are often used for reference, perhaps interactively, as with reservation clerks at travel agencies or airlines, who use such displays for many hours each day. Similarly, in a computer-based learning situation the student may use a screen for an interactive program or in the near future as a surrogate book, particularly as the cost of delivering textual material via computer or video technology declines as compared to the cost of delivering it on paper. The question of *how* text will be displayed on the screens will become particularly important as videodisc technology and computer technology are combined.

In spite of this increased use of screens for displaying texts, the vast majority of screen displays are probably far less effective than they could be. The issues involved include *legibility*, *memorability*, and *motivation*. Increasing a display's effectiveness is not just a matter of improving the screen's resolution or changing from monochrome to color; ideally, we would also take account of users' reading purposes and draw upon the skills of information designers in deciding how information should be presented. We could then see the possibility of aiding and improving the reading process, as in *interactive* reading, a new reading style possible only with the new media. At present, we are rather far from this. Often, the way text appears on a screen is almost an accident, determined either by the programming languages involved, by the computer hardware, or by limiting users' control to matters that have nothing to do with the visual appearance of text. This is perhaps excusable, since little is available in the literature as yet in the way of good, empirical evidence on *how* to display text on a screen; further, there is a scarcity of information designers with experience of the new media, so there is a danger that designers may rely on experience with older media, such as print, and carry over inappropriate solutions.

In our view, all those who work with new media are in urgent need of an appropriate classification scheme. The body of this paper presents a preliminary attempt to draw up such a scheme, in the form of a taxonomy of the various types of textual treatment which are now possible in the computer environment. This may provide a better basis than is currently available for the information designer who has to compare and choose between various presentational options.

Display Medium Versus Print Material

Many information providers treat the screen as if it were the page of a book. This is not surprising, since the book and related print forms are the dominant reading modes now. Yet even a cursory examination of the display screen and reflection about the possibilities indicate that many differences exist.

The *quality* of text possible on most CRT screens is much poorer than the quality of text available in print materials. Letters formed from a limited dot matrix are at best crude. Hence, legibility is likely to be an even more important issue on the screen that it is in print.

The possibility of the control of the time domain is another striking difference between screen and print. Many different time considerations are possible. In this regard the screen has a closer affinity to a film than a book.

Furthermore, the economics of the two situations are very different. One of the most striking differences comes with the question of blank space. *In books space costs money,* since the cost of printing books is roughly a linear function of the number of pages in the book. However, on the computer screen blank space is *free.* Hence, size for size, blank space can be used in a much freer fashion in computer displays than it can be in the equivalently sized printed medium.

I do not wish to imply that all the previous work done with text display in *printed* form is useless for understanding what happens on the screen. In fact, much of the material concerning legibility and readability appears to be directly applicable. But without further work we cannot know if this information extends to the screen. And, as indicated, there are many differences between print and screen.

THE CLASSIFICATION SCHEME

The purpose of this present paper is *not* to describe experimental work showing how the screen should be used. Rather, it is a preliminary attempt leading in that direction, an attempt at developing a taxonomy of the various types of textual treatment which are already possible in the computer environment. Below, I consider both spatial and temporal factors.

The reader should realize that many of the factors discussed could be controlled either by the *designer* or the *user*. Thus, the user might adjust timing delays to suit individual preferences. The issue of which factors *should* be turned over to the user is one of the most interesting and most important topics for exploration. Further, the question of *how* the user is to exert this control is also critical. Both of these may be dependent, as with many of the other factors discussed, on the *type* of use.

The taxonomy presented may not be complete. Nor is current usage of these terms always unambiguous. This paper sets down possibilities with the hope that readers will suggest others I have missed. Once a reasonable taxonomy has developed we can study through appropriate experiments the effects of these different factors in particular situations such as student learning.

For convenience I have grouped the various factors in categories.

The Time Domain

One of the most critical differences between printed material and material displayed by the computer is that the computer can control *timing*. Thus, in a sense the computer is more like a film display of text or a television display of text than it is like a book. Being able to control timing may enable us to emphasize certain material (words, phrases, sentences, sections), to show structure, or to increase interactivity. Several timing factors need to be considered.

Overall Rate of Text Output. In most existing systems text is delivered to the screen at the fastest possible rate, the channel capacity. In communication-based systems (typically timesharing systems) it is difficult to do much about this; the channel capacity or, in computer jargon, baud rate, determines the output rate. But stand-alone (single user) systems allow us to choose our display rate, and to vary the time delay between two characters. Thus, the image can appear instantly or at some slower rate. The rate can be controllable by the user. The relationship of this rate to reading speed may depend on how the text is added to: one complete line at a time or one character at a time, for example (see "Overflow Handling," p. 168).

Of particular interest is how readability is affected by the speed of output and also how attitudinal factors depend on this. My speculation would be that a large amount of text displayed very rapidly would create a negative impression, but this is only a conjecture.

Relative Rate of Text Output. In addition to the general slowing of the display rate just discussed, special delays might apply to particular parts of a document for emphasis. So we could pause both before a key word and after it to give it a particular emphasis. The delays might be of different lengths. Or we could impose uniform delays after *each* word. A similar approach could help to emphasize phrases or even sentences that need special attention within material.

End-of-Line Delays. If lines are revealed progressively, at a fast rate, it may be desirable to have delays at the ends of lines to allow for eye movement to the next line.

Delays Between Writing on Different Parts of the Screen. Pauses may help between writing some material on one part of the screen and then writing some other material elsewhere on the screen.

Delays Between Text and Graphics. Although our major concern is with text, it may be that the text is interwoven with graphic material. Perhaps a few words will appear, then something graphic will happen, then a few other words, then something graphic. This resembles what goes on at a blackboard while the instructor is both talking and drawing. In this situation a possible approach is to delay during the transition from text to graphics and the transition between graphics and text, again allowing a shift in the viewer's attention.

Word-Phrase Emphasis

As already stated in connection with timing, it is often desirable to emphasize particular words or phrases. A variety of other visual tactics which come under the general rubric of types of display are possible. These physical methods of emphasis could be important in aiding reading. Fonts, discussed later, also can provide such emphasis.

Flashing. By flashing we mean that a particular word or a particular phrase appears brighter on the screen for a period of time. This might be done on

some types of displays by overwriting and other types of displays by rapid switching back and forth between bold and nonbold type fonts.

Blinking. A variant of the above is that a part of the text can blink off and on. The *rate* of blinking is a variable.

Reverse Video. A critical part of the text might be, for emphasis, in black on white rather than in the usual form.

Bold. Words or phrases may be in bold. This is discussed further later.

Text Movement. Some display systems will allow an individual word within a sentence or some other larger grammatical structure to move around on the screen independent of the rest of the text. Thus, the material might oscillate. This text animation then would also serve as a way of emphasizing the material.

Color. Another variant in this direction is the use of variable colors such as using different colors for different grammatical categories of words in a sentence. (If color is available, sound may be as well. Although difficult to incorporate in a textual taxonomy, the use of sound can also, in a variety of ways, emphasize words, phrases, or other material. This might be just the ringing of a bell or it could be a much more extensive use. Thus, we could use musical background just as in a film.)

Underlining. Underlining is a traditional way of emphasizing words and phrases in typed material. Underlines can *flash* and *blink* also.

Word-Phrase Spacing. Material can be emphasized by displaying it with more than normal spacing, either horizontal or vertical.

Lines of Text

In one sense the basic unit of text display on most screens is the line. In a book the line is the same for all users, but with a screen it can vary with users.

Length of Line. Some evidence with regard to traditional media suggests that longer lines are difficult to read. Thus, an interesting factor to investigate is the effect of line length. As with many of these items, we can let the user pick line lengths.

Natural Breaks. Often, the positions of carriage returns or line-endings are determined by the overall consideration of page or screen width. Another strategy is to have the line breaks at the ends of *natural* phrases, perhaps combining this with a maximum line length.

Hyphenation. Evidence indicates that hyphenation hurts readability in printed material. Nevertheless, hyphenation is very widely used in electronic media also.

Justification. Lines of text can be arranged in a number of ways. The most common is the typewriter-like situation where the lines start always at the same point at the left-hand margin, justification. Often seen in books (but not necessarily helpful in reading) is justification at *both* the left and the right ends of the line by insertion of spacing in the line. This can be done on display screens too, but often the only variable space allowed is that associated with the *spaces* between words; that is, the spacing between *letters* cannot be varied. Furthermore, even word spacing is controllable often at a rather crude level, a full space. Justification in conventionally printed material involves much more flexible control of space; the technique of letter spacing adds small spaces between all the letters.

A third possibility is to justify only the right margin, letting the left margin be ragged. The fourth possibility is to center the line within the space allocated for it, so that neither the left nor the right margin is justified. A variant of this is to put random amounts of space at the two ends; we might consider this a fifth possibility: random justification.

Number of Columns. Both one- and two-column formats are employed in books, sometimes even more. These possibilities also exist for the screen.

Space

A screen contains *both* text and blank space. Although it is perhaps straining a point to put it into this category, I will include such issues as the overall text density on the screen in this discussion of space.

Text Density. This might be defined most simply as the ratio of the screen area occupied with text to the total screen area. Perhaps in making this computation we should include the space at the ends of the lines that would be needed for justification, since that is not typically available for other use.

An important item, difficult to quantify, is *where* the blank space occurs. For example, we may have blocks of text expressing different ideas; the differences can be emphasized if the blocks are separated and placed on different parts of the screen. The question there is whether the blank space can be simply *randomly* determined perhaps by the machine itself, or whether it should be determined by a competent graphic *designer*. One might call this the issue of statistical blank space versus controlled blank space. Control could be thought of as referring either to the placement of the material or to the blank space.

Space Between Letters. Normally, letters are not written directly next to each other; some amount of intervening space is left, usually small. The space between letters is an interesting variable to investigate in connection with the present problems. It might also be described as the size of the letters in relation to the space in which they are put, and so could be indicated by the same type of ratio expression indicated above.

Space Between Lines. Another specific consideration is space between lines of text.

Characters

Comparative Character Size. Letters can themselves be of different size. Many current screens allow only a single size letter or only a few static sizes, but the possibility of variable size letters is not hard to imagine and is already possible with some systems. An additional possibility is the mixing of letters or various sizes in the same presentation, perhaps for word-phrase emphasis or for other reasons.

Fonts. In print media a variety of fonts will be used. Thus, a heading font may differ not only in size from the body font, but may be a bold or italic variant or a different type face, perhaps for emphasis. The font can be a conscious choice, but this is rare on today's screens.

Character Aspects Ratio. The same font of characters can be displayed with varying aspect ratios, the ratio of a letter length to its height.

Quality of Characters. Most computer displays still have very primitive, almost barbaric, characters. These characters are often made up of very limited dot matrix formats. But some displays, such as the Xerox Star system, allow better type fonts.

Page Aspect

The traditional printed page was higher than it was wide, with a variety of ratios. CRT screens also show a variety of ratios, but except for a few word processing systems the tendency is to make the width the larger dimension. Many of these screens are TV-based, having the aspect ratio of 3 to 4. Some systems have a square screen. Although this factor may not be important in our consideration, it would be desirable to determine that through actual usage rather than speculation.

Overflow Handling

Eventually as text is displayed on the screen, either the entire screen or the window or viewpoint in which the current material is being written will be full. The points raised in this section have to do with the action taken under these circumstances.

Scrolling.   Most of the common, inexpensive displays use a simple scrolling mechanism. That is, when the user gets to the bottom of the screen every line jumps up by one line, and the new line is displayed at the bottom. Thus in this circumstance (if the screen is not cleared), most of the time associated with any long text output will be spent reading the bottom line, which may appear instantly, character by character or word by word.

A useful variant under many circumstances is to allow scrolling of more than one line at a time; the number of lines scrolled can be chosen either by the program designer or by the user. Another variant is that scrolling can either occur automatically, or it can

occur after the user is queried as to whether scrolling *should* take place.

Scrolling can be a property of the full screen. But we can also scroll individual areas of the screen. Thus, some material can remain on the screen while other material is scrolled. Several textports (areas of the screen) can be manipulated separately.

An alternative to scrolling is a complete clearing of the screen, with text written at the top of the screen once more. Again, this can be done optionally with the user requesting it, or it can be done automatically when the end of the page is reached, possibly combined with some suitable delay, as indicated in the section above.

A special case of scrolling might involve only a single line of text. The material thus is constantly being erased and rewritten.

Panning.   In scrolling, the lines always move by an integral number of lines, typically one as indicated. In panning (or smooth scrolling), the text moves upward or downward at some steady rate. As with other items considered, the rate can be chosen by the designer or can be under the control of the user.

Crawling.   A small amount of overflow can be handled by having the entire text move to the left, as in some news signs on buildings.

Aids to Browsing

Books are seldom read completely linearly. Some books are almost never read in this fashion! The typical situation for browsing or searching might be where the reader wants to find a particular piece of information or wants to obtain a general impression as to what a book is all about. I use browsing to include both of these categories, although they might be split or perhaps better terms might be developed. Convenient browsing is a very important property.

Indexing. Most books, and much other printed material, contain indexes. They vary greatly in completeness. An index can also indicate the degree of importance of a particular reference, the level of treatment, etc. Indexes can be selectively displayed on the screen.

Free-Form Indexing. An alternative to an index is the ability to search for *any* word or phrase, possible in a computer environment.

Page Flipping. Page flipping is the facility to be able to move either forward or backward rapidly in gulps of pages at a time. The rate can be selected by the user. In a variant on page flipping, on each page key words or phrases (perhaps user-selected) can be highlighted by one of the processes discussed above in word-phrase treatment.

Hypertext. "Hypertext" is a word invented, I believe, by Ted Nelson. The notion is to allow a type of superbrowsing capability, where the *depth* of browsing can be controlled from everything to a very brief summary of the material to the full text material. An intermediate stage might offer a summary of each page or each group of pages, so that one could decide whether that was the page at which the material was likely to be usable. The user must be provided with some easy way of controlling this situation. I should hasten to say that the word "hypertext" also includes other concepts besides this, ones that are not directly relevant to our present interests.

Marginalia and Cross-Referencing

Notes in the margin, and other similar devices, can be very useful. These notes might be private, or they might be made available to other readers.

Notes. A common procedure with printed text is the writing of notes in the margin, a capability also related to hypertext. Although this has seldom been done with textual material displayed directly via computer displays, it represents a possibility. Such notes could be later modified or expanded. (See "User Interaction" section below.)

Pointers. The user can also enter pointers from one passage to another.

User Highlighting. A related feature is to allow users to impose their own word-phrase control. This is similar to underlining or using markers in print material.

User Editing. The user may want to change the text for his or her later purposes. Implementation of such a facility will also have to consider privacy factors. The user should be able to state whether a particular note or pointer is to be readable by other users of the same text (if that is possible on the system), or if it is to be restricted in some way.

Viewing Environment

Displays are often viewed in non-ideal environments. Studies in the area should see how environmental factors such as room illumination, screen contrast, distance from the screen, etc., affect readers. Factors such as the wearing of glasses may be important.

User Interaction

So far we have been considering the usual reader, a receiver of information. But the computer allows the reader to play an *active* role. In the best case we can have full interaction, as in the best computer-aided learning material. But with little work for us beyond just employing existing print material on the screen, we can occasionally invite the user to type in a *summary*, with the idea understood that such optional input would not be analyzed.

Design of the Screen

I mention finally the possibility of special graphic treatments set out by a competent graphic designer, as opposed to simply using some (random) combination of the factors indicated.

USER CONTROL

As we have been noting in our previous discussion, one unique aspect of the computer-driven display, as compared with the print medium, is that many of the functions which normally are completely determined in advance *can* be turned over to the user. The reader can be provided with many degrees of control which are not available in the print medium. Almost all the aspects of screen display discussed so far *can* be under the control of the reader.

But with all these new degrees of freedom come new uncertainties about how to employ them. At least four interrelated issues need to be discussed—the dependence on user characteristics, the question of which variables should be turned over to the user, how user control is to be provided, and the issue of training users in the effective use of this new type of facility.

Different users may have very different needs with regard to the type of control provided. So our characteristics cannot be ignored. One would expect, for example, that a second grade student might best be provided with different types of control over the display than that provided for a good university student or an industrial trainee. Although little research is available as yet, the situation might well be very complex, with many different user properties affecting readability and other issues.

In a given situation it might be entirely too complicated from the user viewpoint to turn *all* of the user controllable capability over to the reader. Hence, the issue of which variables should be under user control is one that requires study. At least two issues are important. First, if the user can modify the situation in some particular way, *will* the majority of the users or any users actually use that capability? If something is never used, it should not be given to the reader. But a more important issue is which user-controllable variables will actually make a difference to the reader, either in terms of the ease of readability of the material or in terms of affective issues.

The question of how the user is to exercise control is a fundamental one. How is the user to make the decision as to how to do these things, and what is the mechanism by which the decision is conveyed to the computer? These issues are not simple.

At least three overall strategies are possible, and combinations of these could also be followed.

1. Initial choice. When someone first comes to the text or program it is possible to offer the option that they could alter the conditions in some way beyond the default conditions. This would mean that the assumed conditions would need to be told to the user, and then the user could alter these if desired. Some methods for this initial alteration are possible. One is a menu-like approach where one points with the cursor to a line that is to be altered, and then the user is led step by step through the altering procedure.

2. Verbal commands during reading are the next possibilities. It is possible that readers could be entering commands indicating changes. Thus, if readers wanted the entire program to go faster, they might type faster, while the output is appearing on the screen. The advantage of being able to use English is clear. The difficulty is that the user would have to learn something of the vocabulary needed for these changes, although the built-in vocabulary could be quite extensive and therefore flexible. Or this could be allowed only at certain specific places in the material.

3. The third possibility is to allow the user some special mode of interrupting what is happening, to make changes. Thus, a particular key might be reserved for this purpose. When the user presses the key, a menu-like situation similar to that described in (1) could then ensue, or a query routine could be started.

These possibilities are not intended to be mutually exclusive, but could all be used. Experimental study could determine which ones and what combinations are more desirable. In any case, the careful picking of the method of user control could have a profound effect on the issue of readability. It may be, too, that the user may not want to use *any* such control, but would find it easier to stay with the default settings. Again, only carefully done experimental work would determine whether this is the case or not.

The final issue is also a critical one— the process of training the user to use the facility. This interacts with the other factors; a training procedure could be rather simple if only a few alternatives are turned over to the user. The question of the type of user is critical as to what one could provide; less training would be needed for the one-time user than for someone who is going to be reading large amounts of material at the screen.

The training process could involve off-line material in written, slide-tape, or other media; or it could be done directly at the display, using the best techniques of modern computer-based learning. My general preference would be the second possibility.

six

VIDEODISCS

Developing Interactive Videodiscs

ALFRED BORK

Abstract: *Several modes of developing videodisc materials are discussed. The process of starting with excellent existing visual material is described.*

The notion of combining the personal computer with the videodisc player was first suggested several years ago.[1] The potentialities of this combination for improving learning at a great variety of levels and tasks still seems very impressive. But, in spite of the lapse of years, very little highly interactive material that combines the two media is currently available. Further, little experience exists in the developmental process and almost no experience in the use of such materials with students. A number of projects are currently working on producing a variety of teaching aids, either for the videodisc alone or for the combination of computer plus videodisc.

Our group in Irvine has not yet produced any material that combines the computer and the videodisc. However, we have produced very large amounts of highly effective, highly interactive learning material[2] at a variety of levels, and we have thought carefully about the possibilities of an intimate combination of computer and videodisc. We have been particularly concerned with the production process, the process of beginning with crude ideas to final development. It is our belief that the production process involved with producing intelligent videodisc materials, combining with computer and the videodisc, is a straightforward extension of the production process that we have already developed for computer-based learning material. Literature is available describing this situation for computers.[3]

It should be emphasized that my primary concern is in producing the best possible material at a reasonable cost. Strategies which limit the *capabilities* of the material are inadequate. Many of the projects have not proceeded with full knowledge of the instructional design process as it would be represented by any media. The key to this process is that a group of people, with a range of talents, is usually necessary to the process.

Perhaps the best example in the world for effective generation of learning material is in the work of the Open University in England with its very careful course production involving such a team. Similar developmental activities have also been conducted at the University of Mid-America and in a few commercial and industrial training establishments in the United States. But

175

this scale of effort has seldom been seen in the computer-videodisc developments. Hence, we have at the present time little experience in development and usage.

TYPES OF DEVELOPMENT

At least four possible strategies present themselves in developing computer-based learning materials. All three of these strategies are likely to be important in the next few years. However, the largest gain eventually is likely to be from the fourth strategy. The first strategy, one that will be discussed in much more detail in the present paper, is that of starting with excellent educational film material and adding interactive computer capabilities to enhance the learning experience. Not all existing film material is worth such a treatment. The education film market is not distinguished for the quality of its products. A few excellent films do exist, and often these films could be made much more effective by making them part of the interactive environment of the intelligent videodisc.

The second strategy is almost an opposite one. This strategy would start with excellent, well-tested, computer-based learning material and ask what slides, video sequences, and sound could be added to increase the learning effectiveness of the material. The computer-based learning material that served as the basis would have to be carefully chosen. Even if it were effective learning material, it might not be possible to enhance it with the other media. But there would seem to be many interesting possibilities in this direction.

A third approach would be to start with material that is already available in videodisc form and to add the computer capabilities. We are currently discussing a possible project of this kind. The advantage would be that one is a little further along than one is with just film material and that what is on the videodisc would already be a combination of media. Frame numbers would already be known in advance. One could develop different pieces of learning material for the same intelligent videodisc, and then undertake comparison studies.

The fourth and final approach in the long run is the one that we would expect to dominate. In this approach the entire material—slides, video, audio, and computer-based learning material— would all be developed together by the design groups. This approach is also the most expensive, as everything must be developed; that is, the cost of developing the video sequences must be added to the other production costs, for example.

PROBLEMS WITH FILMS AS A LEARNING MEDIUM

To investigate further one of the possibilities, that of starting with an excellent educational film, I will review some of the inadequacies of the film as a learning medium. Such a review is necessary to understand where the computer material might be able to improve the situation.

In the usual environment for showing films or videotapes the user has little control over the situation. It is possible to provide some level of control, particularly for someone who knows how to run complex equipment. But this is typically not the case in the vast majority of situations in which films and videotapes are employed in education.

The first problem with film is that it is strictly a linear experience. It proceeds with no divergence from one sequence to another sequence. It is the same presentation for each viewer and cannot be individualized to the backgrounds or needs of particular viewers.

The second major limitation of film is that its rate is determined. In most situations the viewer cannot say, "Stop and wait a minute while I think about this." The film takes the same amount of time each time it is shown, regardless of what is going on in the mind of the viewer.

The third limitation is that it is very difficult to repeat a sequence. Thus, if one of the viewers of the film happens to be doing some daydreaming at a particular time in the usual group environments, there is no practical way of going back and showing that part over again.

The fourth disadvantage in some ways is a combination of the previous ones. Suppose that in a given sequence in the film the viewer does not fully understand what happened in that sequence. Often films are constructed in a tight logical fashion, so that someone who misses something at a given point has very little chance of being able to get anything from seeing the remainder of the film. In the ordinary film environment there is no way of knowing to what extent the

student has "learned" what was expected at each step of the film. It would be possible to construct films in a looser fashion without such logical connectedness, but this is extremely rare not only in films, but also in lectures and textbooks. Lectures and textbooks suffer to some extent from the same problem. But at least in the textbook environment, the student is not driven through it at a uniform pace.

This list of the disadvantages of the film is certainly not exhaustive. It should be remembered that I have assumed the best educational films available today, so that I have not reviewed many problems of typical films.

AN INTELLIGENT VIDEODISC BASED ON AN EXISTING FILM

In this section I consider the process of taking a film and converting it into an interactive learning experience by adding computer-based learning capabilities to the film. As indicated above, this is not the only strategy which can be followed. But for the next few years it does represent one way of producing videodiscs which could be very useful in a variety of learning and training situations and which would be less costly than materials produced entirely from the beginning. The existence of such material would give some interesting opportunities for research, comparing learning with the film alone and with the intelligent videodisc.

The first step is the choice of what film to use. The vast majority of educational films are *not* good learning experiences for students. In general, the quality of production has not been superb, to say the least. Relatively few first-rate filmmakers have made films for learning purposes. They are mostly made in studios where the quality is distinctly inferior to that representing the best possible use of the medium.

Nevertheless, there are a few excellent films. We can suggest criteria that might be used in choosing the film. First, one wants a film that *is* a good film considered just a film. I will not discuss these criteria, since they are reasonably well known. Second, one wants a film that has actually had some use with students and has already shown some potential in aiding the learning process with these students. One wants a visual film rather than an extremely verbal film. My own test is to turn down the soundtrack on a film and see how much is understandable with no voice present. (If there are English messages on the screen, one should also resolutely refuse to read them.) Another way of testing it is to listen only to the voice and see if one can pick up almost all the content of the film. A strong learning film does not depend heavily on the verbal information, but makes use of visual information in a strong and purposeful way. So the vast number of "talking head" films, people giving lectures on tape, often with some auxiliary aids in addition to this, are unlikely to be useful. An occasional film of this kind, given by a superb lecturer and handled by a first-rate director, might be worth the attempt to convert it to the intelligent videodisc form.

The next stage will be to study the existing film carefully and to derive from many viewings an outline of each of the modules involved. We also need to time these modules. Several people, with a variety of backgrounds, should independently engage in this process, and then a composite structure chart should be compiled from all the results. This work is necessary to determine where the computer-based learning material *might* go within the film structure.

The next stage would be to take the preceding information and to produce something like a learning tree out of it. Here the issue is what items are essential for later understanding. Sometimes material in the film will move off in different tracks and some things presented may not be critical for following a later section of the film. But in many cases there is this strong linear dependence. Such sections need to be handled particularly carefully in the intelligent videodisc. If a student does not learn the material in those sections, then the rest of the learning experience is of little or no value. Note that we have implicitly determined the learning objectives of the film. It may be that these were previously available in some other form, but in many cases this would not be true.

The next step is the overall design of the intelligent videodisc module. The previously prepared lists and structures will be vital at this stage. This design may be departed from when we complete the details. But a design is essential to guide the process.

The design and the implementation to

be discussed next are best done in groups of two or three individuals. Within each group we like to have at least one individual who is very familiar with the learning capabilities of the target audience. We would also like to have an individual familiar with the computer-based learning and visual possibilities inherent in learning; in some cases this might be two individuals. We would like at least one subject matter expert involved in the design team. This process, the pedagogical design of the intelligent videodisc material, is the heart of the activity. All the details are specified: What visuals are to be shown, what is to be displayed by the computer, text and graphs, what questions are to be asked of the student, how the replies are to be analyzed, what branches and outcomes are followed in this process. Authors at Irvine develop in a loose script format. The specification must include how the visual information is used as well as how the computer information is to be employed. Naturally the developers will have to have seen the film and will have available the products of the previous stages.

The quality of the eventual product is extremely dependent on this stage. Hence, the best possible people should be involved. We bring in people from various parts of the country for a week at a time to engage in such work with us in our production of computer-based learning materials. Our experience has been that one can produce a reasonable chunk of material in an intensive one-week work group of this kind. These people need not have any experience

with either computers or films. In fact, except for the media people particularly suggested, it might be better if they did *not* have experience of this kind. We want people who are extremely good teachers and who understand students and their learning problems.

The next stage is the visual design of the computer materials. One cannot affect the visual design of the film because in this process we are not planning to make new films. But one still has the question of where the visuals generated by the computer are to appear on the screen. In many computer-based learning situations this is given no attention and is left almost as an accident of how the software or hardware performs. But we believe it is a critical component of producing good material.

The type of person who can best do this is a graphic artist. The environment best for this person is one in which the designer can work directly at the display to create each of the screens. Much of traditional "coding" can be handled by such a person provided with the appropriate software tools, even though that person has little or no familiarity with computers generally. This process is further described in our literature on developing computer-based learning materials.

The next stage is the implementation of the computer materials. Here we are dealing with a typical programming task. The task is not a trivial one. Good material uses a wide variety of logic and control structures. Information on what has happened with the student early in the program may play a critical role in what happens later. The approach in general need not be a linear one in this environment.

We regard the coding of any complex material as a similar process, whether that material is computer-based learning material or other material. The lessons learned in the past two decades about how to program, gathered under the general rubric of "structured programming," should be utilized. We want to work within a language that reflects structure, such as Pascal or Ada. Auxiliary software is needed in order to make the process reasonable. For example, the input and output software contained in almost all the existing programming languages is barbaric for the purposes of working with a casual user of such learning materials, a person not at all familiar with the usual ways of handling computers. The quality of auxiliary software may have much to do with how efficient the process of developing the material can be. Once the necessary underlying software is available, however, it can be used over and over in a variety of situations. The software is primarily that needed for computer-based learning material alone. Only a relatively few additional commands are needed to handle the searching and displaying activities associated with the videodisc player.

I will not discuss in much detail the production of the videodisc itself, since that is the component likely to be best known to my audience. But mention should be made of one important set of possibilities. One possibility is to have

the videodisc contain only the visual material and to have the computer code, including the code that refers to particular tracks on the videodisc, on some other medium such as a floppy disk or a ROM cartridge. These procedures are almost universally followed at the present time. But it does mean that two different media must be involved. For large-scale use this is probably impractical for logistic and other reasons. The other possibility is to place the code on the videodisc, along with the pictorial information. It seems clear to me that this is the better ultimate solution. But there still appear to be technical problems associated with doing this, and I have seen very few examples that follow this approach, except for small amounts of code to drive the internal videodisc processor.

The question of how the material is to be tested and improved, usually through several cycles of increasingly large groups of target audience users, is also important. Many educational activities fall down here and do not go through the necessary revision cycles. But any learning material is based on a set of assumptions by the developers which may or may not be found in full detail with the actual users. Hence, the testing and revision process is a very important component. With current costs of mastering videodiscs, it seems impractical to go through many videodisc masters at this stage. Hence, a likely possibility for such evaluative and improvement cycles is some type of simulation of the computer plus videodisc system by means of a computer plus *videotape* system or by means of more secondary storage so that at least some of the visual computer material can be stored digitally in magnetic form and rapidly accessed. Thus, a very large backup disk might enable us to test at least pieces of the material. I raise this issue to indicate that it still must be solved before one can proceed to large-scale production of effective, intelligent videodisc learning material.

The process described for producing an intelligent videodisc learning package based on excellent existing film material follows the strategies we developed for implementing computer-based learning at the Educational Technology Center at the University of California, Irvine. I do not wish to imply that this is the only strategy that can be followed. But we believe it is a very effective strategy and one that should be pursued along with others in our further studies in this area.

1980

REFERENCES

1. Conference on Intelligent Videodisc Systems, *Proceedings of the 16th Annual Conference for AEDS,* May 1978; Graphics, "Videodiscs and the Personal Computer," NCC, June 1976; "The Educational Possibilities of Intelligent Videodiscs," ACM77, June 1976; "The Intelligent Videodisc," SALT, 1980; "Videodiscs—The Ultimate Computer Input Device?" *Creative Computing,* 2, 2, March–April 1976.
2. "Interactive Learning," *American Journal of Progress,* 47, 1, January 1979; Educational Technology Center at the University of California, Irvine, IFIPS, Summer 1979.
3. "Preparing Student-Computer Dialogs—Advice to Teachers," February 1979; "Limitations of APL as a Language for Student-Computer Dialogs," September 1974; "Student Computer Dialogs Without Special Purpose Languages," CCUC/6, January 1975; "Large-Scale Production and Distribution of Computer-Aided Learning Modules," October 1978; "Single Versus Multiple Authorship of Computer-Assisted Learning Dialogs," *AEDS Monitor,* 17, 7–9, January–March 1979.

The Intelligent Videodisc

ALFRED BORK

Abstract: *The combination of the small personal computer and the optical videodisc, with suitable interface, presents the educational community with major new possibilities and challenges. Although some prototype projects are already started, involving hardware and curriculum development, they only address a very small range of learning possibilities, and they will not provide enough experience on which to base a production system for producing sizable amounts of learning material. Previous experience with either film production or computer-based learning production can be important in furnishing necessary background and providing basic materials to work with. A major question for the future concerns media choice. For some situations, the computer alone will be the delivery system of choice. For others, the intelligent videodisc will be important. Economic factors will play a role in this decision.*

About seven years ago, when I first saw early demonstrations of early optical videodisc systems, I was at the University of California, Irvine, heavily engaged in extensive development of a wide range of computer-aided learning material. A limitation of such material was that it could not call upon, except in rather crude and difficult ways, a full range of multimedia learning capabilities such as films, slides, and sound. When I saw the videodisc, I realized that it offered the possibility of providing such a range of media. At that point I coined the term "intelligent videodisc" to represent the intimate combination of the videodisc and the computer, combined to provide an effective educational delivery system for a wide range of students.

Now, a number of years later, the possibilities of such a combination are being widely discussed, and all over the world a number of active projects are proceeding to develop the initial materials using this capability. The intelligent videodisc presents us, I will argue, with great promises and great difficulties. It will be many years before we are in a position to fully use the technology, and in the present paper I hope to show you why this is the case. I will assume familiarity with the general notion of the videodisc.

Some review of major features is desirable. We can view the videodisc from either a technical point of view or from a pedagogical point of view. The important technical features are (1) the possible storage of a large amount of information on the disk; (2) a variety of types of information, including video sequences, slides, audio, and computer code; (3) the possibility of random accessibility for any of these segments in a short time; and (4) an inexpensive medium, less expensive than magnetic tape. I do not wish to imply that all the problems have been overcome in placing these media together on a single disk. In particular, problems with combining computer code with the other media still need to be solved.

The most important pedagogical feature of the videodisc has already been mentioned, the fact that it allows us to bring in all the learning media within the same learning situation, allowing us to pick the best possibilities for each student and for each situation. The major contribution of the computer component is interaction. The intelligent videodisc can provide a medium every bit as interactive as that provided by the best current material which employs the computer alone.

INCORRECT APPROACHES

The intelligent videodisc can be used in a wide variety of ways. It seems a reasonable approach initially to start by saying that certain modes of using the disk debase the possibilities, and perhaps even could freeze us into unfortunate choices and so affect later uses of such systems. Many possible errors are ones that have already been made with computers or with other new learning media as they have been introduced.

The first problem with any new

medium is that people tend to produce materials that are imitations of those produced with older learning media, with minor variants and additions. We see many examples of computer-aided learning which are like a book, with only occasional use of the basic interactive capabilities of the computer and with no use of the dynamic capabilities of the computer with regard to such aspects as text and pictorial display. Perhaps this is only natural. We are all prisoners of our past efforts, particularly when these efforts have been successful in the arena in which they were developed. One example of a poor imitation of older media is to repeat lectures in newer media, such as films or on computer displays. This can be done in a variety of forms. The film, for example, can just show a lecture, or it can show a "blackboard" with someone talking. Unfortunately, many learning films are of this "talking head" variety. Even if one does not see the lecture, but sees effectively a "blackboard" on the screen, we still have a highly imitative medium. We can allow students to review a particular section as often as possible, but most of the interactive capabilities of the computer are lost in a lecture-type presentation.

Another incorrect approach to learning materials is to place technological considerations first. There is a great tendency to do this, since many of the developers are fundamentally technologists and only secondarily educators. It is easier to specify and build hardware and software than it is to tackle the tough problems of providing the best possible learning environment. So it is not surprising that often technology will dominate. But this is the wrong approach. We should always begin with the learning problems and allow the authoring team the greatest possible freedom in coping with these problems. Authors of computer-based material or intelligent videodisc materials must not be given a straitjacket situation to operate in, with only limited capabilities, but should be given almost complete freedom.

Another possible incorrect approach, perhaps not as critical as some of those mentioned, is that of ignoring one of the two capabilities, computer or intelligent videodisc. Thus, it is possible to produce video material with a minor overlay of computer, or to produce computer material with a minor overlay of the visual medium added. In some situations this may be the best approach, but such a tactic often represents the limitations of the developers, the type of background they have had.

Finally, a major problem is that an approach may well be an unreasonable or incorrect approach because it is underfunded. Many of the present projects are underfunded in terms of the tasks which they should be carrying out.

POSSIBLE REASONABLE APPROACHES

What can we say in a more positive vein? In many cases we have already laid the groundwork in discussing incorrect approaches to producing intelligent videodisc material.

The first important lesson is that we should put our emphasis on the learning situation, starting with real learning problems and considering the possibility of *all* media to aid in their solution. The question of media choice is still a difficult one, as I will comment later. The computer plus the videodisc—the intelligent videodisc—may not be the best choice or in many cases will not be the only choice. If we begin with learning problems, we will not freeze ourselves into an unfortunate media choice at the very beginning of the operation.

In every case in the design of good material for the intelligent videodisc, we will need *more* than an individual designer. In the cottage industry stage that has very much characterized much of what has happened in the early development of computer-based learning material, often a single individual carried out the entire operation. But in the present situation too many skills are involved to expect any one individual to be excellent in all of them. We certainly must involve good teachers, good screen designers, good film designers, good photographers, good editors, good programmers, and good evaluators if we are to produce highly usable material. Thus, we need a team approach, a group of people working together at each stage. Even at the pedagogical stage we believe it is not reasonable to assign this to a single individual. Rather, the experiences of a group of individuals, typically two or three in our case, need to be pooled to produce highly effective modules for a wide range of students.

The team approach, of course, is not new. We see it exemplified in major curriculum development efforts around the world. The most impressive is that at the Open University in England. While one might quibble with what they have done (and they have certainly not produced any intelligent videodisc material), the general strategies and the scale of effort conducted at the Open University seem highly appropriate to the task we are considering. Other good examples also exist. In this country the University of Mid-America also engages in the full production process needed for good intelligent videodisc materials.

The view just discussed implies that an efficient production system, one that will produce extremely good material at the least possible cost, is a critical aspect. To some extent we could also compare the process to that used in producing books, where again a production system involving many individuals from the author through typesetters, printers, etc., is necessary in the process.

The production team can start in many ways. One possibility is to begin with existing, extremely good computer-based learning material. In this situation the design team would then ask where visual information, slides and films, or audio information, would improve the learning situation for students. It appears that none of the existing projects is taking this point of view. It should be expected to produce highly interactive material, if the initial computer material is good. So such an approach has great promise, particularly for computer material that has been well evaluated.

The contrary approach begins with extremely good visual material. Unfortunately, the standards of design of many educational films and video materials have very poor visual quality. Only occasionally have the great filmmakers been involved with educational material. Yet good materials which have proved effective for students do exist. These can then be chopped apart and fitted into a computer–based learning sequence which allows their interactive use. The added computer sequences can query students as to what they are learning at each stage, perhaps with small on-line tests, and will provide alternate learning sequences for those people for whom the visual information alone is inadequate. This is the approach taken at WICAT, where an existing biology film was the basis of the activity. Robert Fuller's activity at the University of Nebraska is making use of such effective teaching materials in physics as the Tacoma Narrows Bridge film loop.

Finally, the obvious next possibility is the full approach, where we design both the visual materials and the interactive computer materials from the beginning as part of the same design process. The process of carrying out a fully competent job here would be a more difficult one. It would involve the costs of producing extremely good film material that one has in the best educational films, and so would not be inexpensive. This approach is an important one to pursue.

PROBLEMS TO BE CONSIDERED

It must be insisted that we are a long way from producing the best material that we will eventually be able to produce for the intelligent videodisc. Many major problems are still to be overcome. Some of these are the more obvious technical problems already referred to, but the most important and interesting problems are related to pedagogical aspects. It is those problems which I will now consider.

First, we need more research. Several different types of research are needed. We need fundamental research into the learning process, research which is independent of a particular learning medium. We have a number of competing theories about how learning takes place in the literature today, and none of these theories gives a complete view of the learning process. Nevertheless, some of these approaches are proving to be extremely fruitful. For example, the insights provided in modern cognitive psychology in understanding the manipulation of material within the brain in terms of models of the information is important. Another important set of insights comes from the study of developmental stages in progress and the resulting effect it has on such factors as providing a wide range of experience for students to learn. A third set of insights comes from the mastery learning enthusiasts, insights which insist that detailed feedback for each student is critical.

In addition we need media-oriented research on the unique capabilities of such learning media as the videodisc and the computer. As mentioned, we tend to use these media without too much thought in ways that are similar to the older media, but they are very different media.

As an example of the differences I consider one problem, how the material is to appear on the screen of an intelligent videodisc. I discuss primarily the material stored in computer code form, but similar considerations apply to other visual components. The computer screen is *not* a page of a book. It differs in many ways from a book. For example, blank space on a computer screen is free and can be used as a pedagogical element. In a book, blank space costs money. The book has no timing considerations. When the page is turned, the full page stares at the student. We can control the time in many different ways on the screen, providing a dynamic reading medium which we could never do in any other form until the advent of the modern computer. We still do not understand all the factors involved, and much research is needed even in such a specialized area as this.

The unsettled commercial situation again presents problems, although of a different nature from those discussed. We already have a number of competing videodisc systems on the market, and we do not have anyone yet marketing a full combination of the computer plus videodisc (although we might expect that the newly formed company between MCA and IBM might have products in that direction). One of the videodiscs that looks as if it may be a major contender on the market, the RCA system, looks as though it may not be usable in the combination suggested. It has a needle which rides on the groove, making it unlikely that one will be able to do rapid random access. The wear on such a system may make it an expensive medium. Optical systems, although related, are to some extent incompatible with each other. Thus, the MCA system, the Magnavision (Philips) system, the Thomson CSF system, and the Ardev system are by no means identical.

A problem with any new medium is that little practical experience is available in instructional design employing such a medium. Naturally this experience must be gained slowly, with many attempts. Thus, although we have been developing computer-based material for twenty years, it is only recently that we are beginning to gain the experience which leads to effective production systems. Unfortunately, the lack of such practical experience can become extremely limiting, restricting greatly what can happen. Many proposed authoring systems do not allow the full range of capability in the medium, but restrict the medium in ways which are unfavorable in terms of the possible results.

Little experience in developing materials and therefore little material developed imply that we have very little student experience in using such material. Using material with a few students in very selected environments with the developers present and consciously or unconsciously offering aid is very different from full formative and summative evaluation of the material with widespread student use. Even with computer-based learning sequences, with their much longer period of development, relatively few full-scale classes in the United States or anywhere in the world routinely make heavy use of computer-based learning material. Recently I put together a session describing such courses at a meeting of the Association for Computing Machinery, with courses at Irvine (physics), University of California, San Diego (computer science), and Stanford (logic). But there are not too many other examples of such full-scale courses, and so even there student experience is limited. With intelligent videodiscs, it is almost nil. I am unhappy about proceeding to any type of full-scale production without extensive student experience. Developers of material have often been wrong in the past; it is the students who keep us honest.

Finally, we still have little reliable information about the effective choice of a delivery system. It seems only reasonable that the intelligent videodisc system will not always be the system of choice of a particular application. Rather, we would expect the media choice to be application- and student-dependent, with choices differing in different situations. In many places in science education, for example, little would be gained by adding the visual medium. In these situations the computer alone, a cheaper delivery system than the intelligent videodisc, would probably be a better choice. On the other hand, I can conceive of situations where the visual information does play an important role.

For example, many areas of biology, where one can see things that aren't available to the naked eye through instrumentation or through changing time scales, offer interesting possibilities. With students who are in the concrete operational stage, we would expect too that real-life examples, video sequences of actual phenomena, would play an important role in materials, and so we would need both the computer and the videodisc. As with many of the other problems raised, the final need is for greater experience and based on this, effective ways of choosing appropriate media.

THE FUTURE

Each of the problems discussed suggests routes we need to explore for the future and raises the question of whether we will indeed have time to explore carefully all these routes. The press of developments may overtake us and force us into precipitous choices, choices which will have long-range effects on the educational system.

We are moving into an entirely new educational system. During the next twenty-five years we will see changes not only in the typical delivery of educational material, but in the whole nature of the institutions that we refer to as schools. The major mechanism for this change will be the computer, sometimes alone, sometimes in combination with the videodisc.

One problem with this future is that there is so little vision at the present as to what would be a *desirable* future. We cannot expect to move toward effective futures without consideration of what we would like an educational system to do. Some efforts of this kind exist, but far too little.

The critical factor in determining this development will be that of the entry of large companies or government-supported institutions into the production and distribution of computer-based learning materials or intelligent videodisc learning materials. This still is perhaps five years away, although it is difficult to say exactly. Many companies are interested, and some are already actively working. With the entry of many large companies at a sizable level, our freedom of choice is likely to be very much restricted. They will determine later directions.

The possibilities for improving the educational system are great, but we have a long way to go, and our future is not necessarily a bright one.

February 1980

Aspects of Marketing Intelligent Videodisc Learning Material

ALFRED BORK

Abstract: *This paper explores the current problems associated with intelligent videodisc material and makes some suggestions intended to lead to successful marketable learning materials in this area.*

First, it must be noted, in spite of the title of this paper, that there is now almost no marketing of intelligent videodisc material. I have been using the term "intelligent videodisc" to indicate an intimate combination of the computer and the videodisc. Material for such a hardware hybrid could be viewed as either providing a variety of visual media as additions to computer-based learning material, or it could be viewed as making television an interactive as opposed to a passive medium. But the intelligent videodisc is effectively a new medium, one that combines capabilities that could not be easily combined before. So probably we will discover that both of these descriptions are inevitably inadequate.

A number of very difficult questions could be asked about marketing intelligent videodisc material. Is there a market? Where is the market? When? Where would we expect the videodisc alone to be competitive? Where would we expect the computer alone to be competitive? Where would the intelligent videodisc be the delivery system of choice?

In any new area where no direct marketing experience already exists, it is very difficult to answer questions of this kind. The typical types of marketing surveys usually work best in an area where there already is some experience, some type of product that gives the potential audience some clue as to the new product. Here almost no experience is available, and so answering such questions is very difficult. I have touched on some of these issues in previous papers and will not try to answer these questions. But I do believe I can make some contribution toward the beginning of answering these questions and can point to some directions which will be important as preliminary to answers.

"THE FACTS"

We can ask ourselves, as preliminary to discussing ways of progress at the present time, what are the essential pieces of information we need to keep in mind. Most of these refer to the current situation, and some of them may well change with time.

189

1. **Storage.** The videodisc provides a very large, random, access storage, very inexpensive compared to other modes of storage. The storage, as is well known, can contain video sequences, sound (either in video or compressed), slides, and computer code. Typically the systems available today do not combine all these on one disk. Although the systems allow random access of any of these components, the access is slow compared to access to floppy disks, for example.

2. **Hardware Situation.** There are a number of videodiscs being marketed. The optical ones appear so far to lend themselves best to an intelligent videodisc system.

   Perhaps the most significant piece of information about hardware is that so far we have no *unified* intelligent videodisc system (videodisc and computer) on the market. The systems that are on the market are pieced together from some particular computer, plus some particular videodisc. Some videodisc materials use the built-in computer present in most videodisc players, but that capability is a very limited one.

3. **Volume Medium.** The intelligent videodisc is a volume medium. Because of the expenses in preparing material that includes both computer and visual information and because of the nature of the production process for videodiscs, we would expect that marketing will occur only in areas where there is a sizable market. In particular, the videodisc is not likely to be satisfactory for use by a particular individual or for use by only a few people. Much of the literature seems to ignore this fact, I am afraid. So in looking for markets we need to look for sizable markets.

4. **Little Developmental Experience.** Relatively few intelligent videodiscs have been made and most of these, frankly, are less than impressive. Many of them fail to use the capabilities of the medium and are often of very limited scope. This is not too surprising, because in the early stage of the use of any new learning media there is often slow progress. It took something like 250 years to use the printing press as a learning medium.

   The situation is rather drastic at the present time. Much of the experimental work has been supported by either the National Science Foundation or various military sources. The educational activities of the National Science Foundation have been almost destroyed in the new budget, so it is extremely unlikely that that source will be available for further developmental experience. Military support is unclear. Much of the military support seems to have gone in very specialized directions, such as the "Journey Through Aspen" type of videodisc.

   Furthermore, the United States in general is weak on sizable curriculum development involving *any* medium. The large National Science Foundation programs in curriculum development stopped around 1972, with the MACOS controversy. We have had in the elementary area, the secondary area, the university area, and the adult education area almost no major sizable curriculum development projects for more than ten years in the United States. For example, we have nothing like the kind of expertise that is found in the United Kingdom Open University in curriculum development. However, we do have some competent commercial concerns that have grown up in response to military and training needs and have been very good at a full-scale developmental process. But these companies so far work in very limited areas.

The conclusion is that not only do we have little recent curriculum development experience so far, but there is presently little possibility of sizable experience of this kind unless some new moves are made. I will suggest one such move in a moment.

5. **Little Student Experience.** The test of any learning medium comes with using it with actual people, whether those people are second graders or Bell Telephone operators. At the present time very little student experience is available. I know of only one sizable test of videodisc material, based on the WICAT-NSF disk, which has had experimental studies on its actual usage with students. Although that report is promising, it hardly covers the full field that needs to be explored with students.

6. **Inadequate Current Materials.** Many of the few examples of production of material we can find do not come close, in most cases, to recognizing the potential of the intelligent videodisc medium for learning with any type of learners. Curiously, because video is involved, many of the materials seem to be ones where the television people have been dominant. The computer-based learning components of these materials often use technology that was outmoded a dozen years ago. Few intelligent videodiscs use reasonably current strategies that are available in the best current computer-based learning material. It is not too strange that this is the case. Successful developers from older media often come into the newer media carrying all their old habits, and it takes some time before the nuances of the newer medium become obvious.

This problem is made more difficult if one takes into account the fact, already noted, that we have had so far not only very little developmental experience, but that current sources of funding for such developmental experiences are very uncertain.

SUGGESTIONS

The factual information just stated, often without the full support it deserves, leads me to a number of suggestions which will be important for progress toward fully marketable computer-based learning materials.

1. **Highest Standards.** We must move toward bringing together the

highest standards of video material and the highest standards of computer-based learning materials, if we are to achieve the combined product. I do not mean to imply that we can simply work with a combination. But the full use of the videodisc demands that we, particularly in this early age, not be satisfied with material that "runs," but that we must demand material of the highest quality and material that is tested with actual students. If we set our standards low now, we will get to the point where we are willing to market poor material, and we will find market disasters.

2. **Support.** The unclear aspect of government support, given the policies of the new administration, have already been pointed out. While we could have expected continuing developmental efforts through the National Science Foundation, particularly in the Developments in Science Education program, it seems now very unlikely this program will continue to exist. Indeed the present indication (July 1981) is that nothing in science education will exist. Other federal educational programs have been severely cut also.

The corollary is that if we are to make progress in this area, we must look to other means of support beyond the support of the federal government. State funds, too, are likely to be limited. It seems clear that there is only one possible source that will supply the funding at the level necessary to lead to fully marketable products. The *industry itself*, both the computer industry and the videodisc industry, must provide this type of support, if we are to make progress.

Furthermore, the problem is too big for any single company. We cannot expect one company to provide the range of support, talent, and strength needed, unless it were one of the major research laboratories of a very large company. The indication is that this activity very likely will need to be a group effort.

3. **Nonprofit Institute.** How can various industrial sources cooperate in stimulating developmental and research activities in connection with computer-based learning, the activities I have argued are essential for successful marketing? The suggestion I will make is the formation of one (or several) nonprofit institutes that will stimulate a wide range of research and development in connection with the intelligent videodisc. These institutes would be supported by a range of companies with interests in this area, each contributing to the institute, but the institute would have its own separate management to make it independent of any particular company.

The program of these institutes should have a strong, practical flavor. It should emphasize what works, and so move toward marketing aspects. The research involved would not be theoretical learning research, but practical, product-oriented research and development. The institute should be large enough so that it could sponsor a variety of projects, mostly carried out elsewhere, in a coherent program planned to lead to successful intelligent videodisc products.

4. **A Proposed Marketing Area.** The question of where to market these materials is certainly a much broader question than can be answered in this paper. Many markets are eventually likely. But it does seem to me that one class of activities will lead to marketable products and will deal with important problems that are critical to the future of education in this country and eventually in the world.

A number of such problems can be pointed to. I will concentrate on areas that seem particularly important in viewing the future of this country as a major force in the technological world. An extensive report conducted at the end of the Carter administration looked at the current status of science, math, and engineering education in the United States. Unfortunately, because of its timing, it received little publicity. This report, *Science and Engineering Education for the 1980's and Beyond,* prepared by the National Science Foundation and the Department of Education, October 1980 (Superintendent of Documents, U.S. Government Printing Office, Washington, D.C. 20402), among other things, compared the science and math education in the United States with that in many other technologically important countries, including most of the countries we compete with from both a military

and technological basis. It concluded that our program was already very weak in both the quality of courses and in quantity. While the report was mild, it made an effective case for the current weaknesses of our system and pointed out the long-range consequences of such weaknesses.

Although I would think that the state of science and mathematics education would be extremely important to the future of the country, the new administration chose to make one of its major budget cuts in precisely this area. The National Science Foundation had a well-conceived project in science education, with a strong component of research and developmental activities (the RISE and DISE programs) that supported much of the early work with intelligent videodiscs, as well as in many other areas. But as indicated, this program has ceased.

Our relative decline in science and math education has a number of important conclusions. It means that our companies will have an increasingly difficult time in finding graduates adequate for their activities. The military, with its increasing reliance on sophisticated, technologically based equipment, is having enormous training problems with many of the current recruits. Both of these problems can only continue to accelerate as our science and math education deteriorates.

Many current movements, such as the "basics" programs in many elementary schools, are leading to far less emphasis on science. The intelligent videodisc could make a major contribution to improving science and mathematics education.

Furthermore, products in this area would be highly marketable, simply because so many students would need access to them. I do not mean to imply that this is the only major problem area, but simply to point to one where there are major problems which could be aided by a full-scale development involving the intelligent videodisc and to one where the market would be sizable.

July 1981

seven

COMPUTERS AND THE FUTURE OF EDUCATION

Learning, Computers, and Higher Education

ALFRED BORK

Abstract: *This paper concerns the current and likely future situation with regard to the use of computers in the* instructional process in colleges and universities. *It begins with a discussion of some major problems facing education, the background for the computer discussion. It then considers the current and prospective situation with regard to both computer hardware and the computer as a learning device. It considers the issue of who owns the computer, and discusses the current direction toward very large numbers of personal computers on campuses, often individually owned. Then it focuses on what I regard as the most critical question, one that has received far too little attention: Where and how is computer-based curriculum material to be generated and distributed. Finally, I end with brief comments about the changes in universities that computers are likely to promote.*

THE NEW UNIVERSITY TODAY

The American university, like universities all over the world, is rather content with itself. But it faces a number of important problems. Furthermore, instructional technology is changing and growing rapidly. These changes will, I maintain, create great differences in the way universities function. In this section I review current major problems of universities, in preparation for the discussion of how the computer can be used to alleviate some of them.

Data about declining enrollments is well known and has received considerable attention. While predictions abound in the literature, perhaps the most carefully done study is that of the Carnegie Commission as reported in *Three Thousand Futures.*

The decline, on a national basis, is considerable. Optimism is shown in the graph at the point where the data become less reliable; students on the rising part of the curve are not yet born! The situation will vary greatly in different parts of the country. The overall national decline in enrollments seems inevitable because it is based primarily on demographic data. Universities in the past have argued for increasing funds on the basis of increasing enrollment. In some cases explicit legislative formulas will reduce funding as numbers of students go down.

Most universities believe that they will

be able to avoid enrollment difficulties by more vigorous recruiting. The trouble is that not everyone can avoid them. The steps that are being taken to maintain student populations are amazingly similar from place to place.

Coupled with this decreasing enrollment in some areas for the next fifteen years is the fact that our student body is growing more heterogeneous; students have increasingly different backgrounds. Mostly our ways of handling students are based on assumptions of homogeneous groups. Even remediation programs usually occur at the whole-course level, running everybody through the same material. Yet as our population is more heterogeneous, the needs of each student, particularly in building up missing skills, will be widely different. Learning resource centers on campuses have tried to cope with this, but their resources are limited compared with the magnitude of the problem.

Another problem for universities is the steady deterioration in our school systems.[1] In many cases the courses that we assume for universities, such as advanced mathematics and physics, are not even available for many high school students. Relatively few students have the possibility of taking adequate advanced placement courses in any academic area. Science and mathematics courses are particularly affected. The number of competent science and mathematics teachers for high schools is declining; very few of these are currently coming out of our schools of education.

Data from the National Science Teachers Association show that over a ten-year period the number of students in both science and math education in our schools of education have decreased by a *factor* of about four or five. Hence it is not surprising that many students do not receive adequate science and math courses in our schools. Other areas of our school systems have troubles too, but science and mathematics are particularly dramatic.

Another serious problem is the imbalance of faculty. In some areas universities seem to have more faculty than needed. In other areas, computer science and engineering, it is now difficult to hire faculty. Almost all major computer science departments have openings at the present time which they are not able to fill, even among the best departments. The problem is that few Ph.D.s in computer science are coming from graduate schools, and of these industry is also seeking to hire many. Universities do not compete well with major industries in most instances.

The situation in computer science is particularly bad. Because universities have trouble hiring the needed numbers of faculty members, they often react in ways which can only compound the problem. In many cases they restrict the number of students in computer science, not because of the lack of suitable applicants, but because of the lack of faculty and facilities. Furthermore, part-time instructors are brought in from the community, often leading to courses of variable quality.

COMPUTERS AND UNIVERSITIES: HISTORICAL SITUATION

Computers are very common in American universities, and indeed the available computer power in these universities continues to grow at an astounding rate. Nevertheless, computers are little used at present in the *instructional process* in *any* university in the world. The situation perhaps can be made clear if we examine *student learning time.* In almost all universities, the major component of student time goes into the use of books. Probably lecture time is second. The computer accounts for only a small fraction of the student learning time. Very few courses are based *primarily* on the computer (Stanford logic course, the Irvine beginning quarter of physics). With all of the talk about using computers in education, all the conferences, all the papers, ironically the actual present educational use is trivial.

This is not too surprising. Computers came to universities because of their usefulness as research devices. Research users still remain the heaviest users on most campuses. Administrative use has also grown extremely rapidly. And while educational use has grown, much of this use is extremely simplistic; furthermore, its growth has not matched that of other computer uses.

Although university faculty and administrators seldom admit it, the vast majority of all courses in all universities are *almost entirely* based on a small set of textbooks. The introductory calculus course, for example, differs little from university to university, with a few rare exceptions, because most universities use the same three of four textbooks, and most of these textbooks are quite similar. A few textbooks dominate any one area, and new books today are mostly imitations of currently successful books.

Extremely few existing textbooks recognize the role of the computer as a learning device, and very little computer learning material of any quality is currently available. Much of the current commercial available material is of very poor quality, employing tactics which were primitive even fifteen years ago.

COMPUTER TECHNOLOGY IN EDUCATION

During the last decade, amazing advances have occurred in computer technology. These advances have led to a strongly decreasing cost of computers; furthermore, this rapid decline in hardware costs will continue for a long time.

The university administrator and faculty member often do not recognize how dramatic the change in computers has been. One figure frequently seen in the industry is that computers go down in cost by 25% per year for equivalent computer power. Computer technology is still young and vigorous, so we can expect a long period of cheaper, smaller, and more powerful computers.

Today's personal computers, such as the IBM Personal Computer and the Apple Macintosh, represent computer power that was almost undreamed of by most institutions fifteen years ago. This power is often in the hands of the individual student. However, current capability is very small compared to that now under discussion, and being considered by a number of universities. More computer power and extensive amounts of computer memory are no longer issues of any doubt in the computer field.

This dramatic decrease in cost, increase in capability, and decrease in size should be compared to what happens elsewhere with learning systems. It is this factor *alone* which assures that the computer will eventually become the *dominant delivery system at all levels of education.* It will be increasingly cheaper to learn via computer than to learn in any other way whatsoever.

This conclusion, the likely dominance of computers in learning, does not address the *quality of learning.* Computer learning material can be poor, just as lectures, books, discussion sections, and laboratories can be poor. Emphasis on hardware is the major *problem* with the way computers are viewed in universities, not one of the strong points. Having great quantities of powerful computers, and little high-quality computer instructional material, is not conducive to progress in education. Indeed, the universities moving in this direction may be courting disaster.

WHO OWNS THE COMPUTERS?

One of the major issues connected with hardware, receiving a tremendous amount of attention recently, is whether the computers are owned by the university, or whether the computers are owned by students. A related issue is the possibility of every student having a computer.

Until recently it was unthinkable that students could own computers. Computers were too expensive. It is a consequence of the steadily decreasing cost of computers that now a very sophisticated computer costs very little. The schools in the initial Apple Macintosh University Consortium are selling the Macintosh to students and faculty for about $1,000 each. The Macintosh is a powerful recently designed computer, equivalent to computers costing hundreds of thousands of dollars only a few years ago. While this is a "special" price, not available to everyone, it dramatically illustrates how much computing power students can now own.

A few universities, mostly private, and many with an engineering bent, require all students to have computers, either supplied by the university or purchased by the student. It is also conceivable to require computers not in a university as a whole, but only in selected departments. Universities with these policies include Brown, Carnegie-Mellon, Clarkson, Drexel, MIT, Rochester Institute of Technology, and Stevens. Indeed, the list grows rapidly; it is even difficult to say who "belongs" and who does not, because of the variety of arrangements.[2] From a curriculum point of view, the most interesting situations are those that either *require* all students to own a certain computer, or provide enough computers themselves for this to be possible for all students.

Few publicly supported universities, such as the major state universities in the United States, have moved toward "one computer per student." It is not entirely clear why this is the case; perhaps they have less freedom, because of legislative bodies, and are therefore slower to move. It is very likely that, as the prices of computers continue to decline, policies of this kind will become almost universal.

The "one computer per student" point of view is, in the more advanced schools, also coupled with advanced computers, beyond those currently used, and with the notion of providing powerful resources that all of these small computers can access, through both local and remote networks. These resources are likely to include large computers, doing extensive calculations, very large file storage devices, with major student usable data bases on them, high-speed and high-quality printers such as laser printers, special graphic plotting devices, and other facilities. Carnegie-Mellon's hardware plans are particularly far-reaching.[3]

However, the Achilles' heel in this rapid increase in hardware, made possible by the decreasing cost and increasing capabilities of the personal computers, is the area of developing the necessary curriculum material which *really* uses these computers. *At the present time, even in schools where every student owns a personal computer, very little significant use of the computer is occurring in standard courses.* Indeed,

students in these schools presently have, I believe, considerable right to complain! Although the university has required that they buy the equipment, no university has as yet altered its courses and curriculum to make any effective use of these computers.

Universities, both the faculty and the administration, are extremely naive on this issue of modifying courses. I will address course development in more detail later, since it is the most critical step for the future prospects of the computer in education. Unless we develop high-quality learning material for most of our university courses, the computer is more likely to hurt education than to help.

THE PROBLEMS AND THE COMPUTER

I would not want to suggest that the computer can "cure" all of the problems that face the American university. But it *could* play a sizable role in helping us with these problems, leading to increasingly effective educational systems. It is not clear that this will happen. Indeed it may well be that while the computer will be the dominant delivery device for higher education, the standards for education will be poorer than they are at the present time. There is nothing magical about any learning technology. The quality of learning depends fundamentally on the quality of the instructional system, including the quality of the learning modules.

To illustrate the possibilities of solving some of the serious problems of

American education, let me consider two subproblems, student weaknesses in mathematics relevant to introductory science and mathematics courses, and the shortage of competent instructors in computer science. These are not the only problems the computer can address, but they illustrate the types of solutions which are possible. The reader can extend these strategies to other situations.

We have noted the increasingly heterogeneous background of students coming to universities. Universities effectively assume, in our curriculum, that "prerequisites" and other admissions standards assure that students are the same, stamped out by the same cookie cutter. This has never been the case, and the differences among students are growing. A student coming from an excellent suburban school is in a very different situation than a student coming from a small rural school. Teachers, equipment, quality of the instruction often are extremely different in different school situations.

One place where this heterogeneity manifests itself is with mathematics. Many college courses, such as physics, chemistry, and calculus, depend heavily on students' intellectual backgrounds before coming to college. Many universities have "admittance exams" to calculus, barriers which send students into remedial courses before allowing calculus. For example, at the University of California, Irvine, where such an exam is given, about 50% of the students who wish to enter calculus are asked, based on an exam, to take a remedial course.

The University of California accepts the upper 12% of high school students in California, so we would expect that this situation would be worse in many other schools.

Current courses are extremely inflexible, and do not take into account differing mathematical needs of courses. The mathematical background a student needs in a beginning physics class is different from the needs of chemistry. Within the University of California and the California State University and Colleges systems, we developed mathematics exams where we correlated performance on each question with performance in courses. These exams were developed for four courses, precalculus, calculus, physics, and chemistry. The questions related to success were very different in each of the courses.

Not only are needs different for different courses, but students have a variety of educational backgrounds. To put everyone through the same course, assuming that the deficiencies of all students are the same, is very wasteful of student and faculty time. We may not even touch the most critical problems of the particular student. We need a much more flexible learning approach that can react to the needs of each student.

Such an approach is possible with computers. We can develop good computer-based learning material which first tests students, based on the needs of the intended courses, and then provides interactive learning material in areas where the student needs it. Such material is relatively simple to develop at the present time, although, like all curriculum material, it is not inexpensive to develop and test. Good computer-based learning could be used very effectively on a national basis. Currently only odds and ends, often of poor quality, are available. But universities would need to cooperate in such a development, difficult to arrange at present.

The second issue is introductory computer science. The number of students desiring to take courses is much more than the available slots, and the situation is deteriorating. Universities *cannot* hire enough qualified science faculty. Furthermore, in many places existing courses are of poor quality, reflecting old strategies for introductory computer material. If good universities cannot hire adequate faculty, we can deduce what courses are available in community colleges. Few community college courses in computer and information science are adequate. Indeed they are often positively harmful, teaching habits which do not correspond to decent contemporary practice. This situation is even worse in the high schools.

How can the computer help with this important national problem? The solution lies in the careful and methodical development of a full-scale *computer-based* course for the introductory year of computer science. Almost all of the learning material would be available on the computer, in a highly interactive fashion. It could be given in situations where *no,* or very few, teachers were present, and could still provide a good modern introduction to computer science. Such a computer-based introductory computer science course could be, on the average, superior to most current courses.

I emphasize that the development I am suggesting in these two cases, and by extension for many other situations in higher education, is one that *cannot* be undertaken by two or three faculty members, or even by a single university. Such a development is expensive, and so probably needs national support, perhaps with a consortium of universities. These universities who supported development are likely to find such materials a considerable source of income.

Support might come from a variety of sources, including the universities. Federal support, foundation support, support of computer vendors, and support from publishers are possible.

OTHER UNIVERSITY CURRICULUM DEVELOPMENT WITH COMPUTERS

In addition to the examples described, university education could be improved in many other situations by the use of personal computers as part of the learning environment. Indeed, it is probably true that almost all courses could be greatly improved.

The key to the computer's effectiveness is the interactive learning environment, the possibility of making learning an active experience for the learner, rather than the passive experience so often provided by lectures and books. Because of interaction we can also utilize the individualization possible with computers. So we could build more versatile courses for our universities, taking into account a wide range of individual differences between students. Some of this material can be used in conventional courses. We can also develop computer material for learning centers to help the students in trouble.

Another interesting opportunity is the chance to improve learning-at-a-distance courses. The Open University in the United Kingdom has demonstrated that learning at a distance can be a very effective and economically reasonable way to learn. We can expect increased interest in this country in such a direction.

I am not attempting an exhaustive treatment of the use of computers in learning situations. I would argue that they present us with extremely interesting, even unique, possibilities for improving university education.

DEVELOPMENT OF COURSES

The real problem is not hardware, as I have tried to make clear. Rather, we must inquire about where all these courses are to come from. At the present time, very little in the way of computer-based learning material at the university level, or any level, is of any value.

Schools that are moving rapidly toward "every student with a computer" are, as a group, weak on curriculum development. The general attitude in these universities and in at least some of the major computer companies is that given the hardware, university faculty members will produce very large amounts of excellent computing material. I claim that this is very naive and unrealistic.

Faculty members have *never* produced very large amounts of high-quality curriculum material, even in the days before computers. A few wrote books, and an even smaller number were involved in instructional films. It is unlikely that the situation with the computer would be any different.

It is clear why so few faculty members have developed extensive curriculum material. First, the reward systems in most universities do not encourage such development. Our strongest universities emphasize research; faculty time spent on extensive development of learning materials does not "count" in the same sense that research counts. Extensive time on curriculum development is likely to hurt tenure and advancement chances. Even in the teaching universities, where research is less emphasized, there is often only lip service to curriculum development. Furthermore, in all types of universities, faculty members are busy individuals, with little spare time, trying to do a variety of different types of activities. Research universities often have a lower teaching load to encourage research. The teaching universities use more faculty time in teaching courses, assigning heavier teaching loads. In neither case is extensive time available for course development.

A major factor that must be taken into account is that almost all university faculty members simply *do not know how* to produce extensive high-quality curriculum material. They have not been trained in curriculum development. Other than their own educational experiences, they usually have restricted views of the learning process. Since faculty typically learn very easily, they have little appreciation of the learning problems that many students have.

So arrangements which dump large numbers of personal computers on universities are *very unlikely* to produce satisfactory curriculum material. Even when groups are funded within the university to explore course development directly, they are often funded at levels which are so low that nothing of any consequence can be produced.

The Open University at the present time, in developing a *single university-level course* (typically now with little use of computers), spends about a million dollars. That figure is a reasonable one to use in judging the cost of curriculum material. A recent paper by Arthur Melmed, United States Department of Education, argued that high-quality curriculum development costs between $5,000 and $50,000 per hour of student material. We estimate about $20,000 for the development of interactive computer material at the Educational Technology Center at Irvine.

The development of computer-based material costs about the same as the development of books. Well-done films are more expensive than computer-based learning material. Intelligent videodisc material will probably be the most expensive medium, since both video and computers are involved; perhaps this accounts for the fact that so little good interactive videodisc material has been generated.

I do not mean to imply that curriculum development is hopeless. Rather, my point is that it must be carefully organized, adequately financed, and involve the best faculty members. *Development of curriculum material is a serious business* and cannot be done in one's spare time. Of all the messages in this document, this needs to be most forcefully brought to the attention of administrators and faculty members.

DEVELOPING COURSES

Many models exist for the process of developing courses involving the computer. The large-scale curriculum projects in the United States in the 1960s and early 1970s show what is necessary. At the university level, the most successful curriculum development has taken place in the Open University, in the United Kingdom, already mentioned. We know the process of producing textbooks, the current major curriculum efforts. Another point of view is furnished in the development of industrial and military training material.

At the Educational Technology Center at the University of California, Irvine, we have, over the past fifteen years, developed a full-scale production system for computer-based learning. This system has been employed in producing a wide range of materials at both pre-university and university levels.[4] The emphasis is on stressing pedagogical design in the early stages.

The pedagogical design is done by groups from all over the country, the people most experienced in helping students to learn in a particular area. It is silly to believe that all the best people for designing curriculum material happen to be in the same geographical location! We want to bring the successful teachers, the researchers in how people learn in a given area, and those with great experience in educational technology into a single design group, and we want them to plan the material with little concern as to how it is to be implemented.

Implementation involves several sets of specialists. First, graphic designers plan the computer screens, in space and time. The important issue is to use the full capabilities of the computer, avoiding the booklike or filmlike approach as seen in much commercial material. The coding process must follow the same standards of good code that are generally accepted for producing any complex program developed in modern software engineering and programming environments.

An important aspect of developing learning modules is evaluation, particularly the evaluation stages associated with improving the materials during development. The computer provides unique capabilities to assist in review and evaluation, enabling us to do more careful evaluations than with other types of learning material. The computer can gather very detailed information on student performance; it is an interactive medium. We are "talking" to the students constantly, and letting students reply. We have an almost moment-by-moment account of what is going on in the student's mind, gathered by the computer, and so we can often make major improvements using this rich information. Other techniques are also useful in evaluating computer-based learning modules.

WHERE IS THE MONEY TO COME FROM?

The development suggested in this paper will require considerable funding. Universities will not be able to fund any extensive development out of their own funds. This implies that some national, or conglomerate, source of funding will be necessary.

The federal government is an important possibility, although at the moment, even with recent additional funds to the National Science Foundation for development, little university-level material is being sponsored. Another possibility is a consortium of universities, a group that sees common problems that they wish to solve together.

Universities are at the moment, in curriculum, very much at the mercy of the textbook publishers. While there are advantages to that situation, there are also disadvantages. In a few situations, such as the formation of TIAA, university faculty and administrators have banded together to support their own interests. The suggestion of doing this with regard to computer material has been made, but so far I know of no efforts in that direction.

Another possibility of support is from major corporations. At least one computer vendor has already begun to spend sizable amounts of money for curriculum development, naturally material involving the computer.

FINAL COMMENTS

The extensive changes proposed cannot take place without structural changes within our institutions. Those changes are not discussed here. I have already mentioned the possibilities of distance learning. It is likely that it will become much more important in the United States educational system than it is at the present time.

Bold leadership too will be needed to bring about the necessary reorganization of universities required by the availability of this new and extremely powerful learning medium.

May 1984

REFERENCES

1. *A Nation at Risk,* National Commission on Excellence in Education, Department of Education.
2. Barbara Wierzbicki, "College Students Learn to Live with Computers," *InfoWorld,* January 16, 1984, p. 35.
3. Douglas Van Houweling, "Information Processing Factors for Higher Education," *EDUCOM Bulletin,* Fall/Winter 1983, p. 35.
4. Alfred Bork, "Production Systems for Computer-Based Learning," *Instructional Software: Principles and Perspectives for Design and Use,* Decker F. Walker and Robert D. Hess, Editors, Wadsworth Publishing Co., Belmont, California, 1984; Alfred Bork, *Learning with Computers,* Digital Press, Bedford, Massachusetts, 1981; Alfred Bork, *Personal Computers for Education,* Harper and Row, New York, 1985.

Computers and Information Technology as a Learning Aid

ALFRED BORK

It is a pleasure to return to Holland to both renew old acquaintances and to participate in the opening of your new center for the computer in learning. Centers of this type are increasingly important in the world, and Holland is to be commended for moving in this direction.

The computer will become the dominant way of learning in our society over a relatively brief period of time. That is, more people in the near future will learn more things from computers than from any other learning modes, including books and lectures. We are at the beginning of serious development of computer-based learning material. In this paper I look at some of the key factors involved in this massive change in our educational systems.

COMPUTERS IN SCHOOLS

First, let me note that computers are appearing very rapidly in schools all over the world. The most reliable figures from the United States, from the National Center for Educational Statistics within the Department of Education, suggest that at present there are approximately 150,000 personal computers in schools in the United States, about an average of two per school. The rate of purchase is approximately 100,000 per year, so this

number will be increasing rapidly. In recent years, roughly speaking, the number of computers in schools in the United States has doubled each year. There is nothing remarkable, however, about the United States's data. I understand that in England at the present time, for example, there are between two and three computers per school. While in the United States many schools still have *no* computer, in perhaps half the schools in England it is the government policy that every school should have at least one.

What happens when these computers appear in the schools is not necessarily favorable, unfortunately. Two major problems, problems which will be important in much of what I say here, affect this. First, extremely little good curriculum material employing the computer is available. This is true whether one is looking at the teaching of programming, the teaching of broader aspects of informatics, or whether it is using the computer and some formal computer-based learning material to learn some subject area not necessarily concerned with computers. The lack of first-rate curriculum material involving the computer is a tremendous deterrent. Although much is now commercially available within the United States, this material can only be characterized overall as poor and often trivial.

The second major problem to be considered is related to this. Not only is little decent learning material using computers of any kind available, but almost all the teachers currently in schools and universities all over the world have little experience with computers, particularly little understanding of how the computer is used in learning situations. Teachers whose only computer background was during a brief workshop or some short period of time are poorly prepared to teach programming because they have likely picked up a style of programming that bears no resemblance to good modern programming, and they often use a language that should not be used.

COMPUTER ADVANTAGES

I have argued (in *Learning with Computers*, Digital Press) that the computer is a very powerful aid to learning in many areas. Although I do not intend to make a full case, it is important to mention the main advantages of the computer in education.

I regard the most important advantage as *interaction*. The computer can provide frequent and highly relevant feedback, based on exactly what the student has been doing. Questions can be asked and responses can be carefully analyzed, all within the common everyday language of the student. As numbers have increased in our educational systems, we have been less and less able to afford a highly competent tutor who works with one or perhaps three or four students. Rather, we have moved toward mass production methods, where students play a passive role in the learning process.

For the first time, by using the computer we have the possibility of providing an interactive education for *everyone*, not just the children of the very wealthy. This issue is extremely important not only in the developed countries of the world, but in underdeveloped countries which need to make rapid improvements in their educational systems.

The two key issues in interaction are how frequently the student does something and the quality of each of these student-learning interactions. Not all interactions are equally useful in learning. Thus in our activities in the Educational Technology Center we avoid almost entirely the use of multiple choice, even in quizzing situations. We consider this to be an unpleasant form of interaction, one that has many negative aspects in learning situations.

One consequence of interaction is the possibility of individualizing the material. Most learning material delivered today in books, the typical classroom situation, treats everyone the same. But one person may want to move through the material at a different *rate* than another person, or one person grasps the material quickly, but another needs other pedagogical strategies to understand what is happening besides the one used initially. Some students have weaknesses in background. Thus a student in a science class may not be able to use, in a functional sense, some critical mathematical technique. Lip service is paid in education to the notion that different students learn in different ways, but unfortunately our current learning structures do not permit us to react reasonably to this. The computer, because it is interactive and therefore pays attention to what the student is doing, *can* with well-developed material individualize the learning experience.

This paper, examining the computer in education, will be concerned primarily with computer-based learning. However, I wish to make it clear that this simply is a restriction in content, not a philosophical position. The computer can be used in many ways in learning situations. We have already mentioned the learning of programming and the learning of informatics. There are also very important tool-like uses of the computer, such as those employing word processing systems. In all these areas, good curriculum material is necessary for effective usage. But I will concentrate, as indicated, on computer-based learning.

SOME EXAMPLES OF COMPUTER-BASED LEARNING

I examine briefly several examples of the computer as a learning device. The examples from the Educational Technology Center at the University of California, Irvine, show learning in the sciences with different levels and techniques. The first example is about six years old, a beginning quarter of physics for science and engineering majors.

Students are offered a choice of a noncomputer version and two computer versions which differ in content. About three-quarters choose the computer.

The course follows a mastery organization. For each unit, the student has a list of learning resources and a description of what is to be learned. Students cannot continue to the next unit until they have demonstrated, through on-line quizzes taken directly at computer displays, that they know the material in a given unit perfectly. Four hundred students in the computer course take about 15,000 quizzes in the ten-week period, with the computer generating each quiz uniquely and giving immediate feedback. All the recordkeeping and much detailed aid to the student, aid which is highly relevant to an error that the student has just made, are available. Students agree almost unanimously that the quizzes are learning material. Testing becomes a learning mode. In a sense, the tests *are* the course, in that they are the major learning facility for almost all the students. This way of organizing courses is possible only with the computer; it has considerable promise. It resembles the situation of pre-testing and post-testing, except that the two forms of tests plus the learning all take place with the computer-based format.

The development of this material was funded by the National Science Foundation.

The second set of computer-based learning modules concerned scientific literacy, the nature of science. It is aimed at a broad audience, from young children through adults. The material has been widely tested in schools from junior high school through universities, and within public libraries and science museums.

When the science literacy units are used in the library, no one is there to "help" the student, with either the computer details or with the subject details. Thus the materials are completely self-running, and therefore also suitable for the home environment. The dominant pedagogical approach for the literacy materials was suggested by Robert Karplus a number of years ago—the learning cycle. Karplus derived these ideas from his study of Piaget in connection with the Science Curriculum Improvement Study materials. The learning cycle suggests three stages in the learning process. The first is experiential; the students have experiences which lead to better insight and which prepare the way for the more formal learning activities of the second phase. In the third phase students demonstrate what they know through testing or some other way and receive additional help if necessary. The student should also be able to apply the ideas to other areas. Karplus sees these three features as essential to learning.

There are six units available, each taking a student between one to two hours to complete on the average. Each of the modules has a subject area in science and mathematics, but, as indicated, the emphasis is not on the subject matter itself. The units are broken into fifteen-minute modules, so the students can move around within the materials. The project was funded by the Fund for the Improvement of

Postsecondary Education within the Department of Education in the United States.

The Educational Technology Center develops many types of materials, such as the two indicated here. We also are involved in research in using the computer more effectively in education, and we also consult with schools, universities, and companies on computer-based learning. Some of this consulting involves the workshops to train people to prepare such material.

PRODUCTION OF COMPUTER-BASED LEARNING MATERIALS

A key factor for the future will be a system for producing very high-quality computer-based learning material at reasonable and estimatable costs. One of the difficulties with so much of the material available at present is that material is produced by cottage industry procedures, and therefore often does not reflect the standards necessary for good learning material.

The major point to emphasize is that developing good computer-based learning material is fundamentally no different than developing good curriculum material of *any type*. Thus, to make an educational film or to write adequate text material is a long, difficult, and expensive process. It it foolish to believe that there are shortcuts to developing computer-based learning material which would make it much cheaper than other competently done material. Many of the details of producing adequate computer learning material are similar to the details associated with other curriculum developments. Thus the pedagogical development stages and the various evaluation procedures are similar, no matter what the medium is, although we will point out some differences.

In understanding the question of computers in education, I find it illuminating to consider the history of textbooks. Textbooks revolutionized education, changing the major learning mode in almost all areas. Like our current interest with the computer, the textbook was based on a technological innovation, the invention of printing. In the early days of the printing press, if a teacher wanted to use one of these newfangled things called a textbook, the only possibility was to buy a printing press and a set of type (undoubtedly the teacher was told that there was an easy way to use the printing press!) and to proceed to learn the art of printing. The teacher was probably not very good at this and only produced a few rather mangy books for use primarily in the teacher's own classes. Eventually a system developed and an industry developed around that system which removed the necessity for teachers to use the printing press. Today an author of a book is usually concerned just with the pedagogical details, as reflected in the preparation of a manuscript. A very similar situation exists with the computer, with many close parallels.

I now make a few brief comments about the stages involved in developing good computer learning units.

Pedagogical Design

Two important aspects must be considered in connection with pedagogical design. The initial planning session may involve people from all over the country, engaging in a brainstorming activity; they create a specification document for each of the modules to be developed. It is important that research on learning and teaching in the subject area be examined. For good curriculum material, we want to employ the best people in the entire country. This design specification can be sent out to competent individuals who did not draft if for review and for subsequent improvement.

Next is the detailed pedagogical specification of each unit. We generally do this in groups of three to five individuals. One or two people in the group will be highly competent teachers who have had much experience not only in teaching the area, but also in reacting to individual student problems. One other person in the group might reflect the research background, and another person should be highly experienced in producing computer-based learning material. In the case of the Educational Technology Center, this last person is usually a staff member of the center; other people involved may typically come from outside our group from other locations.

We find it desirable to do the design work in intensive one- or two-week sessions in pleasant isolated locations, avoiding constant interruption from telephones or other people. We want our designers to concentrate intensely on the activity. I will not discuss the strategies we use for recording the results of the design group. The specification of the units can be given to the screen designers and coders in the next stages in the process. This document can be reviewed, as with the preliminary design document. That is, it can be sent to others with instructions on how to read it; changes can be made based on the suggestions received.

Some training of the detailed design group is needed, usually the first morning. The critical aspect is to understand the nature of the computer as a learning medium, mostly by looking at many examples of good and bad practice. We do *not* believe it is valuable to teach these people anything about computer languages whatsoever; the issues of the technical details associated with computers and the issues of how to use the computer effectively in a pedagogical sense are unrelated.

Nothing has been coded in this stage. One of the keys, we believe, to effective material is to separate pedagogical issues from technical or coding issues. The issue of how it is to be programmed should not influence the pedagogical design, the critical factor in producing high-quality material.

Screen Design

An important aspect of computer units is how they are structured on the screen,

both in space and time. The instructors, in some design groups, may make detailed design suggestions, but these suggestions usually do not give a complete specification of the screen. Instructors, indeed, may not be the right people to do it. Ideally, a good graphic designer, sensitive to educational issues, should be involved, working with interactive software particularly prepared for such individuals.

Often, however, in our projects at the Educational Technology Center we have not been able to afford such a graphic designer. In such a case, a series of general principles will be useful, such as the following:

1. Use blank space freely—it is free on computer systems.
2. Remove any information not needed—the screen should not be a history of what has happened in the last five minutes.
3. Use as much visual information as possible to aid the student weak on understanding verbal information.
4. Use timing and other devices to stress key words or key phrases. Thus a key phrase might blink.
5. Use timing to aid readability. Stop when you have periods or question marks.
6. Use short lines to avoid reading errors.
7. Keep the natural phrases together on the lines, if possible, rather than splitting them across several lines.
8. Use a variety of textual styles, such as the occasional use of a text which is right-justified but not left-justified.

Screen design furnishes another stage where review and evaluation can be important. That is, the screen designs, created on-line by the designer, can be reviewed directly at the screen by other designers, and they can suggest changes to be made.

Writing the Code

The next stage in the development process is to write the necessary programs to carry out the logic indicated in the scripts produced in pedagogical design. If there has been a separate screen designer, it will be not necessary to enter text material, as that will all be present. Simple graphics will already be done, but the coder may need to do complex graphics, such as that involving animation.

The basic principle in coding is that, as these are large, complex programs which will need to be modified frequently (in the formative evaluation stage to be described later), and possibly transferred to a variety of machines, it is necessary to follow the best practices of modern software engineering. I do not review those practices in detail, since they are amply described in the programming literature. Unfortunately, most computer-based learning material developers seem to be completely unaware of these practices, and so a number of unfortunate directions have become common.

Programs should be written in such a fashion that they are as readable as possible. They should be written in a highly modular fashion. They should be

amply commented. Variable names should be meaningful. Data types should be carefully specified and should be natural to the area involved.

As with any other well-done complex coding activity, codes should be *designed,* perhaps by the use of such devices as structure charts, before any actual coding is done. This design can be reviewed and improved before the coders themselves work. A long program will probably have several different coders employed, and one of the important aspects of this initial design is to coordinate their activities and to assure that the interfaces between their work are appropriate. After it is written, the code should be reviewed, again following good modern programming standards, and revised.

Given these factors, almost any knowledgeable computer scientist would suggest that the programming should be done within one of the powerful, higher-level structured programming languages. Currently our materials in the Educational Technology Center are all coded within UCSD Pascal, a variant of Pascal very common on personal computers. Other good possibilities, although little used at present for this purpose, would be Modula 2 or Ada. The particular language used is not as important as the fact that the language reflects modern programming standards; if it does not or if it is not used in satisfactory ways, the problem of improving the materials and transferring them may become insurmountable for an extensive set of learning materials. Some special procedures are useful in helping the coders here. Particularly, we find existing languages extremely weak on the issues of organizing the screen, and so we found it necessary to augment Pascal with a whole set of procedures for this purpose.

Review Evaluation of the Running Program

At this stage, we now have the first running program. Two types of review and evaluation activities are critical at this stage, the internal review of the material and an external formative evaluation.

In the internal review, the material will be run over and over by staff members of the project. They attempt to find out where the program does not work by trying many alternative branches. They will also see where the pedagogical ideas which seem good in the discussion group and on paper do not seem to be adequate in an actual running program. Emphasis on improving the interaction is important at this stage. Usually the program will go through many versions because of internal testing before it is available for full-scale testing with the target audience.

The formative review process is the first time that the units are used by the people they are intended for. The formative evaluation is perhaps the most critical of all the stages, except for the detailed pedagogical design, in assuring the eventual effectiveness of the material. One of the great advantages of computer-based learning material is that it is still possible to make changes at this point, because computer programs *can* be easily changed if they are well written.

With books, for example, change is almost impossible after the book is printed.

The computer can collect much of the information in this initial testing with typical students. The student responses can be stored selectively, and so we can find where the program is not responsive to the student language. The students can be allowed to make comments. We can keep data on different paths taken through the material. We can do testing on-line to determine what the student has learned.

Other evaluation procedures are also useful. A skilled evaluator can interview students or can observe students' behavior. Detailed studies can be conducted using videotapes of students using the materials.

Several cycles of formative evaluation are useful. As increasing numbers of students are used in each cycle, the evaluations may become quite expensive, so budgetary considerations may restrict how much may be done at this stage.

The final summative evaluation is a more difficult issue. Good summative evaluations are expensive. They should be done outside the initial group by competent evaluators and with adequate unding, so that sizable numbers can be involved in these tests. They should also not be performed until well after the materials are developed to allow the maturing of the product.

Authoring Languages and Systems—A False Direction

Before leaving the issues of producing computer-based learning material, I wish to contrast a system of the type just discussed with another commonly used system which, I would argue, has been one of the main deterrents to producing effective computer-based learning material thus far, the use of specially designed authoring languages or authoring systems particularly for such materials.

Hundreds of millions of dollars, and perhaps even billions of dollars, have been spent on developing such systems. With few exceptions, languages with large financial support (such as Tutor) have been used in writing materials. That alone should indicate that something is wrong with the approach.

The *initial* philosophy behind many of these languages is a "Renaissance man" philosophy. Instead of the careful separation of tasks by using people of different abilities necessary for the type of production system envisioned in the last section, one person does it *all*. It is as if we were back to owning one's own printing press and preparing books! Developing curriculum material is a complex activity and cannot reasonably be expected to be carried out by a single individual, regardless of the medium involved. Inevitably the pedagogical issues become, in authoring languages, confused with the necessities of programming, and the primary decisions are *not* made on pedagogical grounds.

Although many of authoring languages and systems start with this single-person philosophy, some recognize its limitations and begin to use a strategy more like the one reflected in the last section. Then the author no longer uses the system, but

separate individuals are involved. Then the objections to the authoring languages and systems become quite different. They are then programming languages and they can be evaluated as programming languages with the same modern criteria we would use for evaluating any other programming language. The authoring languages and systems are mainly very primitive compared with modern programming standards. They do not take into account what is known in modern software engineering.

Consider, for example, Tutor. Tutor is an old, creaky language, dating from about fifteen years ago. Its structure is essentially that of an assembly language macro language, with a label field, a command field, and an argument field. It has a vast number of very complicated commands, over two hundred. No experienced language designer today would ever develop such a language! Yet Tutor has been the most widely used of all such authoring languages and probably also the most widely imitated.

Most authoring languages and systems allow one to use standard programming languages too. When this is the case, then often much being done within that language really *does* use a standard language, so the authoring system becomes less and less necessary. In the early days of Coursewriter I looked at an interesting program in physics concerning Gauss's law. However, in getting the code, supposedly written in Coursewriter, I discovered 90% was in Assembly code for the IBM 1500.

Authoring languages and systems are often particularly weak for revision, a critical aspect of development. Indeed, with many of them the only possibility for revising a section of material is to redo it. The facility must be re-created on each new machine, often an expensive job, so transferability is not easy.

Eventually, a language for computer-based learning must have as a minimum *all* the capabilities of a general-purpose language. So the writer ends up re-creating a general-purpose programming language with a few additions. It makes sense, therefore, to start at the other end with a good language and add a few special capabilities in the form of procedures.

Many of the developers of authoring languages and systems are not highly experienced with learning material. They often have a simplified view of how the computer can be used in learning, and the language they develop is restricted to that simplified view. As the view expands, under pressure of new materials, the language may be extended if funds are available. But then it becomes clumsy, as these new features were not taken into account in the initial facility.

There is a tradeoff, too, between how easy the language is to use and how restrictive it is on what it lets the author do. Thus, languages that are advertised as very simple, easy to learn by everyone, can usually produce only the most trivial material. This will become boring even within a single long program. Given the future needs for sizable amounts of computer-based learning material, authoring systems are an unfortunate direction.

I now wish to move from this discussion of the current situation to consider the future of computer-based learning material. In an area where the technology itself is changing rapidly, it is particularly important to think ahead.

FUTURE HARDWARE

The computer, particularly the personal computer, is evolving very rapidly. Computers are not only becoming cheaper, but their capabilities are increasingly rapidly. New systems will not necessarily be cheaper than they are today. Vendors will give us some balance between decreasing costs and increasing capability. Central processing chips are becoming more complex and faster, as we move to larger instruction size and larger data paths. Memory is also becoming cheaper and more compact.

Certain new facilities for the computer are important in connection with the future of education. Some are already available, but need to be further refined or made more available. Others are future possibilities, existing to some extent in research laboratories, but with much still to be learned.

Voice output is already available today, but needs further work. A variety of strategies—analog storage, digital storage, and phonetic re-creation—are in use. Except for analog storage, the voices still have an artificial sound generally not desirable for education. Voice is important in the learning process, so better voice output will be of some value. Music, particularly for motivational purposes, will be useful.

Graphics is still relatively crude, although typically available on personal computers. We can expect much better graphics—more choices of color, resolution, shading, and intensity control, and even general-purpose animation—as personal computers begin to use special graphic chips or use more powerful chips and more memory. Text too needs to be improved beyond our current rather crude text; choices of font and size of text should be available to the designer of computer-based learning material.

Networking, at the local level and nationally, is just reaching the stage where it is practical. For years we have been hearing about the ethernets, and they are sometimes commercially available now!

The combination of the optical videodisc with the computer, which I referred to many years ago as the intelligent videodisc, is a curious one. Although this technology has been around for about a dozen years, and although many people have recognized its potential in education, it has been so far relatively little used for the development of educational material. Much of the material that has been developed, particularly for industrial use, is relatively crude, with very weak forms of interaction. Full multimedia is an interesting possibility, and undoubtedly one that will be pursued further in the future.

Other forms of input will undoubtedly be developed. Painting input is becoming more common and undoubtedly will be improved. Voice input is possible for discrete speech, but still is beyond our capabilities for continuous speech. However, it is being vigorously pursued in the research laboratory. If we can solve the problems of voice input we may not need it, since from the computer's standpoint the analysis of complex voice patterns and the analysis of complex brain wave patterns are not necessarily that different.

WHERE WILL THE CURRICULUM UNITS COME FROM?

If we are to move from our current state, where the computer is relatively little used in learning, almost at the level of trivia, to a state where the computer is very heavily used, we need to ask where the new courses and curricula will come from. The production system outlined is intended to be adequate to produce sizable amounts of curriculum material of high quality. But many other issues are involved.

The Producers

Who will produce this new computer-based learning material? At the present time, some of it is being produced by individuals, teachers and university professors, and other materials are being produced within companies—textbook companies, computer vendors, and new companies which have been developed particularly for this purpose. Another possibility is the development of national centers, perhaps with government support, for such developmental activities. The Carnegie Commission report about a dozen years ago, *The*

Fourth Revolution—Instructional Technology in Higher Education, proposed that seven such centers should be established in the United States and that they should receive 1 percent of the total budget for higher education. Such centers now seem politically unlikely within the United States, but they have greater possibilities within some other countries.

The interest of the publisher is in protecting existing educational markets, so many publishers are already making investments in this direction. But they remain relatively uncertain about how to proceed, fearful of making mistakes in an area where little marketing data or experience is available.

The computer companies too are fearful, but perhaps less fearful since they are familiar with the technology. They see the production of computer-based learning material as a way of making certain that more hardware is sold and of developing another market in software as the cost of hardware continues to go down. Initially there were some alliances between publishers and computer vendors, but the interests of each were different. So such companies are often not satisfactory.

The Distributors

The issue of who will distribute the materials is a different issue. All the same "players" already mentioned are possible, but a given group might decide to play a role either in production or in distribution or in some combination of the two.

Distribution brings in questions of protection from copying, either through technical means or through legal means. We do not know if the copying of computer-based learning material will be a serious problem or not, since our experiences are so small. We do know, however, with other kinds of software, that a market may exist in spite of copying. Spreadsheet programs have sold well over half a million copies, although they are on floppy disks that could easily be copied.

The Home Market

In considering educational materials, it is very important to take into account the growing home market. The home computer will need a variety of applications-oriented programs to make it marketable. One of the categories in which such materials will be developed is education. Products of this type will be widely available and will affect what happens in the schools. There may be products usable in both home and school.

EDUCATIONAL INSTITUTIONS AND ORGANIZATIONS

It is impossible to imagine a change of the magnitude predicted here, the computer becoming the dominant educational delivery system, without anticipating massive changes in our current schools and universities. These changes are not likely to occur from internal pressures, as educational institutions are very conservative, slow to change. Even educational institutions most in favor of changes promote relatively trivial changes that do not fundamentally affect the institutions. We can expect, due to the current severe problems in education, including both financial and public opinion difficulties, that very strong external pressures will encourage change, particularly regarding the use of the computer. These changes will be particularly accelerated in the United States if such radical systems as the voucher system come into widespread use.

We already see a number of nontraditional ways of organizing universities. The most interesting are learning-at-a-distance institutions, such as The Open University in Great Britain. Within existing institutions there will be changes, particularly in the way the courses are run. The notion that a course should take a fixed amount of time will probably vanish as flexible, individualized computer-based learning material becomes available. Computers will be more used in schools at all levels. Changes in grading systems, made possible by the fact that much more is known about the student and the student's problems, may well happen, shifting from norm-based grading to competency-based grading.

It is quite possible that with the new learning materials there will be a shift in the *arena* of education. That is, less education will take place within formal schools, and more will take place either in public environments, such as public libraries, or the home. The learning-at-a-distance institutions already represent a move in this direction. Not all education

will move out of the school, but certain components are good candidates for such a move.

THE FUTURE—GOOD OR BAD?

Although it seems clear, for reasons not fully discussed, that the computer will become more important in education, it is not yet clear whether the computer will improve education, helping to overcome some of our current problems, or whether it will lead to further deterioration in the educational systems of many countries. The effectiveness of the use of the computer in education may be an important factor in determining which countries will succeed in the future.

There is nothing magical about computers. Like all technological developments, the computer itself is not good or evil. Rather, it is the way it is used by humans which is the critical factor, in education or elsewhere.

The poor quality of much existing computer-based learning material and the widespread acceptance of this material by teachers and administrators give us cause to worry about the future. If publishers distribute third-rate material and this material is eagerly gobbled up, publishers have no incentive to develop better material. It is critical to educate teachers to understand the quality of the materials, to look at computer materials critically, just as they might look at other kinds of educational material.

This material is "reviewed" to some extent today. Most of these reviews are in magazines which are heavily dependent on the vendors for advertising. So it is not surprising that most of these reviews are positive. I remember seeing a review recently, for example, about a new Pascal. The person had just studied Pascal and had taught BASIC for years, hardly the person one would want to review Pascal.

If we are to move toward a better future in education, we must look at new ways of organizing our entire educational system. Yet relatively few such visions of the future are available, and the vast majority of teachers with computers have no view of where they would like education to move.

One view that I recommend to readers is in George Leonard's book, *Education and Ecstasy*. Two chapters portray a school at the beginning of the next century. While the technology that Leonard portrayed has been to some extent surpassed, because of the quick rise of the personal computer, the educational ideas are worth looking at.

This presents only one view of the future. It is hoped that readers will develop their own visions and that they will take an active role in moving us toward a better educational system.

June 1983

Statements About Computer Futures for Education

ALFRED BORK

Education in the United States is in trouble. We are besieged by reports of the difficulties. Many parents realize that things are not right in our schools. The unhappiness with our school systems is unlike anything seen in the past. These problems have been documented in many reports, over at least a dozen years. But remarkably little happens to improve the situation, other than cosmetic changes.

It is not my intent to dwell on these very serious problems of education in our country. Rather, I want to consider the role that the computer may play in solving these problems, and leading us toward future educational systems.

My tactic will be to present a series of *statements*. The purpose is to make my views clear, and to focus on the major issues. Most of these issues are discussed in much more detail in my book *Personal Computers for Education* (Harper & Row, 1985), in *Learning with Computers* (Digital Press, 1981), and in papers developed at the Educational Technology Center.

GENERAL STATEMENTS CONCERNING COMPUTERS IN EDUCATION

1. The computer is the most powerful new learning device since the invention of the printing press and the textbook.
2. The computer is important as a learning device because it allows us, for the first time in hundreds, perhaps even thousands, of years, to move toward situations in which *most learning is interactive.* As we have educated larger and larger numbers of people, essential in a democracy, we have adopted undesirable passive modes of learning. With the computer, we can create active learning environments for *all* students.
3. Interactive learning has important consequences. Because the computer is constantly interacting with the student, we can *individualize* the learning experience to the needs of each student. When education is individualized, it can be more effective. We need not "teach" something already known, and we can work in ways that are most efficient for each learner. Interaction, used well, also implies a high level of motivation, and thus can be an important feature in increasing time on task, an important factor in determining how much students learn.
4. As with any technology, the computer can be used well in the learning process or it can be used

poorly. Moving computers into the educational process is no guarantee that learning will be improved. There is nothing magical about the computer.

5. Computers will continue rapidly to decline in cost, and improve in capability.

6. Because hardware will become cheaper, and because we are becoming more skillful in developing computer-based curriculum material, the computer will eventually become, in almost every area of education, the cheapest learning delivery system.

7. We should not seek the "best" way of using the computer in learning. The computer can be used in many different ways to aid many different aspects of the learning process. None of these should be eliminated at the present time, when our experience with first-rate use of the computer is still extremely limited. Decisions should be made on empirical grounds, rather than on the basis of philosophical positions. We need to use the principles of science in deciding where computers can best be used in the learning process.

8. Because the computer is a revolutionary device in education, it will lead to new educational structures. To think of computers in terms of current schools, and current universities, may be very misleading. New possibilities, such as learning-at-a-distance environments, become much more practical in an educational system heavily dependent on the computer.

STATEMENTS ABOUT THE CURRENT SITUATION WITH COMPUTERS IN SCHOOLS

9. Computers are appearing very rapidly in schools. Although estimates vary, it is reasonable to assume more than 300,000 computers in United States schools. Recently the number has doubled, or better, each year. Strong parental pressures assure that even in a time of financial strain, schools are still buying computers at an amazingly rapid and increasing rate. Parental feeling is that "My child has an inferior education if the school doesn't have computers."

10. A recent study at Johns Hopkins (Becker) indicates the schools that have computers do not necessarily use them, or may very much underuse them. Even when computers are given to schools, the school district may not actually let them be used in the schools.

11. The educational use of computers is often a disaster. One might reasonably argue that computers in schools at the present time are more harmful than helpful in the educational process, almost independent of the type of use. Students are, in some situations, being harmed by computers.

12. Teaching of programming in schools is a particular disaster area, building up bad habits which are almost impossible to overcome in later life. The major problems are BASIC and teachers who do not understand modern programming style.

13. Almost all commercially available computer-based learning material for school use at the present time is *poor*. Much of this material is trivia.

14. United States teachers are poorly trained to use computers effectively. Brief workshops are entirely inadequate for producing teachers who understand educational uses of computers. Teacher training is a major problem; few school districts are approaching it adequately. Training about computers in many schools of education is worse than no training at all. A few rare exceptions offer excellent training.

15. Schools depend on curriculum material. Good education demands that well-tested learning modules be available to the schools. Very few teachers have the time, energy, resources, and know-how to develop their own learning units, except in very small ways. The notion that teachers can develop their own computer-based learning modules is not reasonable.

16. Computers have the *potential* for helping with the major difficulties that confront education. But it is not certain that potential will be realized.

STATEMENTS CONCERNING THE PRODUCTION OF LEARNING MATERIAL EMPLOYING THE COMPUTER

17. The development of good learning material of any type is a nontrivial process. It demands competent people who know what they are doing.

18. Learning material must be carefully evaluated and improved in one or more formative evaluation cycles.

19. The development of good curriculum material, regardless of the media involved, is costly. To develop a single college-level course, the Open University (United Kingdom) typically spends about a million dollars. We can develop courses for less money, but quality is seriously affected.

20. Many of the stages for developing good curriculum units are independent of the subject area, the level, and the media involved. Developing good print-based learning material has many similarities to developing good computer-based learning material.

21. No effective shortcuts are available for developing computer-based learning material. Although beginners in this field often assume curriculum material can be produced at little cost, experience shows that good material is almost never produced this way.

22. Authoring languages and systems are almost useless. Little good curriculum material has ever been produced using these systems, in spite of the fact that vast numbers of such systems have been developed, and in spite of the vast publicity they have received. I would guess that in excess of half a billion dollars has gone into such systems. Unfortunately, major companies, and even major

countries, continue to support such development.

23. If the vast amount of money spent developing useless authoring languages and systems had gone into quality development of computer-based learning material, we would be much further along. These expenditures on authoring systems continue, draining away resources that could produce useful material.

24. In producing curriculum material, a variety of talents are needed. Most good curriculum material, such as that in the Open University, and in the major curriculum development projects in the United States following Sputnik, used sizable groups of people with different talents.

25. Effective ways of producing computer-based learning material exist and have produced sizable amounts of material, at costs resembling that of any good curriculum development.

26. The ultimate test of any method of producing learning units, including computer-related material, is the learning effectiveness of the materials produced.

STATEMENTS CONCERNING COMPUTERS AND THE FUTURE OF EDUCATION

27. The computer has the potential to solve most of our current educational problems.

28. The computer will play a dominant role in future educational systems.

29. Within twenty years, the computer will be the major delivery system for education at all levels, and in practically all subject areas, replacing books and lectures.

30. The computer may lead to a better *or* worse future educational system. At present, this issue is very much in the balance.

31. The federal government should fund vigorous research efforts to learn how better to use the computer in education. Current efforts are inadequate and often motivated by very specialized points of view. Diversity is the key to these efforts. There should be no national policy; the quality of the research should be the key factor in determining grants. Development cannot wait until this research is completed, but must proceed parallel to it.

32. Massive development of high-quality learning material involing the computer is essential, and should begin at once, primarily at the full segment or full course level. The computer should not be assumed to be the only medium. Development should take into account possible nontraditional organizations of schools and nontraditional delivery modes. The emphasis should be on *quality,* and on nontrivial amounts of material.

33. This curriculum material cannot be produced by cottage-industry authoring strategies. Production is a serious activity, and must be considered carefully. Further research on production strategies is needed.

34. The new learning material may follow modes impossible without

the computer, because the computer suggests new ways of organizing the learning experience, new ways of organizing courses, new ways of organizing schools, and new ways of organizing learning.

35. Learning-at-a-distance possibilities deserve further study. In many cases, the new computer-based learning materials may be able to follow distance-learning strategies. This implies that in learning systems of the future, fewer teachers may be needed.

36. Some of the uses of the computer in education will involve teachers. Teacher training, understanding how to use the newer materials and the newer media, is an essential component of curriculum development. Few teachers at any level, from earliest childhood to adult education, are prepared for the computer. Conventional methods of teacher training, pre-service and in-service lecture and textbook courses, are inadequate.

37. The computer should be the principal learning device for teachers in training programs. Curriculum development in courses where teachers are to be involved must take this into account, producing the teachers' material as well as the students' material. Teachers must have direct exposure to computers.

38. Large funding is essential for new learning material. There must be federal leadership and federal funding. Funding can also come from the states, from possible commercial vendors of the materials, from foundations, and from interested industries, particularly those with a technological basis.

39. Centers should be established all over the country for both research and development. While these centers should work together, in the sense of talking with each other and cooperating on some projects, a friendly rivalry between centers should assure diversity of approaches and materials.

40. Decisions of the next five to ten years will heavily influence our educational system for a long time in the future.

41. We have little time to alter the future. Many factors already suggest a "bad" direction. The question is one of establishing suitable models and directions, hard to change once they are fully in place.

42. The time to begin quality development is NOW.

February 1984

Education and Computers: The Situation Today and Some Possible Futures

ALFRED BORK

A remarkable aspect of education in the past few years, both in schools and in universities, has been the rapid increase of computers as part of the instructional process. All indications are that the educational presence and influence of the computer will continue to increase. Yet many disquieting factors exist about what is currently happening with the computer, and many uncertainties about what will happen.

Often people, and articles, are either totally supportive of computers in education, accepting the computer as a magical device to improve the educational process, or they are totally negative, seeing the computer as an inhuman evil. My aim is to present a balanced current picture, and based on that picture sketch several very different futures for education. Many aspects only mentioned are explored in more detail in my books and papers.[1]

NOW

In looking at the current situation of schools and universities, I discuss these under three topics of *increasing* importance: the equipment now available in schools, and the trends; instructional material available for use with the computer; and the classroom situation with regard to computers. In all, I stress possible future trends, to understand better where we might be going.

Computers

Student accessibility to computers has grown very rapidly. While estimates vary, it seems likely that in April 1984, approximately 350,000 computers were in the first through twelfth grades in schools in the United States, an average of about four computers per school. In the schools for the past few years, the number of computers has been roughly *doubling* each year.

While it is more difficult to come up with college data, counting computers that students own themselves and those the universities own, computer access for students continues to grow. Perhaps the most interesting hardware trend in the college situation is the move in colleges and universities toward "one personal computer per student." In some cases, entire classes have been required to buy a particular computer (freshmen at Drexel have been required to buy Apple Macintoshes this year). In other cases, vast numbers of computers have appeared at the school, either gifts (IBM gifts to MIT, Berkeley, and Austin) or special projects (the advanced computer system for Carnegie-Mellon University).

Thus, at all levels the amount of raw computer power accessible to students, in one way or another, is increasing rapidly. Even in the high schools, particular courses may require a student purchase. I know of situations where students are told that to take an advanced placement computer science course they must own computer X.

One wonders, looking at schools and universities, if this large recent rate of increase in computer capabilities *can* continue, or even increase; for how many years can we expect the doubling effect in schools? Doubling has occurred when schools were in poor financial condition, and the United States economy was poor. Less and less funds were available from the federal government for education. But, in spite of this, numbers of computers grew rapidly. In many situations, parents demanded this growth. It is not clear how long we can expect an exponential increase in computer availability to continue, but we must consider rapid growth a distinct possibility, at least for several more years.

The consequences of doubling are interesting. It means, that if this should continue for another several years, the computers *currently* in schools will be a very small minority of the machines in schools. Much of this increase in sheer computing power for students has occurred during a time when *almost no interesting learning materials were available* to use with these computers!

The availability of *decent* curriculum material, a possible future event, may have a considerable effect on the continuation of hardware purchases.

Another factor must be mentioned in connection with the increase in computer power available per student, in all areas of education. The computers available are also becoming more powerful. The transition from Apple II to an IBM PC or an Apple Macintosh is an important increase in computer power. Newer systems in schools and universities are almost inevitably disk-based, they have more memory, they have faster processors, they have better graphics.

Computer Programs for Education

The situation becomes, however, less favorable for education when we begin to observe what has happened with the production and distribution of software to aid the learning process, learning modules. The *amount* of software for education, at all levels and all types, has increased greatly, particularly commercially available software. But the *quality* of this learning material has consistently remained remarkably low. Thus while the hardware has improved in both sheer numbers and in the power of each unit, the curriculum material available on the computer has *not* kept pace with regard to quality.

Although it is widely said that current commercial educational materials for computers are poor, seldom is there much careful discussion of quality issues. It is not difficult to see the use of many unfortunate tactics. We *know* how to produce decent computer-based learning material at the present time. But most of the available programs have not been produced by any careful process, and very little has undergone careful evaluative study. Our increased capabilities in producing material have largely gone unused.

While almost no learning software was available a few years back, now dozens of companies are distributing modules. Some of these companies were already involved in related activities; thus many of the major textbook companies have established electronic publishing subsidiaries, and now have catalogues of computer-based learning material.

Computer companies are also increasingly involved in this market, seeing it as a way to strengthen their hardware sales, and as a promising new market. Many new companies have arisen, both for the production and for the distribution of computer-based learning material. In some cases, a single company will undertake both production and distribution, but in other cases, they are separate activities. One group of companies resembles bookstores; they do not themselves publish computer materials, but list in catalogues material available from a wide variety of sources.

While the amount of material has increased rapidly, it is not easy to measure this increase. But, given the low average quality, there is no point in determining hours. In addition to commercial modules, we also have other materials available, perhaps only from the developers. Many of these will become commercial products.

One often hears it argued that certain computers are used in schools because of the vast array of available software. This is a very peculiar argument, one that seems to say that large quantities of educational garbage are superior to small quantities!

I mention some factors which characterize poor software, not attempting a complete discussion of the process of examining and evaluating or reviewing software.

Failure to use adequately the interactive capabilities of the computer

Failure to use the individualizing capabilities of the computer

Use of extremely weak forms of interaction, such as multiple choice

Heavily text-dependent presentations

Heavily picture-dependent presentations, where the pictures play no important role in the learning process

Screens treated like the page of a book

Material that is entertaining or attractive, but with no, or vague, discernible educational objective

Material which does not fit anywhere into the curriculum

Games which are nothing but games

Long sets of "instructions" at the beginning of programs, difficult to follow even by the teachers, and even more difficult to recall

Dependence on auxiliary print material

Small pieces of material, lacking context

Material which does not hold the student's attention

One does not have to be an expert to notice many of these factors in much available computer learning programs.

It is hard to determine the funds going into curriculum development by *all* companies. I suspect it is, compared to the amount of material that they are marketing, small. Funding coming from publishers into development *is* increasing, but relatively few large companies are spending "real" money thus far.

So far most of these companies have looked around the country, found already *existing* material, and then put it out under their label. Note how very different this is from the way textbook companies proceed with books.

There are some bright spots with regard to funding of curriculum development. Several large computer companies, IBM and Digital Equipment Corporation, for example, now *are* spending sizable sums for serious curriculum development. The recent IBM sponsorship of the Writing to Read program is a good example.

Federal involvement in the development of computer-based learning material was important in the period of the 1970s. Projects such as Plato and Ticcit received millions of dollars of government money, and then generated commercial spinoffs. Many other groups,

such as my own Educational Technology Center, depend primarily on federal support, in our case from the National Science Foundation and from the Fund for the Improvement of Postsecondary Education.

This federal funding was reduced drastically, overall, in 1980, with the new administration. In 1984 federal funding is again growing, but it is difficult to determine what directions it will follow. Private foundations have so far put relatively little of their funds in this direction. Some funding is now going on from states.

The case of the computer vendors and support for development of learning materials is curious. While certain vendors are providing such support, no *full* realization of the eventual close tie-in between the availability of good learning material, and the sale of hardware, is present. Curriculum units will be in the future the driving force in the educational hardware market; people will buy computers because they run extensive, well-prepared learning material.

Although little good computer-based learning modules are currently developed, we do know *how* to develop such material, and by a variety of strategies. The Educational Technology Center at the University of California, Irvine and other groups have been particularly interested in the *process* that leads to sizable amounts of very high-quality computer-based learning material. We think that we have a good understanding of that process.[2]

Recent examples of computer-based

learning material illustrate the great potential of the computer as a learning device.

The hallmarks of such development are the use of groups; the use of a well-designed development process, including evaluation; and sufficient money to carry out the development. All useful development, I argue, starts with clear pedagogical purpose. The approaches which start with the computer, and produce a little bit of jazzy material, are not likely to be of long-range effectiveness.

Furthermore, this area is fraught with *false* directions. The development, for example, of authoring languages has been an enormous waste of money; perhaps at this point billions of dollars, which could have gone into useful development of materials, have been spent on developing authoring systems. Hardly anything of any consequence has been developed with any of the authoring systems or languages which have been developed. (Tutor was an exception, possibly because of the almost infinite amounts of money that Control Data was willing to spend.)

Distribution of both the computers and the learning material, in education, is becoming big business. Many companies realize that very sizable amounts of money *could* be made in education in the future. We can expect this feeling to continue, leading to strong economic pressure to increase the use of computers in schools. This factor alone will insure greater and greater presence of the computer in the educational process, at least in a country like the United States, where the profit motive is important.

The issue of *why* current software is so poor is interesting, deserving far more attention than I can give it. A tendency in computer science is to blame poor software on the current state of the hardware. The myth is that computers can never be used for successful learning until A1 techniques are very widely used, with much more powerful computers than today's personal computers. I do not believe that. Many interesting examples of computer-based material *already* exist on current hardware. Although we can expect hardware to improve, the notion that we cannot develop good educational material until we have advanced hardware capable of supporting A1 software is wrong.

The Classroom Situation Today

In both schools and universities, in spite of the increased presence of the computer in education, computer use is still only a *very small fraction* of the total instructional system presented to students. If we examine, at almost any level, the total student learning time, breaking this into categories including use of the computer, the computer occupies a trivial percent of the total.

Even in the university courses which make the most extensive use of the computers, the computer occupies no more than half of the total student learning time. And very few such courses are available. I would be very surprised if the involvement of the computer in the instructional process in the entire country is more than 1%.

Most learning is *still* taking place through the passive learning modes dominant for hundreds of years, books and lectures. This is not surprising, considering the lack of high-quality computer material. The typical teacher is dependent on existing curriculum material. While we like to think of teachers as developing their own classes, and this does happen occasionally, statistically it is a small activity in either schools or in universities.

Another factor must be taken into account. Teachers have little knowledge of how to use the computer. Current training programs leave much to be desired.

The vast majority of beginning university courses are standard, prosaic courses with large lecture sections, based on relatively few standard textbooks. Most of the faculty are happy with these courses, because they believe they understand them. After all, the faculty members themselves took and did well in these same courses! Very few teachers or faculty members have ever developed any sizable amounts of curriculum material. Most of them do not know *how* to develop such materials, most of them have little experience in this direction, most of them do not have the resources, and most of them work within a reward system where this is not encouraged.

POSSIBLE FUTURES

Given the current situation, which I have tried to portray realistically, what can we suspect, as soothsayers, might happen with computers in education? What are likely future directions?

The number of computers and computer access will continue to rise, both in schools and in universities. We are already getting predictions of over a million computers in United States schools in just two or three years. We can also predict increasing commercial involvement, both selling computers to schools, and stimulating, producing, and distributing computer-based learning material.

Computers will continue to evolve and improve. Hardware will continue to get better, and costs will continue to come down, stimulating even further the uses of computers in the educational process. Graphics capability and text will improve, with choices of fonts and sizes not provided in most systems today. We can expect better resolution, and larger screens. In the not-too-distant future, videodisc technology will begin to become more used than at present, and such strategies as voice input, and even brainwave input, will become practical.

It seems likely too that current severe problems of education will continue. For example, the shortage of teachers in science and mathematics will not be alleviated by any measures, no matter how drastic, in a short period of time.

In spite of these likely future directions, a wide variation still remains as to how computers might affect the educational system of the future. I would like to sketch, briefly, two general future directions, a "bad" one and a "good" one.

A Bad Future for Education with Computers

One possibility for the future is that we simply continue the way we have been going at present. In this view, the school and university continue to decline.

Commercial forces become more and more dominant in the computer-based curriculum, just as they are in the book-based curriculum. They continue to feed schools and universities little bits and pieces of material, mostly of low quality. As computers increase in schools, the audience for this material will grow more and more. Teachers and administrators will have little chance to understand what is good, because there will be such a flood of what is bad. So they will be "satisfied" with poor material. Classes will continue to be book- and lecture-dominated, supplemented by computer material. Teacher training programs will be of low quality. The true interactive capabilities of the computer will not be realized.

In this unpleasant view of the future, both the public and the private schools, and the universities, continue to grow weaker. Current education problems will not be solved. Parental pressure for educational change will grow, but will often lead to measures such as the voucher system, which will not improve education, but merely transfer it from public to private concerns. Large corporations will see the voucher system as an indication that they can participate in the "education market," running their own schools and universities.

Test scores of American students will continue to drop. The computer may even accelerate this. For example, poor modes of teaching programming, taught by teachers who do not understand programming, and who know little about modern programming strategy, will make certain that very few students are competent programmers. Large American companies will discover they can move to locations overseas to acquire the kind of people that they want, so they are not dependent on the declining quality of American education.

Although the views expressed may seem very negative, I would argue that this possibility is realistic. It *could* happen! I only extrapolate many of the bad features of the current situation, and assume that they will continue to grow as they have been growing. This bad scenario is not intended as a scare tactic, but as a genuine possibility.

A Good Future for Education with Computers

This scenario begins at the present time, or perhaps a very few years into the future. Powerful national leaders agree that the United States educational system must be rescued if we are to maintain our position in the world, and if we are to provide equality of opportunity, the best possible education, for *all* citizens. Strong leadership is brought to bear on the educational issue, from the highest political offices in the country. The major American corporations join vigorously in this activity, seeing the quality of education as critical to their futures too.

A major result of this increased

concern with improving education is large-scale development of new curriculum material, courses which assume from the beginning that the computer will be an integral part of the student learning system. We develop an entirely new set of courses, everywhere from first grade through undergraduate education. To maintain the plurality of our education, we develop *several* distinctly different courses in each area.

Such an extensive development of courses cannot take place instantaneously, but represents a national commitment over ten years. In each of these years, 1% of the total budget of education in the United States supports curriculum development. Commercial forces join in with this massive national effort, contributing their resources also.

Development of new courses is the heart of any successful use of the computer in improving our educational system. Material must be produced on professional standards, using a wide variety of learning theories and approaches. Several courses in each area, done by entirely different groups, will assure a much greater diversity of available learning modules than we currently have with books; now textbook-dependent courses tend to be extremely similar, even though written by different authors and coming from different publishers.

The new courses lead to changes in the organization of schools, and new and more dignified roles for the teacher. It seems inconceivable that such a powerful learning device as the computer could be extensively used in education without profoundly altering the shape of the schools. Many types of activities which currently take place in schools move to homes, public libraries, and other environments. As the computer becomes more and more prevalent in our society, learning based primarily on the computer takes place almost anywhere. But some activities demand groups, and so still take place in schools.

The literature sketches various future school systems which make effective use of the computer. Two of the most interesting come from George Leonard. One of them was in a book called *Education and Ecstasy,* published in 1968.[3] The other Leonard future school, much more recent, appeared in the April 1984 *Esquire.*[4] Leonard's schools, although different, have many interesting features in common. I will enumerate a few common aspects:

1. The computer is the major delivery device, and in many cases the only delivery device, for knowledge-based learning activities.
2. The schools consider the whole education of an individual, so that affective and physical aspects of education are integral parts of the school.
3. Teachers play a major role in the affective areas.
4. Both schools depend on a full computer-based course management system, maintaining complete records of the student's progress. In the original school, the student learning activities are completely determined by the computer. In the later version, the management

system is more versatile, presenting study programs to the student and reaching mutual agreement on the student's responsibilities for a particular day. Humans may also enter into this process.

5. In the original school, *everything* takes place at the school itself. In the new version, the student has the choice, having completed the minimal requirements, to spend most of the time working at home or elsewhere. In both schools, if one examines the knowledge-based components, most of the activities *could* happen away from school.

6. Both of the schools are based on mastery learning. This is perhaps a little less clear with the first one, but is stressed in the second one. That is, it is assumed that the student stay with a given topic until that student can perform at almost 100%.

I do not mean to imply that these are the only two good futures for education with the computer. A good bit of

thoughtful concern has gone into Leonard's future schools, so his books deserve to be widely read. Many of the features would seem to me to be likely in almost any school of the future in which computers were used effectively as learning devices.

June 1984

REFERENCES

1. Bork, Alfred. *Learning with Computers.* Digital Press, 1981. Bork, Alfred. *Personal Computers for Education.* Harper & Row, 1985.
2. Bork, Alfred. "Production Systems for Computer-Based Learning." *Instructional Software: Principles and Perspectives for Design and Use,* Decker F. Walker and Robert D. Hess, Editors, Wadsworth Publishing Company, Belmont, California, 1984.
3. Leonard, George. *Education and Ecstasy,* Delacorte Press, New York, 1968.
4. Leonard George. "The Great School Reform Hoax," *Esquire,* 101, 4, April 1984, pp. 47–56.

CREDITS

part one *Overview*

"The Fourth Revolution—Computers and Learning." Alfred Bork, University of Oregon paper, May 1982.

"Compendium of Bad but Common Practices in Computer-Based Learning." Alfred Bork, April 1983.

part two *Computers and Schools*

"Teachers and Computers." Alfred Bork, *School Microcomputing Bulletin,* September 1983.

"Computer Literacy for Teachers." Alfred Bork, National Computer Literacy Goals Conference, December 1980.

"Don't Teach BASIC." Alfred Bork, Educational Technology Center, April 1982.

"Informatics for Everyone: A Proposed Curriculum for Math, Science, and Engineering Students." Alfred Bork, *Informatics Education for All Students at University Level,* Elsevier Science Publishers B.V. (North Holland), 1984.

part three *Scientific Reasoning*

"Science Literacy in the Public Library—*Batteries and Bulbs.*" Alfred Bork, Arnold Arons, Francis Collea, Stephen Franklin, and Barry Kurtz, January 1981. Proceedings of National Educational Computer Conference, June 17–19, 1981, Denton, Texas.

"A Computer-Based Discovery Module in Optics." Alfred Bork, Arthur Leuhrmann, Barry Kurtz, and Victor Jackson, January 1982.

"Computer-Based Learning Units for Science and Math for Secondary Schools." Alfred Bork, Augusto Chioccariello, Werner Feibel, Stephen Franklin, Barry Kurtz, David Trowbridge, Ruth Von Blum, July 1984.

"Observation and Inference: A Computer-Based Learning Module." Alfred Bork, David Trowbridge, and Arnold Arons. Proceedings of National Educational Computer Conference, June 1983.

"A Computer-Based Dialogue for Developing Mathematical Reasoning of Young Adolescents." David Trowbridge and Alfred Bork, January 1981. Proceedings of National Educational Computer Conference, June 17–19, 1981, Denton, Texas.

"Computer-Based Learning Modules for Early Adolescence." David Trowbridge and Alfred Bork, January 1980. Paper presented at the Third World Conference on Computers in Education, Lausanne, Switzerland, July 29, 1981.

part four *Physics*

"Computer-Based Instruction in Physics." Alfred Bork, *Physics Today,* vol. 34, no. 9, September 1981.

"*Newton*—A Mechanical World." Alfred Bork, Stephen Franklin, Martin Katz, and John McNelly, Proceedings of National Educational Computer Conference, June 1981.

part five *Production and Design*

"Production Systems for Computer-Based Learning." Alfred Bork, February 1982.

"Interaction in Learning." Alfred Bork, National Educational Computing Conference, June 1982.

"Right Justification and Word Processing." Alfred Bork, *Educational Technology*, April 20, 1982.

"Books Versus Computers: Learning Media." Alfred Bork, ASIS, October 1980.

"Graphics and Screen Design for Interactive Learning." Alfred Bork, Stephen D. Franklin, Ruth Von Blum, Martin Katz, and Barry L. Kurtz, National Computer Graphics Association, March 1982.

"A Preliminary Taxonomy of Ways of Displaying Text on Screens." Alfred Bork, *Information Design Journal*, vol. 3, no. 3, 1983.

part six *Videodiscs*

"Developing Interactive Videodiscs." Alfred Bork, SALT, 1980.

"The Intelligent Videodisc." Alfred Bork, SALT, February 1980.

"Aspects of Marketing Intelligent Videodisc Material." Alfred Bork, SALT, July 1981.

part seven *Computers and the Future of Education*

"Learning, Computers, and Higher Education." Alfred Bork, for AAUP publication, 1984.

"Computers and Information Technology as a

Learning Aid." Alfred Bork, June 1983, Netherlands.

"Statements about Computer Futures for Education." Alfred Bork, *Creative Computing*, November 1984.

"Education and Computers: The Situation Today and Some Possible Futures." Alfred Bork, T.H.E. Journal, 1984